# AFTERLIVES OF ENDOR

# AFTERLIVES OF ENDOR

## WITCHCRAFT, THEATRICALITY, AND UNCERTAINTY FROM THE *MALLEUS MALEFICARUM* TO SHAKESPEARE

LAURA LEVINE

CORNELL UNIVERSITY PRESS
*Ithaca and London*

Copyright © 2023 by Laura Levine

All rights reserved. Except for brief quotations in a review, this book, or parts thereof, must not be reproduced in any form without permission in writing from the publisher. For information, address Cornell University Press, Sage House, 512 East State Street, Ithaca, New York 14850. Visit our website at cornellpress.cornell.edu.

First published 2023 by Cornell University Press

Library of Congress Cataloging-in-Publication Data

Names: Levine, Laura, 1955– author.
Title: Afterlives of Endor : witchcraft, theatricality, and uncertainty from the "Malleus maleficarum" to Shakespeare / Laura Levine.
Description: Ithaca [New York] : Cornell University Press, 2023. | Includes bibliographical references and index.
Identifiers: LCCN 2023023300 (print) | LCCN 2023023301 (ebook) | ISBN 9781501772085 (hardcover) | ISBN 9781501772184 (paperback) | ISBN 9781501772191 (pdf) | ISBN 9781501772207 (epub)
Subjects: LCSH: Demonology in literature. | Witchcraft in literature. | Uncertainty in literature. | Contradiction in literature. | Trials (Witchcraft) in literature.
Classification: LCC PN56.D465 L48 2023 (print) | LCC PN56.D465 (ebook) | DDC 133.4/309—dc23/eng/20230623
LC record available at https://lccn.loc.gov/2023023300
LC ebook record available at https://lccn.loc.gov/2023023301

*for my family
and in memory of the
late Harry and Esther Levine*

# Contents

*Acknowledgments*   ix

   Introduction     1

1. Judicial Procedure as Countermagic in *Malleus Maleficarum*     12

2. Broken Epistemologies: Bodin and the Repudiation of Spectacle     25

3. Our Mutual Fiend: Reginald Scot and the Exorcism of the Other     39

4. Strategies for Doubt: Curiosity and Violence in King James VI and I's *Daemonologie*     55

5. *Newes from Scotland* and the Theaters of Evidence     65

6. Spenser's False Shewes     81

7. Danger in Words: Faustus, Slade, and the Demonologists     91

8. Paulina and the Theater of Shame     102

   Epilogue: This Is and Is Not Magic     120

*Notes*     131
*Bibliography*     165
*Index*     173

# Acknowledgments

Chapter 7 of this book appeared in an early form in *Magical Transformations on the Early Modern English Stage*, and I am grateful to Ashgate for permission to reprint it. The discussion of Lambe in chapter 6 draws on a much larger argument which appeared in the *Journal of Medieval and Early Modern Studies*, in the issue *Performance beyond Drama*, and I thank Michael Cornett, Ineke Murakami, and Donovan Sherman for responses to early drafts of the argument. I gratefully acknowledge the NYU Center for the Humanities, the Folger Shakespeare Library, the National Endowment for the Humanities, and the former Mary Ingraham Bunting Institute for providing time to conduct research, as well as New York University's wider support of my work.

Mahinder Kingra has been a wise and generous editor whose insights proved valuable at every stage of the process and both press readers (subsequently unmasked as Jessica Winston and Jesse Landers) offered useful suggestions and correctives. I thank Cheryl Hirsch and Susan Specter as well for their painstaking work on the manuscript. Lachlan Sage Brooks, Zoe Sophia Gray and Audrey Miller provided excellent research assistance and Isabel Dollar's resourcefulness at tracking down documents, including undigitized manuscripts during the worst of the pandemic, was vital to the book's completion. I thank Jennifer K. Nelson, Hans Peter Broedel, and Christopher S. Mackay, each of whom offered generous help on matters of translation. The last two of these, along with Stuart Clark, Lawrence Normand, and Gareth Roberts, have contributed to the explosion of important work about demonology in the last few decades. Although I have differed at points from the conclusions of some of these scholars, I remain grateful for the work they have done.

I owe much to the many colleagues, friends, and family who read and commented on portions of the manuscript, as well as to those who responded to parts of its argument presented at conferences. Of these, I would particularly like to thank Jim Ball, the late Harry Berger, Ann Blair, Claudia Burbank, Charles Donahue, Maria Fahey, Laura Geringer, Elizabeth Hanson, Julia Lupton, Carol Martin, Katharine Eisaman Maus, Subha Mukherji, Katharine Park, Annie Saenger, Mark Sherman, Daniel Spector, and Jane Tylus, the last of whom offered invaluable bibliographical suggestions as well. Lorraine Hirsch listened to large portions of the book and posed questions which forced me to clarify my ideas. Stephen Orgel and Joseph Campana each read the manuscript at early stages of its composition and in different ways profoundly influenced the direction of the book.

Among other things, this is a book about doubt, a condition with which its author is all too familiar. As such, I owe to those readers and friends, who engaged not only with its subject matter but with the conditions of its composition, a particularly large debt: Larry Rosenwald, who not only shared his knowledge of medieval Latin and read key sections of the book but encouraged me to talk out the most difficult parts of the argument; Rubén Polendo, whose generosity sustained me during much of the process; and the late Esther and Harry Levine, whose encouragement and whose own courage made so much possible. My greatest debt is to Peter Saenger for his tireless attention to both the imagined version of the book and its actual details. This book is for him.

# AFTERLIVES OF ENDOR

# Introduction

This book began with a pair of questions, the first about *The Winter's Tale*. In II.iii, threatening to have her burnt, Leontes throws Paulina out of his chambers, calling her a "mankind witch." "I care not," she tells him; "it is an heretic that makes the fire, / Not she which burns in't."[1] In this exchange, the play presents the fantasy of witch-burning from two opposite points of view, that of the witch hunter and that of the woman hunted. Paulina claims that the crime lies in the mind of the man who makes the accusation and lights the fire, not in the actions of the woman burnt. Leontes acts as if the crime of witchcraft is "real" and warrants death. These views correspond roughly to two poles of debate about witchcraft during the period: the position taken by Reginald Scot, in his 1584 *The Discoverie of Witchcraft*, that most witch hunts were scapegoating practices aimed at poor, menopausal women and that the "witchcraft," if there was any, was in the mind of the victimizer; and the position taken by King James the VI and I, Shakespeare's own spectator at the time of *The Winter's Tale*, whose 1597 *Daemonologie* argued for the reality and extermination of witches.

For both Scot and James, as well as for others during the period, a focal point for discussions of witchcraft was the witch of Endor story, from which this book takes its title. In 1 Samuel, chapter 28, Saul, overwhelmed by fear of the Philistine army, seeks out the witch of Endor, who raises for him the dead Samuel. "What really happened at Endor?" scholars and commentators like James and Scot asked.² It would be profane to think the elect in the bosom of Abraham could be raised by every passing witch, but what must have happened instead? For Scot, the witch of Endor was a charlatan using stage tricks like ventriloquism to dupe Saul. For James, in contrast, what looked like Samuel raised by the witch was really the devil in the shape of Samuel. Both explanations imply a "theatrical" conception of witchcraft in the broadest sense of the word in that they involve the creation of illusions. But they do so in different ways. For Scot what is at issue is human "juggling" or "cousening," the construction of an illusion that could (theoretically) be seen through even though Saul, hungry and gullible, failed to do so. For James what is operative is a demonic theatricality, the devil casting much more powerful illusions by assuming different shapes. Scot chose the natural explanation, James the supernatural. The ending of *The Winter's Tale*, with its ability to suggest that Hermione is raised from the dead while at the same time suggesting that Paulina has staged a theatrical trick to make it *look* as if Hermione is raised from the dead, seemed to suggest irresistibly that Shakespeare was invoking the terms of this debate. But to what end?

The second question emerged from one of the demonological treatises this book examines. Toward the end of Jean Bodin's 1580 *De la Demonomanie des Sorciers* (*The Demon-Mania of Witches*), after describing the elaborate rules a judge must submit to in order to prove a suspect is a witch, Bodin admonishes future judges not to make a "sorcery" of justice by turning to spectacle. A skilled judge will neither attempt to recreate the witchcraft he is trying to prove exists nor seek a theatrical display. He will disdain theatrical spectacles, especially spectacles that are in any way like the witchcraft they examine.³ What allowed Bodin to repudiate a theatrical trial? What allowed him to imagine even hypothetically a possible similarity between justice and the crime it examined?

Demonological treatises and broadside pamphlets of the period abound in descriptions of witch trials rich in spectacle. Book 3—the judicial section of *Malleus Maleficarum*, the infamous inquisitor's manual (circa 1486)—is quite literally a set of scripts for future judges complete with instructions for props and sartorial advice.⁴ *Newes from Scotland* (1591), the pamphlet which chronicles King James's own examination of a set of defendants accused of witchcraft, describes James's fascination, even delight, with the performances defendants supply. Twice he has defendants come before him to reenact crimes they are accused of having committed. Geillis Duncane, maidservant to a local deputy bailiff, is summoned to play before the king on a "jew's trump" the reel she is supposed to have played when she accompanied 200 witches to sea in sieves on Halloween.⁵ And on Christmas Eve, the king has the accused conjuror John Cunningham, also known as Doctor Fian, reenact for him before the court a demonic possession he has confessed to throwing a gentleman into, his rival for a girl in the village of Saltpans. All this to the king's delight.

Bodin's admonition to future judges raised a question. Outliers illuminate both the limits and core of phenomena. Here was a writer no more tolerant of witchcraft than James or the inquisitors who was explicitly eschewing a spectacular trial. What made this possible? Michel Foucault's concept of the episteme—that unit of time marked by shared assumptions which organize knowledge itself—has been criticized both for its rigidity and the dates that are supposed to define it, but here the question was a different one: Even granting the notion of episteme, what might account for differences within one?[6] More broadly, what determined whether or not a given demonologist imagined a trial in theatrical terms?

My first thought was that the answer might lie in Bodin's conception of witchcraft itself. The conception of the trial might reflect an underlying attitude toward the crime being examined: to be able to dispense with theatricality at a trial, a demonologist would have to hold a conception of witchcraft itself as incorporeal and therefore incapable of being demonstrated or acted out. This assumption turned out to be mistaken, at least in Bodin's case. He regularly imagines witchcraft in highly theatrical terms—witches dance the volta, blaspheme in rhyme, and utter words and syllables which seem to have the power to effect destructive actions in the world simply by being uttered. It couldn't be the case that Bodin was able to relinquish the notion of a theatrical trial at the end of his book simply because he imagined witchcraft as completely incorporeal, as somehow transcending and thus eluding the ability to be acted out, because there were many indications that he didn't imagine it that way at all.

Alternatively, I imagined the ability to relinquish a theatrical trial might be an expression of one's conception of evidence. The mind that disdained the evidence of the senses might be one that could forfeit a visible demonstration of the truth and so dispense with spectacle at a trial as a means of authentication. But, in fact, Bodin privileges above all other evidence the evidence of the senses, what he calls the evidence of the acknowledged fact. What the judge sees or touches or "appertains" to the five senses outranks all other kinds of evidence. But although he privileges the evidence of the senses, Bodin is equally absolute in his vision of the universe as one that is not fully available to the senses. There are more things in the universe—and therefore in law—than are comprehended by nature, he says. Although Bodin is committed to the notion of "material" evidence, to the notion that material objects can present themselves to the senses in ways that guarantee knowledge, he is equally committed to a universe that does not always manifest itself in material ways, and therefore cannot be known.[7] This kind of epistemological problem, the tension between the need for confirmation from sensory evidence and a world which by definition eludes that evidence, typifies the treatises this book considers. The friction such tension generates points to a problem that haunts them: the need to make visible the invisible world implied by witchcraft and (simultaneously) the impossibility of doing so.

But the question remained: If neither Bodin's conception of witchcraft nor his conception of evidence allowed him to relinquish theatricality at a trial, what did allow him to do so? Perhaps if witchcraft was theatrical, justice would need to be "a-theatrical," transcend theatricality; justice would always have to be an absolute opposite to the crime it examined. In many ways this did seem to be Bodin's position. The disturbing thing was how like each other justice and crime were, how many of the attributes he ascribed to witches Bodin's version of justice seemed to incorporate into itself. One of the subjects of the legal chapters is the female witch's ability to curse. Simply by uttering her wish, the witch is imagined to enact it in the universe. But words have a curious power to constitute rather than describe reality in Bodin's rules of evidence as well. If a mother is found with a slain child in her arms, she is assumed to be innocent though the house is empty. But if the same woman is rumored to be a witch, she is presumed to be guilty of slaying the child. She need not have been convicted of witchcraft. The simple fact of the rumor, of *words being uttered*, is sufficient to establish a legal presumption of guilt. Bodin doesn't simply worry about the constitutive power of words as a property of witchcraft, the ability of words to create rather than describe; he employs that power as part of a judicial tactic. In that sense, his conception of the trial is as "theatrical" as that of the inquisitors or James, if "theatrical" is expanded so that it no longer means "deceptive" or even "spectacular" but rather "performative"— "performative" in a sense that extends, in a very specific way, J. L. Austin's use of the word when, early in *How to Do Things with Words*, he says of the term "performative" that "the issuing of [an] utterance is the performing of the action."[8]

Bodin doesn't acknowledge the power he ascribes to the words witches use. His articulated belief is that language is referential, that words "mean," they do not "do." In this, he and other demonologists in the book are like the philosophers Austin describes who assume "that the business of a 'statement' can only be to 'describe' some state of affairs, or to 'state some fact,' which it must do either truly or falsely" (1). That the barbaric and incomprehensible words ("les mots barbares, et non entendus") of magic could have more power than meaningful words is particularly galling to Bodin. But even as he asserts this position, he belies it in his own behavior. This is most clear in his simple terror of repeating any of the words or formulas which are supposed to lack power, and his fear of describing the images which are ostensibly harmless (the words used to make sieves jump which he "shall not put down" and the circles and detestable symbols which he "shall not write down"). So intense is his fear of repeating these things that one of the central dilemmas of the book becomes how to talk about his subject itself.

It has become almost axiomatic on the part of historians of demonology to repeat what the demonologists said about their own beliefs—that there was (in the words of James's spokesman in *Daemonologie*) "no power inherent in the circles, or in the holines of the names of God blasphemously used, nor in whatsoever rites or ceremonies at that time used, that either can raise any infernall spirit or yet limitat him perforce within or without these circles" (16–17). "To a man," Stuart Clark argues, demonologists were "moderns," meaning they explicitly rejected the notion that the words and images of magic were efficacious or instrumental.[9] *Afterlives of Endor* doesn't dispute this claim. What it argues is that even as demonologists explicitly assert that the words and images of magic have no efficacy, they regularly contradict themselves by *behaving* as if the words and symbols of witchcraft and magic were efficacious. The texts this book examines are like war zones in which the view of language as instrumental (performative, efficacious) and the view of language as communicative (conventional, referential) are in constant and largely unregulated combat with each other. This is what makes them so interesting, so telling.

All the demonologists considered in this book are implicitly anti-theatrical in the sense that they explicitly deny the power of words to "do" things simply by being uttered. But like actual anti-theatricalists, who claimed that costume was a "signe distinctive" between "sexe and sexe" but worried that costume could dissipate the gender beneath, their denial often contains a deep fear of just the opposite possibility, a fear that words, simply by being uttered, can effect material change in the outside world.[10] (Scot is the obvious exception here, but as we shall see, he is a particular kind of exception, a qualified one.) In this way the demonologists this book examines take the notion of what in the wake of Austin we now call "performatives" much further than Austin himself would have. For them, the issuing of a certain kind of utterance is not simply the "performing of an action" but the performing of a catastrophic action, itself able to effect subsequent disasters. In similar fashion James denies the efficacy of images like the ones witches roast to take the lives of their victims, which images he claims have no inherent "virtue" or power. What looks like efficacy is an elaborate charade orchestrated by the devil. But *Newes from Scotland*, arguably official propaganda for and about James, insists on the efficacy of image magic, insists that, had the shirt or handkerchief which "appertained" to the king been dipped in toad venom collected in an oyster shell, it could have bewitched him to "extraordinary paines" without him ever having had to put it back on.

To claim that demonologists exhibit the fear that words and images are efficacious may seem counterintuitive, even perverse, especially in relation to Protestant demonologists, given the number and variety of Reformation attacks on images and rites, but such attacks were neither unequivocal nor without exception. "Compliance should not be taken to imply agreement," says Eamon Duffy (5).[11] "The notion that the appropriate religious ritual would bring material benefit thus lingered on," says Keith Thomas (64); "Fundamental changes are not accomplished overnight" (73).[12] Margaret Aston characterizes reform during the period in terms of "switchback[s]" and "zigzag[s]."[13] Not only did reform happen in stages which often undid themselves from reign to reign (Edward and Mary) or even within a given reign—Henry's *King's Book* took back much of what his own bishops had said about images a few years earlier in *The Bishop's Book*—but individual moments of iconoclasm themselves were often internally contradictory. Elizabeth I kept candles and a cross in the royal chapel long after the royal order of 1561 mandated rood lofts be taken down as far as the beam. Martin Bucer's attack on images vacillated between the claim that the images were dangerous and the claim that the abuse of them was what was dangerous.[14]

Perhaps more to the point, iconoclasm contained within itself a fundamental contradiction, one which iconoclasts themselves often identified. Carlos Eire points out that for the German reformer Andreas Karlstadt it is the "inner image" that leads men to worship falsely.[15] Similarly, for Ulrich Zwingli the need to formulate images is inherent, inevitable, built into man himself. "There is no one who' as soon as he hears God spoken of, or any other thing which he has not already seen, does not picture a form for himself," Eire quotes Zwingli as saying.[16] Since man's tendency to formulate images is inevitable, every inner image or idol, what Zwingli calls a "strange god," ultimately finds expression in a physical, external idol, *the inner always preceding the external image*. In Zwingli's formulation, I would argue, the hammer which attacks the statue is attacking a poor substitute, the iconoclast trying to eradicate that which is internal and can never be eradicated. To say this is obviously not to suggest that reformers subscribe to a formal creed which sees idols as efficacious, but rather to argue that in attacking the substitute they act as if the danger were in the idol and *behave* as if the image were powerful.[17]

One difference in emphasis between this book and many recent studies of demonology which precede it and which it builds on is a preoccupation with and sustained attention to contradiction. This focus on what is contradictory in these texts grows out of the conviction that texts (like individual people) hold mutually exclusive investments within them and that these mutually exclusive investments illuminate what is central to those that hold them.[18]

A case in point is *Daemonologie*. When Philomathes, the questioner in the dialogue, describes the epistemological crisis that would follow if the devil could take the form of Samuel—prophets would never know whether a message was divinely or demonically inspired—Epistemon, James's spokesman, insists that there is no crisis because the devil's shape-shifting poses no "inconvenience" to the prophets. Knowledge is possible to them because it is a function of their spiritual state. In a broader sense knowledge is conceived to be possible because prosecution depends on the premise that it is possible to tell one person from another, a witch from a non-witch. The book is filled with methods for finding "signs" to tell, for instance, a melancholic from a witch, or a frantic person from a demoniac. But even as the book insists on the reliability of these signs and the possibility of knowledge they afford, it registers a rising, if unacknowledged, doubt. Witches confess to things which while not lies are also not true. The devil can "ravish" their senses, creating collective delusions which ultimately lead to confessions that are unreliable. Where for Bodin a conflict exists between his epistemology and his ontology—between what he believes about knowledge and what there is to be known—for James the conflict exists between alternating moments of dogmatism and uncertainty within his epistemology itself. Clark rightly demonstrates that skeptics and believers alike allowed for an element of delusion in confessions and that doubt and belief existed side by side in both camps.[19] But what do demonologies "do" with contradictions like this one? What strategies—rhetorical or otherwise—exist for demonologists to deal with the kinds of affect such contradictions breed?

*Newes from Scotland*, the pamphlet that chronicles James's activities as an examiner of witches in Scotland, provides one way of thinking about this question because it describes what examiners do when faced with parallel contradictions. Toward the end of the pamphlet, the examiners try to find on the body of a male defendant, Doctor Fian, a "devil's mark," the mark that to them serves as proof that the defendant is a witch. It has "latelye beene found," the pamphleteer tells us, "that the Deuill dooth generallye marke [witches] with a privie marke," and "so long as the marke is not seene to those which search them, so long as [the witches] . . . will neuer confesse" (12–13). Early in the pamphlet a mark is found on Geillis Duncane's throat, at which point she confesses and the various thumbscrew and rope tortures cease. Midway through the pamphlet, Agnes Sampson, "the eldest Witch of them al," is shaved and a devil's mark is found on her "privities." But Doctor Fian's body yields no devil's mark. His body, like his testimony, refuses to yield the certainty the examiners seek. Brutal and incessant, even by the standards of this particular pamphlet, the series of tortures he undergoes suggests the degree to which, as this pamphleteer construes it, doubt and uncertainty themselves precipitate violence. Foucault describes judicial torture in the period as being "regulated" in such a way as to imply it exists almost independently from the affects of the examiners who order it.[20] But in *Newes from Scotland*, the pamphleteer, in contrast to the trial records he draws on, centralizes the responses and affects of the examiners in a way that seems to challenge this picture. Here, then, the performances the king commands (and in response to which he registers "delight") seem attempts to coerce the invisible world of witchcraft to become visible, and thus compensatory, responses to a sense of "knowledgelessness."[21]

In itself, none of this specifically addressed what it meant for *The Winter's Tale* to invoke the debate between King James and Reginald Scot, but it did suggest a general principle that might illuminate the relation between the demonological treatises I was examining and certain literary texts of the period. When Spenser has Arthur and Una strip the witch Duessa in canto 8 of book 1 of *The Faerie Queene*, he draws on the same tradition of stripping the witch that we see in *Newes from Scotland*. Like Sampson, the "eldest witch of them al," Duessa is revealed to be "a loathly wrinckled hag," her head "altogether bald" as if in mockery of "honorable eld."[22] As in *Newes from Scotland*, the male spectators disempower her by stripping her and beholding the spectacle of the naked female body. But in contrast to Sampson's naked body with its mark, Spenser makes Duessa's body ultimately unknowable. Twice the narrator reminds us he can't really describe what he saw because his "chaster Muse" won't let him. Duessa's "filth" is ultimately "secret," too secret for "good manners" to tell. In its resistance to being fully described, Duessa's body resists being fully known. Where *Newes from Scotland* exhibits the violence that uncertainty begets, Spenser calls into question the very possibility of certainty itself.

If the examiners stage performances to make visible the invisible world of witchcraft, literary texts by Spenser, Marlowe, and Shakespeare "stage"—in a different way—the anxieties of the witch hunters and, in making them visible, imagine, test, and sort through them. Where Spenser exposes the fantasy of certainty as just that—a fantasy—and Marlowe in *Doctor Faustus* imagines in legal terms what it might be like to have a contract with the devil, *The Winter's Tale* stages the host of male anxieties about witchcraft that animate a text like *Daemonologie*. In Leontes, Shakespeare presents a figure who, like *Daemonologie* itself, vacillates between extremes of dogmatic insistence—imagining his wife has cheated—and the fear that it may be impossible to know anything at all.

This book is divided into two sections, one on treatises and one on literature. Beginning with *Malleus Maleficarum* and ending with Reginald Scot and King James VI and I, the first part offers a series of readings of four of the most influential and important demonological treatises of the period (as well as a pamphlet associated with one of them). In addition to their explicit subject matter (witchcraft), these texts reveal an evolving set of strategies for dealing with an imagined and malevolent "other." In *Malleus Maleficarum*, the inquisitors seek to manage the idea of this "other," the witch, with a set of counterperformances which they call "precautions," which bear striking similarities to the imagined witchcraft they are seeking to neutralize. In *Demonomanie*, Bodin expends considerable energy seeking to conceal from himself any such resemblances, specifically those between justice and the crime justice examines. In *The Discoverie of Witchcraft*, Reginald Scot (for whom the "witch-mongers" are themselves the imagined "other") exorcises any potential similarities between himself and those he attacks by repeating the charms and conjurations he says have no efficacy. In *Daemonologie*, where the imagined "other" is by turns the witch and by turns the skeptic, James shifts back and forth between a variety of different strategies to keep the doubt which characterizes the skeptic at bay, including the central strategy, I argue, of passing doubt, albeit a different kind of doubt, on to the reader. *Newes From Scotland*, the pamphlet which describes James's activities as a witch-hunter, shows what happens when such strategies for handling doubt—doubt in the sense of uncertainty, not in the sense of an active skepticism—break down and suggests the role doubt plays in the torture of defendants.

The second part of the book examines four major literary texts by Spenser, Marlowe, and Shakespeare. These are at once test cases for the claims made in the first half of the book and, perhaps more importantly, sustained meditations on the half-articulated needs and motives that animate the treatises. The literary texts themselves, some obvious candidates and some less so, are not chosen because they have witches in them—*Macbeth*, *The Witch of Edmonton*, and *Henry VI, Part 1* are all notably absent—but rather because in key ways they imagine "what if" situations that dramatize the premises at work in the treatises, testing and interrogating their implications: Does the spectacle of the witch's body really allow the viewer to "know" what the witch is (*The Faerie Queene*)? What are the legal considerations involved in a "contract" with the devil (*Doctor Faustus*)? What really happened at Endor (*The Winter's Tale*)? Is Prospero's magic circle efficacious (*The Tempest*)? My goal in examining these texts is not to establish whether Shakespeare, for instance, does or doesn't believe in witchcraft but rather to identify some of the "afterlives" or traces of the specific problems identified in the first half of the book. Stuart Clark has already begun a project of this kind in his essay on sight in *Macbeth*. Writing about the parallels between the witch of Endor story and *Macbeth*, he says that these have "long been realized in Shakespearean criticism though little seems to have been made of [them]" (242). What has been less attended to is the way plays less obviously about witchcraft take up questions at the heart of the Endor story, imagine variations, and test possible solutions.

Although the book consists of two sections, a guiding principle has been to look at the texts examined in each of those sections as if they were susceptible to the same kinds of analysis and warranted the same kind of attention to both contradiction and detail. Here, some background may be useful. In a seminal article on *Macbeth* in the early 1990s, Stephen Greenblatt approached *Malleus Maleficarum* in large part by way of a series of claims about an anecdote. In the process of explaining the way that in their attempt to reverse currents of "literate disbelief" in witchcraft and produce more than "grudging . . . compliance," and something more like "robust belief," Greenblatt argued that the inquisitors Kramer and Sprenger turned to "the evidence of narrative."[23] By "narrative" Greenblatt actually seemed to mean something more like "anecdote," and the particular anecdote that served as his example—about a man who, having lost his male member, went to a "certain known witch" to ask her to restore it—became in the wake of that article a virtual synecdoche for *Malleus Maleficarum* itself.

In contrast, in a pair of early articles which anticipate the methodology of his magisterial *Thinking with Demons*, Stuart Clark argued for an approach to demonological texts based on reading them through certain conventional features they shared with each other and with other texts "possibly extending beyond demonology itself."[24] The intention to persuade, Clark argued, "presupposes . . . a framework of shared meanings in which certain concepts and rules for applying them in argument have a *conventional* life" (99, emphasis mine). To avoid anachronism and "reductionism," the "range of meanings" we ascribe to a demonological text should be "limited," Clark argued, to this framework of shared meanings and the rhetorical features—features like inversion, contrariety, dual classification—that express them.

Both these approaches have revolutionized the field as we know it, to the point of being constitutive of it. Taken together, though, they raise a question about what it means to read—or at least close-read—a demonological text. If the assumption behind the use of the anecdote is one of synecdoche in which the part (the anecdote) stands for the whole (the treatise), the risk of the second approach is that one text begins to stand for another, leaving legible only convention, only what gets repeated from text to text. Focusing neither on individual anecdotes as units of meaning, as new historicist readings tended to, nor on the repetition of conventional material from treatise to treatise, but rather beginning with the contradictions themselves, I have sought to take seriously the call made by Walter Stephens in *Demon Lovers*, a book that reckons with both approaches, that we need to read demonological treatises "as carefully as we would novels or autobiographies, paying attention to their themes, their rhetorical strategies, their use of logic and their strategic silences."[25] It is to these texts with their strange silences I now turn.

# Chapter 1

# Judicial Procedure as Countermagic in *Malleus Maleficarum*

In the middle of part 3, question 16 of *Malleus Maleficarum*, the section on judicial procedure, the inquisitors Kramer and Sprenger spell out a kind of theatrical finale in which the judge manages to expose the witch as a witch. He is to cut the seven words Christ uttered on the cross in a kind of "schedule" (*cedula*) bound together for her to wear around her neck. And if he can do so "conveniently," he ought to cut blessed wax to the exact length of Christ's stature for the witch to wear against her naked body. Then after ensuring she is brought in backwards, with her back turned toward him—the witch dangling over the ground—he is supposed to read her the depositions of the informers, exclaiming, "See! You are convicted by the witnesses!" (Ecce, per testes coniucta es; 216B–C, 626). And if the witnesses are not afraid, they're supposed to be brought in and stand before her. So that she may be "shamed."[1]

There are a series of local questions one could ask of this scene: Why does the witch have to be brought in backwards? Why does she have to be suspended above the ground? Why is it suddenly permissible to reveal the names of the accusers, when a central tenet of judicial process until this point has been that the names of the informers and accusers must be kept secret? What are the exact benefits of the sartorial advice the examiners offer to future judges? But all of these questions can be subsumed into one larger question: Why do the inquisitors conceive of judicial procedure in such highly theatricalized terms? As a theatrical performance? In the pages which follow I consider three possible answers to this question. The first considers judicial theatricality as a series of tricks, in effect, bad-faith deceptions. The second explanation looks at the inquisitors' conception of judicial process as a response to a kind of "workload" problem—what they call the arduousness of examining witches. The third explanation, and the one I will be advocating, looks at judicial theatricality as a counterperformance. What I suggest in this chapter is that the inquisitors conceive of judicial process as a performance because they implicitly envision judicial process as compensatory—an attempt to neutralize the deeper and less visible performance of witchcraft itself.

Recent treatments of *Malleus Maleficarum* have touched on the "almost sacramental" or "counterdemonic" quality of a number of the precautions the inquisitors tell future judges to take.[2] I want to argue more broadly that the very logic of the judicial section of *Malleus Maleficarum* is compensatory and "antidotal." Far from being in any way exceptions to or aberrations from the rest of the book, these precautions represent extreme cases of the "logic" the inquisitors exhibit through their discussion of judicial procedure and thus provide a key to understanding many of the book's rhetorical strategies as well.[3]

## Judicial Theatricality as Bad Faith, a Set of Tricks

In a sense, the vision of the judge exclaiming "See! You are convicted by the witnesses!" to the dangling witch is simply one of several conceptions of judicial process as a kind of theater throughout the book. There are several ways in which the inquisitors conceive of judicial process as theater, and in a sense the easiest and least problematic to make sense of are those moments in which the inquisitors recommend what are basically theatrical tricks to elicit confessions or extract direct evidence from the accused. (Though there are local differences in tone and style, this kind of theatricality is roughly synonymous with some of what Foucault describes in *Discipline and Punish* when he describes "a whole casuistry of legal bad faith."[4]) Thus, in the context of advising judges what to do when they believe accused witches are holding back information, the inquisitors recommend bringing in the officers with cords and some engine of torture: "Let the judge order his assistants that she be bound with cords or attached to some other instruments of torture and let them obey right away but not with elation, rather as if distressed" (mandet ministris quod ad cordas ligetur vel ad alia instrumenta applicetur, et ibi statim obtemperent, non leti sed quasi turbati; question 15, 212A, 617). The point is to orchestrate a scene creating the illusion of sadness for the soul of the accused, a collective image of honest compassionate men, sorry to have to resort to such things to extract the truth.

Another trick is the ordeal of the red-hot iron, which is not an ordeal in the sense that the witch ever has to undergo it, but rather a trick to see if the witch is willing to undergo it. It is a well-known fact that devils always help witches who undergo the ordeal of the red-hot iron; therefore, the point is to invite the witch to undergo the ordeal, and if she offers to comply she has accused herself as a witch and thereby given evidence.

Or there is the "good friend who comes to prison" charade. In the context of a discussion on how to get a witch to confess, the inquisitors recommend putting her in prison for a year or more "in case depressed by the squalor of prison she may come to confess her crimes" (si forte post annum squaloribus carceris depressa crimina fateretur; question 7, 202D, 598). But if this should fail, judges are advised to send a friend to visit her, some trustworthy person—though not an accomplice—who is to show up at night, encourage her to unburden herself, and then discover he has missed the last piece of transportation home and must spend the night with her in her cell. The judge is to plant spies outside, and if the "friend" or "trustworthy person" is successful in getting her to confess to harming men and animals, he is urged to go on to ask her about incubus devils.

Finally, there is the voyage-to-a-far-off-castle trick. The examiners recommend taking a recalcitrant witch to a far-off castle or stronghold for safekeeping. There the witch must be told that the castellan, the keeper of the castle, is leaving to go to some remote place, though in reality he remains on the premises. In the meantime, the women of the castle are to approach and offer to release her if she will teach them secret arts. One witch cornered this way in the Diocese of Strasburg rightly feared entrapment, but she asked the informants what it was they wanted to know. One wanted to know how to raise a hailstorm and another about "carnal matters." When the accused witch agreed to show them how to raise a hailstorm by bringing in a bowl of water and said to stir the water a little with a finger, a hailstorm arose over the wood near the castle and the witch was convicted by the evidence. Here, then, an elaborate scene is staged requiring transport to a castle, a feigning castellan, and women to play the role of apprentice witches. That is, judicial theatricality is simply in the service of extracting evidence, of publishing the crime. It is itself a bad-faith trick.

In a sense, though, these scenes of explicit deception are the easiest to explain. They are (variously) in the service of a) extracting a confession, b) obtaining direct or indirect evidence, or c) disqualifying the witch's ability to claim that someone who testifies against her is a mortal enemy. But what the notion of judicial theatricality as a trick or deception will not explain is a much deeper and more profound vision of judicial process as performance which is implicit in the text. At the center of *Malleus* is the belief that if you could script the perfect performance and choreograph the exact details of a trial, you could avoid error and arrive at certainty itself.

## Workload

There are a number of ways in which this faith expresses itself in, for instance, the very titles to sections, many of which are formulated as instructions to future agents: "The 20th question: On the first method of pronouncing a sentence" (QUESTIO VICESIMA: SUPER PRIMUM MODUM SENTENTIANDI; 224D, 641) or "The 21st question: On the second method of pronouncing a sentence when the accused is only defamed" (QUESTIO XXI: SUPER SECUNDUM MODUM SENTENTIANDI DELATAM ET TANTUMMODO DIFFAMATAM; 225D, 643). In one sense, of course, these are not methods for pronouncing words in the way we might envision literal instructions to an actor, but in another they prescribe the conditions for legal speech, the conditions which must be met for the speech to occur. The vision of judicial procedure as a carefully scripted performance expresses itself in other ways as well. The chapters of the text are themselves conceived of in theatrical terms as "actions" or scenes: "General Questions for the Witch or the Wizard (and it is the first action)" (Interrogatoria generalia super maleficam aut maleficum [et est primus actus]; 200D, 593) or "Whether the witch should be incarcerated and how to take her (and this is the Judge's third action)" (AN SIT INCARCERANDA, ET DE MODO CAPIENDI [ET EST ACTUS TERCIUS IUDICIS]; 203A, 598).[5]

But in a much deeper way, the inquisitors conceive of judicial process as a performance in the sense that, quite literally, a large portion of the book consists of a set of scripts, lists of questions the future judge must ask the witness or accused. The inquisitors specify the exact script of questions that a judge must ask of a witness: for example, if he knew the accused and how long, what the accused's reputation is, whether he knows this by report or has witnessed actions directly, were the accused's kindred ever burned? And when the accused speaks, what does the witness think is the intention behind those words? And is the witness saying anything out of hatred or rancor or suppressing anything out of favor or love?

Similarly, there is an exact script of questions the judge *must* ask the accused, both a script of general questions and a script of "particular" ones. Thus the judge *must* ask the accused where he is from originally and who his parents are and whether they are alive or dead—and, by the way, did they die a natural death, or were they maybe burned? And where was the accused brought up and why did he move from his birthplace and whether he's ever heard any talk of witches—for example tempests, bewitching cattle, depriving cows of their milk, that sort of thing. And if the accused admits to hearing of such things, he must be asked exactly what he has heard, and if he says he has heard nothing, then he must be asked whether he believes there are witches. And if he says no, the accused must be asked, "Why then when they are burned, are they then condemned though innocent?" (Quid ergo vbi comburuntur: tunc innocenter condemnantur?; 201B, 595). This is the script of questions that the judge *must* ask the accused in a general examination. And a similar script exists which he must follow for the particular examination.

Similarly, there is a list of characters who must be present for the questions to be asked, and a list of rules about who can and must be part of this performance. After establishing who may bear witness against a witch—the answer is just about everyone: convicted perjurers, criminals, family (but only if they're testifying against, not for), disgruntled servants in search of promotion; anyone but a mortal enemy, that is, an enemy who can be proven to have made a prior attempt on the witch's life—the inquisitors itemize who *must* be present at the examination of a witness. At least five persons should be present: the inquiring judge, of course; the witness, whether the denouncing or responding one, or the accused who appears later; a notary (or a scribe when the notary is lacking, and joined to him another honest man, which two take the place of the notary); and two respectable men as witnesses (Adminus persone quinque debent presentes esse, scilicet iudex inquirens, testis vel denunicans respondens vel ipse delatus postea comparens, tertius est notarius [seu scriptor vbi deest notarius, et tunc adiungat sibi alium honestum qui duo supplebunt vices notarij] . . . et duo honesti viri tanquam testes; 200C, 592). Just as the book hands down a set of scripts for future behavior, it hands down a list of parts that must be played. One might dismiss all these scripts as mere courtroom procedure, but to do so would be to miss at least two key rhetorical features of the book: the feature of repetition and the particular moments at which exceptions to these rules occur.

What the judicial-procedure-as-theatrical-trick approach will not explain is this deeper faith in the ability to script an airtight performance, the ability to choreograph a future hypothetical trial. In one sense there is an available explanation for this. One clue lies in the preface to part 3 of the book, which asks in effect who are the proper judges in the trial of witches. The inquisitors make it quite clear that the answer is, categorically, not "inquisitors." Inquisitors were put on earth for higher purposes, which is to say, for the examination of heretics, and though the rest of the book often treats heresy and witchcraft as interchangeable, the inquisitors insist in the preface to part

3 that they are not the same and need not coincide.⁶ Just as not every adulterer is a heretic, unless he or she additionally believes that adultery is lawful, so not every witch who stomps on the body of Christ or baptizes images is a heretic unless she (or he) does so believing that stomping on the body of Christ is lawful or that baptizing images is efficacious. Inquisitors were put on earth to examine heretics, not witches, and unless it can be indisputably proved that a witch is also a heretic, inquisitors should not have to be bothered with them. Kramer and Sprenger are quite explicit about this being a workload problem. The clearest statement of the purpose of the book comes at the beginning of book 3:

> Our principal intention in this work is, as much as God may permit . . . to free from the examination of witches ourselves, the inquisitors of the regions of upper Germany, leaving the punishment to their judges, and this on account of the difficulty of the work.
>
> (Cum principalis intentio nostra in hoc opere sit ab inquisitione maleficarum, quantum cum deo fieri posset, nos inquisitores partium superioris Almanie exonerare suis iudicibus ad puniendum relinquendo, et hoc propter negocij arduitatem.) (186B, 562)

Looked at from the standpoint of workload, then, the obsession with creating an airtight script makes a certain amount of sense. If you are trying to control the outcome of a trial without actually having to be there yourself, then the tighter the script is that binds future judges to your wishes, the more you have exactly defined the behaviors and actions and words they will have to conform to, and the closer you have come to controlling the process without actually having to take any personal responsibility.⁷

This workload explanation, which is really an explanation about control, would have the advantage of explaining another peculiarity of the text as well, which is the way it is actually unable to successfully envision the performance it is in the process of scripting because of the way this future performance repeatedly degenerates into a vision of a series of written documents and texts—not the performance itself, but the textual traces and props of one. Thus, at least four times during the first question alone, the inquisitors, while describing what future judges must do, get distracted, and what begins as a prescription for a future set of behaviors degenerates into the description of a series of hypothetical texts. Thus, in the process of describing the various ways that judges can initiate a process, the inquisitors become sidetracked by describing the citation the judge must fasten to the parish wall to call witnesses to the scene. In the process of describing the citation itself, they become sidetracked in describing the authority for the words in the citation, the canon itself. In the process of describing how the witnesses must be questioned and who must be there to witness them being questioned, the inquisitors get derailed into imagining the hypothetical text of the deposition which the notary will have to write down. My favorite instance of a text intruding on a future set of actions (favorite because of how redundant it is) is that, after providing an exact script of the questions that the judge must ask a deponent—how he knows that his depositions are his, whether he only heard about or saw that which he swears, who else was there—the inquisitors repeat these questions, the ones they have just itemized and stipulated that the judge must ask, as a hypothetical text:

> And the notary or scribe shall set down everything in the record . . . continuing thus . . . the judge . . . did ask him how and in what way he knew or suspected to be true those things which he reported.
> (Et notarius seu scriptor ponat totum in actis . . . continuando sic . . . interrogauit eundem, vnde et quomodo ea que denunciauerat nouerat vel suspicionem habeat esse vera.) (196A–B, 582)

What is striking about this is that the repetition of the questions the judge must ask, *as a text, envisioned as a future document in the hands of a notary*, is almost identical in content to what has come before. And this becomes the pattern of the book, first to identify the script of questions a judge must ask and then to envision it, repeat it almost verbatim, as a hypothetical text the notary will have written down. This oddity, this feature of *Malleus Maleficarum*, makes some sense as well from a workload point of view, which is, of course, really a control point of view. If you are trying to control the outcome of a future trial, enacted by actors whose identities and proclivities you cannot imagine, collecting depositions whose content you cannot predict, written scripts offer a certain consolation, a stabilizing fantasy or illusion of security, for they allow you to focus on the imagined document, the thing or object produced by the trial, rather than on the element of unpredictability implicit in the trial itself.

But this will still not explain the enormity of the faith in these scripts, the almost talismanic belief the inquisitors seem to have in their ability to avoid error. In describing the persons who must be present for a witness to be questioned, for instance, the inquisitors specify that when no notary can be found, the scribe "must join [with] him another honest man" (et tunc adiungat sibi alium honestum; 200C, 592) who will fill in for the notary. But it is not just a procedural nicety that these persons must be present, but rather an insurance or guarantee against the possibility of error itself. That no error may be produced, the inquisitors say here,[8] "two honest people, whether clerics or laymen, must be there" (duas honestas personas siue sint clerici siue layci; 195C,

581). What neither a "tricks" nor a "workload" approach to theatricality in this text will explain is the intensity of the faith in performance.

What is at stake here is more than a practice. Rather, it is an almost magical belief that the enactment of a given performance will avoid error, ensure truth. That the belief in this enactment is almost magical is implicit in the kinds of verbal formulas the inquisitors adopt. Describing the citation that a judge who initiates a process must post on the parish wall, the inquisitors say he must, in his threat to excommunicate any witnesses who will not come forward, specifically say:

> By the authority which we execute . . . in virtue of holy obedience and under the penalty of excommunication, we order and command and in commanding require and admonish, that in the space of 12 days counting from now . . . [witnesses come forward].
>
> (["autoritate qua fungimur . . . in virtutem sancte obedientie, ac sub pena excommunicationis"] precipimus et mandamus ac mandando requirimus et monemus quatenus infra xij dies proxime computandos.) (195A, 580)

I am trying to imagine in what mental universe the verbs "order," "command," "require," and "admonish" would have substantially different enough meanings to each have to be separately articulated. For it is as if the examiners must exhaust every nuance of difference, must anticipate every possible contingency that could lead to an adverse outcome in order to ward off the consequences they fear. This is a mental landscape in which the universe is perceived as so uncontrollable and so malevolent that the inquisitors must always anticipate anything that could elude their control. The words "direct," "command," "require," and "admonish" are not substantially different in a referential way. But this is no longer a referential universe or referential use of language; rather it is an incantatory one, one where language is being invoked not for what it means but for what it can accomplish simply by being uttered. It is in this sense that the faith the inquisitors betray in performance is an almost magical one. What neither a "bad-faith tricks" explanation of inquisitorial theatricality nor a workload explanation—that is, an explanation based on the attempt to control future judges and witnesses—will explain is this faith itself.

What will explain such a faith in performance? What I'm going to suggest is that if we turn to the moments in the text in which the faith in performance is at its most compulsive, its most inaccessible and ritualistic, they will yield a kind of explanation. By looking at those moments when performance seems stretched to its limits, we will see the principle at work in judicial theatricality itself.

## Precautions and Counterperformance

Performance in *Malleus Maleficarum* is at its most stretched and unfathomable and certainly at its most compulsive when the inquisitors describe certain "precautions," certain highly theatricalized procedures that judges must enact. These precautions, most of which are at least as theatrical as the witch in her wax and "schedule," include capturing a witch on a plank or in a basket so her feet don't touch the ground, carrying her backwards into court in a basket, conjuring her (with great ceremony) to cry, shaving her, stripping her, and searching her. They are great displays in their own right, but what is perhaps more striking about them is the moments at which they arise in the text. For they arise at moments when the inquisitors seem on the verge of ideas which have the potential to threaten the whole judicial enterprise itself.

Bizarrely, there are a number of odd moments in the text in which the inquisitors seem about to acknowledge fundamental ambiguities—about language, about deeds, about human choice—which if taken in isolation might make the scripts they spend so much energy designing somewhat irrelevant. In the context of a discussion on how to interrogate a witness, for instance, the inquisitors specify that the witness must be asked very carefully how he could distinguish the accused's motive. He must be "asked if it seemed to him that such a person said or did these things jokingly or sarcastically or idly or whether he said things assertively or with deliberate purpose" (Jtem interrogatus si videtur sibi quod Talis dixerit seu fecerit trufatorie seu recitatorie seu animo indeliberato vel potius assertiue et animo deliberato; 200B, 592). The inquisitors say:

> It is very important to inquire carefully into these things because sometimes people say things citing the words of others or jokingly or in the course of a conversation in order to draw other people out or test them. But sometimes they say things assertively and affirmatively.
>
> (Et de istis est multum diligenter inquirendum, quia nonnunquam dicunt aliqui recitando aliorum verba vel trufando vel conferendo vt alios alliciant vel incitent, licet etiam interdum asserendo vel affirmando.)
> (200B, 592)

The discussion hovers around the recognition that words cannot always be fixed in their meaning. If taken at face value, such an insight would threaten the structure of judicial confession by suggesting the impossibility of reducing words to a strictly true-false axis. The insight cannot be taken in isolation, of course, but perhaps more threatening to the procedure the inquisitors prescribe is the commonplace that deeds—or at least the deeds of witches—are fundamentally undemonstrable. In the context of a discussion on the various ways to initiate a process, the inquisitors advise against the method of initiating a process which involves having an accuser come forward and offer to make good his accusations. The judge should avoid this method of initiating an action, the inquisitors say, because "the deeds of witches are hidden by the work of devils" (maleficarum facta opere demonum occultantur) nor is the accuser able (as in other crimes) to defend himself through direct evidence (euidentiam facti; 199C, 590).[9]

Taken in isolation, the force of this statement would be to expose the fundamental *undemonstrability* of witchcraft and would undermine the whole judicial process itself. For if, like words being ambiguous, actions were really undemonstrable, there would be little point in trying to establish their existence.

But perhaps most threatening to the series of scripts the examiners are trying to construct is the momentary acknowledgment that maybe judges should ignore scripts in the first place. In the context of describing what a judge who thinks a witch is holding back information should do, the inquisitors, in a startling lapse of procedure, suggest he should appeal to his own experience. "Just as there is no one cure for all diseases . . ." (quod sicut non omnium morborum est eadem medicina . . . ; 213A, 619), no single "infallible rule can be described for extracting the silence of a witch" who won't confess (quam tactiturnitatem euellere non potest vna et infallibilis depingi regula; 213B, 619–20). The prudent judge will rather appeal to his own experience.[10] In other words, the inquisitors seem to allow for an unscripted moment. Taken in isolation, this claim wouldn't invalidate the structure of judicial confession, but it would render somewhat extraneous and irrelevant the scripts, the codified performances the inquisitors have been trying to construct. If judges should appeal to their own expertise or the particulars of a given situation, the elaborate scripts that the inquisitors have designed to bind future judges and witnesses to their wills are more or less beside the point.

But just at the moment that the inquisitors are on the verge of acknowledging the value of choice or freedom or unscriptedness, they draw back from this recognition and add a caveat. The judge should appeal to his own experience as long as he obeys the following precautions. These "precautions" are sets of highly stylized codified and theatrical prescriptions for behavior, among the most theatrical in the book. I will describe these precautions in a moment, but there are two points I am trying to make here. The first is that it is exactly at the moment that the inquisitors seem to be acknowledging the possibility of some sort of fundamental ambiguity to language, to deeds, to human choice, some sort of fundamental unknowability about language, about deeds, about methods, that they draw back from this acknowledgment and produce the most airtight script in the book. My second point is that it is precisely this script, this set of highly theatricalized precautions that the inquisitors introduce which cannot be explained either in terms of simple trickery or workload problems, that will shed some light on the faith in judicial theatricality itself.

The most overtly theatrical precaution that the inquisitors prescribe is the precaution of carrying the witch into court backwards. If it can be done "conveniently" (*commode*), the witch "should be brought in backwards, with her back turned towards the judges and the assessors" (Et si commode fieri potest, ipsa a tergo dorsum vertendo ad iudices et assessores introducatur; 214B, 622). "Nor should anyone think bringing her backwards is superstitious" (Nec quis estimat superstitiosum vt a tergo introducatur; 214C, 622). Why must the witch be led in backwards?[11] Not only must judges make sure not to be touched by witches, "particularly on the naked wrist" (presertim super nudam iuncturam manuum et brachiorum; 214A, 621), and not only must they protect themselves from the sound of the witch's voice, for "sometimes through touch or sight or even the sound of the words they speak they are able (by the works of devils)" to bewitch the judges (interdum per tactum, aliquando per visum aut per auditum verborum ab eis prolatorum maleficiare operatione demonum possunt; 214A, 621), but judges must at all costs avoid the witch's gaze, which is imagined to have a constitutive power over the mind of the judge and therefore over the verdict itself. The inquisitors say:

> We know that certain witches detained in castles begged with the most pressing prayers nothing other from the castellan than that at the arrival of the judge or the others presiding they be allowed to direct their first gaze at the judge before they were seen by him or the others, from which gaze such a judge or his other assessors were so alienated in their hearts that they have lost all indignation if they had any, nor presumed to vex the witches but allowed them to go free.
>
> (nouimus quasdam in castris detentas que nil aliud a castellanis instantissimis precibus flagitabant nisi vt in aduentu iudicis aut alterius presidentis eis concederetur vt primum intuitum visus in ipsum iudicem dirigere possent, antequam ab eo vel alijs essent vise, ex quo intuitu etiam sortite quod talis iudex aut alij sui assessores ita alienati in eorum cordibus fuerunt quod omnem si quam habuerant indignationem ammiserunt, nec ipsas molestare quoquo modo presumebant, sed libere abire permiserunt.) (214A–B, 621)

If even the look of the witch is imagined to have a constitutive power over the judge's mind, then of course the witch will have to be led backwards into the presence of the judge and the assessors. This example reveals openly, then, the principle that other precautions are built on. The precaution is an antidote, a kind of countermeasure or countermagic to the witch's power, and if this is so, it allows us to see the other "precautions"—the ones that resist explanation as mere tricks or workload problems—as countermagical in the same way. It suggests that if we want to explain the most obscure kinds of theatricality in the book, we need to adopt the principle that the theatricality is the antidote—the symmetrical opposite of and countermeasure to what it is designed to combat.

One of the most theatrical precautions the judge is advised to adopt is the shaving of the witch. Ostensibly the reasons for shaving the witch are the same as the reasons for stripping her and searching her house. Witches carry magical instruments that give them the power of taciturnity, the power to resist confession. Their houses and clothing and bodies need to be searched for such instruments, which can be hidden in corners, stuffed into clothes, or sewn into the hair of the armpits or genitals. In Ratisbon, a whole coven of witches was convicted by their own confession but would neither burn nor drown. People began to worry that perhaps they might be innocent, and the bishop, concerned for his flock, ordered a three-day fast which revealed a magical charm sewed between the skin and the flesh of one witch's arm. When it was removed, they all burned. Ostensibly, stripping and shaving are only the logical extension of searching a house: the making open of what is closed and impenetrable, in order to yield up the "thing" in which the power for silence is invested. But if we apply the principle that the theatrical action mirrors and neutralizes the power the witch is imagined to have, searching, stripping, and shaving take on a different meaning. For if the witch's gaze is imagined to be so powerful that it can reconstitute the mind of the judge, then stripping and shaving restore to the inquisitorial court the power of being the looker rather than the thing looked at and make the witch back into the object of the gaze.[12]

But how will any of this help explain the obsession the inquisitors register with creating the perfect script for the judge? How will it help explain the obsession with framing each detail down to the way he articulates a question or frames a sentence? If we think of the "precautions" that judges are supposed to adopt as specifically and symmetrically designed to neutralize given actions of witches, the obsession with inquisitorial scripts and their articulation makes perfect sense. There is nothing new about saying that one of the deepest powers the witch is understood to have is the power to curse. Or, differently put, the witch is imagined (with the help of the devil) to wield a language that is fully and at all times performative, capable of effecting as material change in the physical universe the wish it embodies. Thus, in one of the commonest kinds of anecdotes in the literature of witchcraft, but interestingly, one of the few anecdotes told at all in the judicial section of *Malleus*, the inquisitors tell the story of a certain "honest man" of Spires who would not come to an agreement with a woman (subsequently accused as a witch) over an article for sale. She angrily calls after him, "Soon you'll wish you had agreed" (Jn breui optasses vt annuisses; 210B, 613). He looks over his shoulder to see her, and his mouth is stretched so "that he could not draw it back" (nec retrahere potuit). He remains in this deformed state "a long time" (multo tempore; 210B, 613). For the inquisitors, this is direct evidence of witchcraft, the evident "deed exposed (made known) before the judge" (Hic euidens factum iudici proponitur; 210B, 613), and in fact, had the consequence followed "not so suddenly" (non ita subito; 210C, 613) "but some time after the witches' threats" (sed processu temporis illatis, per minas tamen etiam precedentes; 210C, 613), it would still have constituted a kind of evidence, though a more indirect kind.

The assumption here—less a theological point than an unacknowledged fear—is that language is performative, capable of bringing about a change in the material world.[13] This is implicit as well in what the inquisitors have to say about what is called the "second line of defense" for the witch's lawyer. If he admits that the witch said what she is accused of saying, but argues that the words didn't cause the harm that they are being said to cause (the deformed face, the cow who won't milk, the sick child), the judge is to tell him that if he can prove the existence of natural causes, fine, but if he cannot, the default assumption is that the charge holds and the witch is responsible. The default assumption is, in effect, that language is performative, is *always* performative, when one accused of witchcraft has spoken.[14]

From this point of view, the inquisitors' obsession with choreographing the perfect script, the perfect articulation of speech for future judges, makes sense, for they seek to create a judicial language, a speech that neutralizes and stabilizes the language of the witch. They seek to stabilize the witch's performativity. From this point of view, the meaning of judicial theatricality becomes clear as compensatory and recuperative, not simply a series of tricks or a response to workload or a way of controlling future unknown judges but a way of creating a counterperformance to the deeper and more invisible theatricality of witchcraft itself.

Under what circumstances might a demonologist with an interest in judicial procedure be prepared to relinquish such a script or relinquish such theatrical procedures? These questions are the subject of the next chapter.

CHAPTER 2

# Broken Epistemologies
## Bodin and the Repudiation of Spectacle

Toward the end of book 4 of his book on witchcraft, *De la Demonomanie des Sorciers*, Jean Bodin, after describing the elaborate rules of evidence a judge has to submit in order to prove a suspect is a witch, reneges and says that everything hinges on the discretion of the judge (Tout cela depend de la discretion d'un Juge prudent et bien entendu; 214r).[1] The skilled judge must combine all the clues to register the truth, provided he doesn't behave like so many judges in Germany do, "who seek other witches to make sieves jump in order to learn whether the accused is a witch" (qui cherchent d'autres Sorciers qui font danser les tamis, pour savoir si celui qui est accusé est Sorcier; 215r). The skilled judge neither seeks a theatrical display nor tries to recreate the witchcraft he is trying to prove exists. He does not, for instance, employ children to smear shoes with pigs' grease in church—apparently a popular custom for almost literally sniffing out witches. Nor does he tie the witch's hands and feet up and throw her in water to see if she sinks. He disdains spectacles, especially spectacles that are in any way like the witchcraft he examines, for in turning to such spectacles he allows "the devil to make a sorcery of justice which ought to be holy" (Car le Diable faict par ce moyen une Sorcellerie de la Justice, qui doibt estre sacree; 215r).

The moment is an extremely unusual one, both in the context of Bodin's own book and, even more importantly, in the broader context of treatises and pamphlet accounts about witch trials during the period. For if contemporary accounts of witch trials during the period tell us anything, they tell us that the model trial was a spectacle. The author of the sixteenth-century pamphlet *Newes from Scotland* describes two performances that King James VI and I witnessed: that of Geillis Duncane, who plays on a "iewes trumpe" for the court the music she played when she sailed out to sea in a sieve to meet the devil, and that of a male conjuror, John Cunningham, also known as Doctor Fian, who reenacts before the court a whole demonic possession, throwing a man into a trance to the "great admiration of his Maiestie."[2] Almost a hundred years earlier, as we have just seen, the inquisitors Kramer and Sprenger construct a different kind of performance for future judges trying to extract confessions.

Bodin's explicit censure of this kind of spectacle, then, is unusual enough that it raises a pair of questions. First, what is it that allows Bodin to relinquish the notion of a spectacular trial?[3] And second, given Bodin's zeal for putting to death those accused of witchcraft, what is it that allows him to admit even the hypothetical possibility of justice becoming uncomfortably like the crime it examines?[4] Bodin is not in any way tolerant when it comes to witches. But his warning that justice can become a kind of sorcery raises the broader question of under what circumstances justice can even hypothetically see the possible resemblance between itself and what it examines. In this chapter I consider three possible reasons for why Bodin might be able to forfeit a spectacular trial and then return to the broader question of what might allow justice to consider the similarities between itself and what it examines.

## Barbaric Words

In theory, Bodin might be able to relinquish a highly theatrical trial, a trial that sought to reproduce the crime before spectators, if he thought of witchcraft itself as something that just wasn't susceptible to being "acted out" or performed. If witchcraft were undemonstrable, Bodin's suspension of theatricality at a trial would be a predictable reflection of his conception of the crime.[5] But, in fact, there are a variety of ways in which he describes witchcraft as specifically theatrical. In an extraordinary set of passages in book 2, Bodin associates witchcraft with dance. At nocturnal sabbaths, one husband reports, witches are accustomed to dance in a circle facing outward rather than inward, so that they can't see each other and won't be able to turn each other in when they are investigated in the morning. In another description, Bodin virtually defines witchcraft as dance and dance as witchcraft. The description is of the volta, a dance brought from Italy which is characterized not only by "indecent movements" (mouvemens insolens, et impudiques; 98v) but by the tendency to cause spontaneous abortions in women and murder in men. There is no assembly where witches do not dance, Bodin says (98r). It is the highest matter for the state to prohibit such things (or at least to teach everyone to dance more slowly the way they do in Germany).

In Geneva, where the state takes such issues very seriously, Satan responded to a prohibition against dance by teaching a girl to dance in a way that made anyone she touched jump and exhibit a St. Vitus–like disease. The prohibition against dance in these anecdotes is so clearly a prohibition against witchcraft and vice versa that it suggests in a crude way the anti-theatrical bias operative in this book, the way that witchcraft is an implicitly theatrical phenomenon. There are other ways in which the text conceives of witchcraft in vaguely theatrical terms. In book 3, the witch Trois-eschelles, who passes in and out of the discussion, is a good illusionist. Later in the book, there is a rhyming blasphemer. But by far the deepest and most intense conception of witchcraft as theatrical lies in Bodin's conception of language, language as it operates both in the witch's capacity to curse and in the formulas and symbols of witchcraft. This is a conception of words as "performative," to use J. L. Austin's term—but one that goes beyond Austin's conception in its fear of words as things that behave and act and precipitate catastrophes out in the universe.[6]

When I say that Bodin holds a conception of language as "performative" I should say right away that Bodin energetically denies he thinks this, and it is in fact the belief he most energetically attacks when he sees it in others. From the very beginning, *Demonomanie* is striking for its articulated belief that words have no performative power, its insistence that language is referential, that words "mean," they do not "do."[7] Bodin tells the story of another sieve-mover, a Parisian witch who made a sieve jump ostensibly just by reading a series of words. But the proof, Bodin says, that the words themselves didn't really make the sieve jump and that the power lay instead in the presence of the devil was that when someone else recited the very same words, he failed. Witches often try to make us believe that words alone can work magic as part of the snare they use to draw us in. But this is just "demonic trickery which spirits use to trick the ignorant" (une piperie Diabolique, de laquelle les malins esprits ont accoustumé d'user, pour attraper les ignoras; 59v). It is a trickery which typifies witch defenders as well. Thus Johann Weyer *purports* to hate the symbols of magic but then perversely reveals them to his readers, an atrocity which even his master, Agrippa, wouldn't have dared to perpetrate. Pico della Mirandola, especially, offends Bodin by claiming that the "barbaric and meaningless words" (les paroles Barbares, et non signifcatives; 59v) in magical formulas "have *more* power than those that mean something" (ont plus de puissance, que celles qui signifient quelque chose; emphasis mine, 59v).

Bodin wants to reveal what he calls the "impostures" in this kind of thinking—in Pico's aim to work magic through the force of letters and symbols and Agrippa's belief in the efficacy of meaningless and barbaric words. What really enrages Bodin is the idea that these meaningless words could have *more* power than meaningful (i.e., referential) ones, the idea that "barbaric and incomprehensible words" (les mots barbares, et non entendus) "in magic have more power than those that are understood" (plus de puissance en la Magie, que ceux qui sont entendus; 59v). In other words, he explicitly asserts that words are *more* referential, more inclined to mean, than they are performative, inclined to behave. And this is not just a claim he makes about words, but about images as well. Those who believe that representations can work magic are as deluded as those who think that diabolical formulas can. In relation to "codpiece-tying," the traditional art of tying the strings of a man's underwear to produce impotence, Bodin says that "neither the words nor the codpiece string do anything" (les paroles ny les esguillettes n'y font rien) but that it is all due to the "artifice et malice" of the Devil (63v). In claiming that it's not the image (the codpiece as a representation of the male genitalia) that has the effect but the devil, Bodin insists on not only a referential theory of words—language in the narrowest sense—but a referential theory of images and figures. What does not "mean" has no power. It doesn't behave. It doesn't alter.

But even as Bodin intensely asserts this position, he belies it in his own behavior. This is most clear in his simple terror of repeating any of the words which are supposed to lack power. Even as he is insisting that the words of diabolical formulas have no power, he is afraid to repeat them. Even as he is insisting in effect that language is referential, he behaves as if it were performative. Describing the various ways that witchcraft imitates religion, Bodin is striking for his fear of writing down and repeating those things which are supposed to be harmless. He attacks the "protector of witches" (protecteur des sorciers) for drawing the "circles and detestable symbols" (cercles, et caracteres detestables) "*that I shall not write down*" (que ie ne mettray point; emphasis mine, 19r). He talks about those who, "to achieve something else *which I shall not say*" (parvenir à quelque autre chose que ie ne mettray point; emphasis mine, 19r), write out four sheets of parchment (19r–v). He alludes to "other wickednesses that *I shall not name*" (autres meschancetez, que ie n'escriray point; emphasis mine, 19v) for which they repeat the 108th Psalm. He alludes to Germans who wear what he calls the "shirt of necessity made in a detestable way it is *not necessary to name*" (la chemise de Necessité faicte d'une façon detestable, qu'il n'est besoin d'escrire; emphasis mine, 19v).

Not only is Bodin afraid to name and repeat the practices that these witches and their defenders employ, the words used to make the sieve jump "which I shall not put down" (que ie ne mettraie point), he is afraid to name the witches and their defenders themselves. Thus he lambastes the Master Sorcerer "who does not need to be named" (qui ne merite d'estre nomé; 19v) and "the great doctor in the diabolical art whom *I shall not name*" (du grand Docteur en l'art Diabolique, que ie ne nommeray point; emphasis mine, 56r). If words have no power to effect terrible consequences simply by being uttered, why is Bodin so afraid to repeat them?

In one sense there is an obvious answer to this question, and Bodin is quite explicit about it. At the beginning of book 2 he identifies the central dilemma of the book: How do you expose the practices of witchcraft without inadvertently teaching them to others? He wants, he says, to expose the practices of witchcraft (described as "les moyens qui sont illicites") "as soberly as possible" (le plus sobrement que fere se pourra) for the sake of future judges (58v). But how do you expose such practices without inadvertently teaching them? For to show "the words and practices one has to use" (les moyens, les parolles, desquelles il faut user) is "to teach what ought to be buried in oblivion" (ce seroit enseigner, ce qu'il faut ensevelir d'une eternelle oubliance; 58v). Bodin is therefore always in the situation of having to compromise that which he would reveal: "This is why I have as much as possible covered and hidden what should be buried in oblivion" (C'est pourquoy i'ay le plus, qu'il m'a este possible, couvert et caché, ce qu'il faut ensevelir d'oubliance; 59r). His announced solution to the problem is to write down *only what has been written down before* in the form of existing trials and written records, as if the writtenness of the words, and their place in the genre of historical record, would rob them of their dangerous power: "I will write down what I have read about *in writing* or from trial records" (ie mettray quelque chose par escrit de ce que I'en ay leu par escrit, ou és procez qui se sont presentez; emphasis mine, 58v). Like the inquisitors who turn to scripts to stabilize future unpredictable actors, speakers, and events, Bodin takes refuge in the idea that drawing only on what is written, and written as a *record*, will protect him from replicating what he attacks and fears.

## Codpiece-Tying in Poitiers

But the fear of teaching these practices cannot be all that keeps Bodin from repeating the words and names which he says have no power. And the evidence for this is that he glamorizes a teaching relationship with a mysterious woman who knew more than all the doctors and philosophers did and taught him many of the secrets of witchcraft. If it were really the fear of teaching the practices that he is trying to criminalize that made Bodin so afraid of repeating the formulas of witchcraft, he would not be so quick to glamorize the woman who taught him so many interesting practices and facts. No sooner has he announced his intention of sticking only to what has already been entered into the historical record, than he undermines this strategy in his evocation of this murky woman who taught him so much, a hostess he stayed with while serving as a substitute prosecutor in Poitiers.

Bodin and a clerk were hard at work investigating a series of difficult cases of "codpiece-tying," the traditional art of tying a codpiece string to make a man impotent. After a few introductory comments on the despicable frequency of the crime—even children do it; even children who have no knowledge of witchcraft; a child was once seen doing it in church, right in the middle of a wedding ceremony—Bodin warms to his theme, which is the skill and expertise of a local hostess at the inn at which he and the clerk are staying. Not only is she rich in expertise ("fort sçavante"; 62v) about codpiece-tying (she knows more than all the doctors who have written on the subject) but she is a fount of colorful stories, many of which Bodin repeats, his fear of passing on secrets operating, apparently, in a selective fashion. The hostess knows, for instance, of many ways to tie a codpiece: in order to afflict for a lifetime or for only a year, before or after marriage, to only one partner or both, to prevent procreation or only copulation or even urination. She tells him a story, which he repeats in lurid detail, about a man who nearly died because his codpiece was tied and he couldn't urinate. Then the witch who tied it untied it in public in order to shame him.

Or there is the story of the couple from Toulouse who came together each night to make love and clawed each other to bits, an illustration of the principle that both partners can still love each other and yet be afflicted. Perhaps most graphically there is the image of the codpiece with boils on it, each boil reflecting the life of an uncreated child. As Bodin grows more animated, his writing gets more detailed, more graphic, more anecdotal, more imagistic. He repeats, that is, not for the historical record, but out of a fascination with the material for its own sake. This is not, admittedly, repetition in the service of incantation or charm; but it is not quite mere archive or record or proof either. It is not in a deliberate way performative, but it is not quite inert description either. In a telling passage later in the book, Bodin raises the question of how the intention behind an utterance affects its propriety. Is it, he wonders, okay to recite part of a psalm and to utilize its holy properties, for the purposes of waking up early in the morning? He concludes that it is not, because the "force" or intention behind the repetition is not what it ought to be. In his reminiscence of the hostess at Poitiers, the "force" or intention is not simply to prove that witches exist and that they should be punished, but rather to *recall* in an almost literal way, or bring back, precisely the kind of relationship he is supposed to be attacking—that of a female expert on witchcraft passing down secrets, practical tips, to a male apprentice or novice. In one edition of the book she even tells him what kind and color of leather to use to tie a codpiece.[8]

Bodin's fear of repeating the formulas of witchcraft cannot then be purely a fear of instructing us, for at points in the book, he gets pretty excited about the possibilities of instruction itself. He seems afraid not just of teaching the practices of those he is trying to criminalize but of inadvertently replicating them in the process of repetition: "to pass on in an incomprehensible word the impiety" (Et de passer aussi en un mot non entendu, l'impieté; 58v), he says, does not benefit anyone, either the judge or the ignorant man. Although he claims that the formulas and barbaric words have no power, his anxiety about repetition suggests the opposite possibility—the possibility that he shares (in the form of a worry) the belief of those he is so busy attacking, the belief that the words and symbols of magic have enormous power, that they can behave and destroy just by being uttered. In fact this is just what emerges at the end of his description of the hostess.

There are, the hostess tells him, words not derived from Greek, Latin, French, or in fact any other known language that pertain to each "liaison" (ligature) of the body (63r). This is what makes codpiece-tying possible. These words "pertain" to the ligatures of the body, not only in the sense of describing or referring to them but in the sense of governing, actually controlling them, each word corresponding to a connective tissue or limb. Buried in the text is the notion of a language with the capacity to alter the body. The next chapters take this thought a step further in the form of a fantasy of a language that is physically embedded in the body itself. The witch Trois-eschelles reveals on other witches marks shaped like paws or claws, marks that go so deep they penetrate to the bone itself, marks that constitute a kind of language, for they identify the witch as a witch. Demoniacs are even more deeply "inhabited" and penetrated by language, for the demons who possess them speak through specific and inappropriate organs, "the stomach, when the woman's mouth is closed" (comme dedans l'estomach estant la bouche de la femme close), "sometimes the tongue half a foot out of the mouth" (quelquesfois la langue tirer de demy pied hors la bouche), sometimes through the "shameful parts" (les parties honteuses; 83v). These passages suggest a partial basis for Bodin's deeply held fear of a word which can govern or alter each limb. It is possible for Bodin to hold such a view in part because he already holds a reciprocal view of the body itself as inhabited and penetrated by language—tongues and marks—to begin with.

Although Bodin insists that words *mean* rather than perform, he himself acts as if they behave, invade, inhabit, penetrate, alter. It cannot be the case then that Bodin repudiates a theatrical trial, a theatrical demonstration of the crime, because he lacks a sense of witchcraft as being theatrical. For far from eschewing such a conception of witchcraft, *Demonomanie* is virtually animated by one, if by "theatrical" we no longer mean "spectacle" but words as actions, aggressively changing material substances. Any explanation of why Bodin imagines a trial without theatrical spectacle will have to contend both with the fact that he does think of witchcraft in theatrical terms and with the *kind* of theatricality with which he endows witchcraft.

## Judicial Strategy

But if it isn't Bodin's conception of witchcraft that allows him to relinquish theatricality at a trial, what is it? If the answer doesn't lie in his conception of witchcraft itself, perhaps it lies in his vision of justice: a vision of crime and the organ that prosecutes crime as two essentially separate and different activities. If witchcraft is theatrical, it is necessary for justice not to be. The two must, by definition, be opposites. Bodin virtually says this himself when he talks about the danger of justice becoming a "sorcery." One problem with this explanation, though, is how terribly alike justice and witchcraft are in Bodin's discussion.

One of the central subjects of the legal chapters, and a hallmark of female witchcraft throughout the period, is the female witch's capacity to curse. It is, Bodin says, a great presumption when the female suspect is accustomed to curse, "make threats" (d'en menacer; 212r). The "impotent nature of women burns . . . and she can't hold her tongue if she has the power to harm" (le naturel des femmes impotent brusle . . . et ne peut tenir sa langue, si elle a puissance de nuire; 212r). In this vision of female speech, language is performative in the most obvious sense of the word, in the sense that simply by uttering her wish the witch has the power to enact and effect it in the universe. The witch's words are constitutive in that they make happen what they describe.

But the fantasy that words have a constitutive power is one of the animating ideas of the book not only in the sense we have seen, that Bodin is afraid to utter the practices of witchcraft lest he teach or even worse replicate them, but as a judicial tool. This becomes clear in the context of Bodin's discussion of what counts as evidence. Ideally, to tell a suspect guilty of witchcraft from one merely accused, one wants as evidence one of the following: the evidence of what Bodin calls the "acknowledged fact" (du fait notoire; 193r), the evidence of confession, and the evidence of the testimony of witnesses. But in crimes like witchcraft, Bodin says, indisputable evidence is hard to come by and the maxim of the law is that less must suffice when more is unavailable.

In the absence of indisputable evidence, one must settle for "presumptions," that is, things which simply allow one to presume the suspect is guilty. And in the absence of strong presumptions, one must work with weaker ones. There are many widely recognized presumptions, many things which allow one to presume that the accused is a witch. These include the inability to cry (as is the case with a witch cited for her ability to get only three tears out of her right eye), parents who are witches, associating with other witches, and inability to look one in the eye. But the chief presumption, in the sense that Bodin refers to it the most frequently, is simply the existence of the rumor that one is a witch. The example is a mother found with a slain child in her arms. In the absence of any other evidence, she is presumed to be innocent of murder though the house is empty. But if the same woman is found with a slain child in her arms and she is rumored to be a witch, the presumption is that she is guilty of murder. The sheer fact of *words having been uttered* is enough to incriminate her. She need not have been sentenced or even convicted of being a witch but only to have been *said* to be one. Which is to say that in this way of looking at things, words have a constitutive power, since the sole difference between the two situations is the existence of words having been uttered. When it is a question of witches, rumor ("le bruict commun") is almost infallible, Bodin says (quand il est question des Sorciers, le bruict commun est presque infallible; 210r). In this way, he not only attributes the capacity to constitute through words to witches but employs it as a judicial strategy.

The sense that language operates in performative ways animates not only Bodin's understanding of witches but the way he treats them. Language is performative not only in the way witchcraft operates but in the system of justice that examines that witchcraft.[9] There is a theatrical component to justice at the trial then, but that "theatricality" lies in the ability of words to "make" and "constitute" the accused, rather than consisting in a visual reenactment of the crime for the purposes of authenticating testimony. We really need to ask, not why Bodin is able to forfeit theatricality at a trial, but why he is able to forfeit a kind of theatricality or spectacle per se. What allows him to forfeit a visible spectacle as a kind of authenticating testimony? What concept of evidence and what epistemology are being presupposed?

## Broken Epistemologies

One might imagine that to relinquish the theatrical demonstration of a crime at a trial, one needs a real skepticism about the evidence of the senses, the evidence of what the eye sees in particular. For the mind that needs no visible demonstration knows that the evidence of the senses lies. But, in fact, Bodin privileges the evidence of the senses above all other kinds of evidence. Hierarchizing the various kinds of evidence available to a judge in a courtroom, Bodin privileges above all else what he calls the evidence of the acknowledged fact: fifty witnesses swear that Pierre is dead, bewitched by the accused, but Pierre shows up very much alive in the courtroom in front of the judge and this takes precedence above all the witnesses and confessions on earth. Bodin's explicit criterion is the evidence of the senses, "what the judge sees or knows or touches or what he perceives by one of the five senses" (Il faut donc s'arrester à la verité du faict permanent, que le iuge void ou cognoist, ou tousche, ou perçoit, ou cognoist par l'un des cinq cens; 193v).

But although Bodin articulates an absolute faith in the evidence of the senses, he is equally absolute in his vision of the universe as one that is not available to those senses. Discussing the kind of improbable narratives that come up in confessions of those accused of witchcraft, he cautions us not to confuse what is legally possible with what is *naturally* possible, because there are more things in the universe—and therefore more things in law—than are comprehended by "nature."[10] "For what is impossible by nature is not impossible" (Car ce qui est impossible par nature, n'est pas impossible):

> For the grand works and marvels of God are impossible by nature, and yet true. The actions of Intelligences and everything Metaphysical is impossible by nature which is why Metaphysics is entirely distinct and different from Physics, which touches only on nature. One must not then measure the actions of spirits and demons by the effects of nature.
>
> (Car les grandes oeuvres et merveilles de Dieu sont impossibles par nature, et toutes-fois veritables: et les actions des intelligences, et tout ce qui est de la Metaphysique, est impossible par nature, qui est la cause pourquoy la Metaphysique, est du tout distincte et differente de la Physique, qui ne touche que la Nature. Il ne faut donc pas mesurer les actions des esprits et Demons aux effects de nature.) (204v–205r.)

Although Bodin is committed to the notion of "material" evidence—to the notion that material objects can present themselves to the senses in ways that guarantee knowledge—he is equally committed to a universe which does not always manifest itself in material ways, to one that cannot possibly be described or known by the kind of evidence he believes in. There is a discrepancy between his epistemology and his ontology, between what he believes about how we know and what there is to be known. He is committed to the idea that the senses can deliver knowledge, but equally committed to the idea that the universe is not finally knowable by these senses. He is committed to the notion of empirical evidence but equally committed to a metaphysical (and therefore nonempirical) world.[11]

What would be the consequence of living in such a mental universe? One possible consequence might be an overvaluation of what is experienced by the senses themselves. Some indication of this exists in the premises of Bodin's own argument. Apropos of how we know witches exist, he asks, how do we know that fire is hot? It is, he says, calling upon Aristotle, because "it seems that way to the Indians, the Gauls, the Scythians, and the Moors" (qu'il semble tel aux Indois, aux Gaulois, aux Scites, et aux Mores; preface, 13r).[12] Here, the perception of the thing is evidence that it exists. But in an example even more central to the book, perception of the thing is not just evidence that it exists but what makes it exist. It is constitutive of the thing itself: Bodin says that what differentiates his book from all others written on witches is his definition of a witch itself. A witch, he says, is someone who *knowingly* utilizes diabolical means to accomplish things: if a sick person takes a diabolical formula from a witch, thinking he is taking it from a good person, he does so in ignorance, so he is not a witch. It is the mind's perception of what it is doing that constitutes the crime. In its most limited formulation this amounts to an emphasis on intention; intention, says Bodin, is the foundation of the hearts and minds of man. But more extreme formulations occur, like the paradoxical claim that those who believe in false gods but blaspheme them are blasphemers not because they believe in the wrong gods but because they believe they are blaspheming the true God. The tendency to look at things this way might begin to provide an explanation for how Bodin can believe in the constitutive powers of language, for if you believe that thought can construct reality it is only a step to the idea that the articulation of that thought in words can do so as well.

If one possible consequence of living in a belief system in which the senses are believed to guarantee knowledge but the universe is believed to elude those senses is an overvaluation of the mind's ability to constitute reality, another simpler consequence might be intense frustration, even rage, over the discrepancy between how we know and what we are trying to know, a rage over the whole issue of knowledge itself. We can see glimpses of this in the sequence of frustrated knowers who parade through the book.

In the most extended of these (often read as an autobiographical disclosure), Bodin tells the story of a "friend" who is visited by an angel in his thirty-seventh year. Ostensibly the story is an illustration of the mitzvah, the blessing of certainty which only the most fortunate figures in history have had in the form of guaranteed revelation from a spirit. But though the story is supposed to illustrate the blessing of certainty, what it dramatizes is the impossibility of ever really knowing anything definitively.

## CHAPTER 2

After reading the *Book of Sacrifices*, Bodin's friend begins to pray that he be visited by an angel. He gets what he prays for and each night a spirit knocks at the door at three, maybe four in the morning, but when the friend goes to the door, no one is there, and he becomes afraid. The more afraid he gets, the harder he prays, thinking it is an evil spirit. The situation repeats itself. From the very beginning, then, the experience that is supposed to deliver certainty has itself become an occasion for uncertainty, doubt, misinterpretation.

No sooner has this uncertainty been cleared up than the situation repeats itself in a new way: the spirit sends admonitory dreams, warning the friend if he's in danger, warning him if he's about to commit evil, instructing him how to behave. But now the friend, the dreamer, does not know how to tell which dreams are the ones sent by the angel and which are normal dreams or even dreams that are merely the result of indisposition, so the two work out a system in which the angel knocks first early in the morning and the dream which follows the knocking is the real dream, the guaranteed one.

The angel works out another system of signs as well: it tugs the friend on his right ear if he is in danger of committing evil, reading an evil book, eating an unhealthy food, thinking an evil thought, and tugs him on the left ear if he is about to do something spiritually valuable. As the story progresses, communication between the angel and the friend comes more and more to be characterized by such systems, methods of containing uncertainty, as if the relations between angels and men were characterized by the same semiotic problems, the same gaps in communication which characterize relations between humans. When Bodin asks the friend if he has ever communicated with the angel more directly the friend tells him that he tried once and the spirit expressed its displeasure by knocking and banging loudly. The closest he's ever come is hearing an indistinct voice like an unarticulated sound and seeing a bright light like a disc. In half sleep he once dreamt of a child in a robe growing purple. Knowledge is always mediated, compromised, partial, and if this story dramatizes the distance between the fantasy of certainty and the frustration of that fantasy, the stories that follow suggest the increasing rage that such frustration engenders. For those who seek knowledge either exhibit or are the victims of an escalating violence.

Thus there is the tyrant who, to seek prophecy from the dead, beheads a firstborn child and, consulting the head for the outcome to an important battle, is told only "Vim Patior" (I suffer violence). Or there is the sorcerer who summons up a devil and is immediately killed. When his assistant asks the devil why, the devil says it is because the sorcerer *neglected* to ask a question and that Satan needs to be beseeched. Or there is the "acquaintance," a kind of parody of the friend, who is pursued not by an angel but by a devil and pulled not on the ear but on the nose and incited not to do good deeds but to wreak revenge, and who ends up empty-handed. Or there is the sorcerer of Noyon who knows the day of his own death and who goes to his friend, a bishop, to try and ward off what is coming. But while he is dining a man comes to the house demanding to speak to him and crushes the sorcerer between two doors. Again and again, knowledge is sought by violence, precipitates violence, fails to ward off violence. And this suggests that some of the violence that characterizes the book is engendered by uncertainty itself. This is not to suggest that the book fails to distinguish between those who seek knowledge by licit means and those who seek it by illicit means, but rather that the fantasy of certainty is dangled only to be frustrated over and over again in the text, and Bodin himself seems to be one in the company of frustrated knowers the book presents.

Perhaps the uncertainty at the heart of the text is epitomized by Bodin's version of the "devil's mark." This is the mark purportedly made by the devil on a witch's body that in demonological treatises normally guarantees to the examiners that the witch is a witch.[13] But in Bodin's discussion such marks have the capacity to erase themselves or disappear. The witch, Trois-eschelles, turned in some witches with devil's marks to verify their witch status, but later the witches thwarted the court when those marks disappeared. Even the traditional badge of certainty in other discussions of witchcraft, the devil's mark, has become an emblem of uncertainty. The text is punctuated again and again by the fantasy of certainty, but this fantasy is repeatedly frustrated and exposed.

How can this help to answer the original question: Why is Bodin able to relinquish spectacle at a trial? It suggests both the need to make visible the invisible world and the impossibility of ever doing so.[14] For if Bodin lives in a mental universe that insists on, on the one hand, the veracity of the senses and, on the other, the invisibility of the universe to them, then no amount of reenactment will make this invisible world of witchcraft appear. In some sense, despite its physical manifestation as the volta or as a jumping sieve, witchcraft *is* invisible, incapable of assuming a displayable form.

But this is really only part of the story for, as we have seen, there is a *kind* of theatricality to Bodin's conception of witchcraft. And there is a kind of theatricality built into his conception of the way words work at a trial, if by "theatrical" we no longer mean merely spectacular but performative. As the book progresses the rules that govern words at a trial become steadily more involved with the capacity of those words to create effects than with the capacity of those words to mean. Things said in court are more damaging than things said outside court; things said voluntarily are more damaging than things said under pressure; equivocations are more damaging than out-and-out lies; and silence is more damaging than equivocation. Bodin's view of language at a trial is "theatrical" in the sense that it is deeply strategic, pragmatic, and tactical rather than wrapped up in the capacity of words to mean.

We need to ask then not why Bodin forfeits all theatricality but rather under what circumstances justice would adopt this style of theatricality, a strategic deployment of language, rather than a visual reenactment of evidence. One answer may lie in what it is justice seeks to find out. If you believe that witchcraft *is* the volta which causes abortions then it is possible to get a set of witches in to dance and see what happens. But if you believe that the volta is just the outward manifestation of an invisible world, an invisible world that includes that intention that constitutes the foundation of the hearts and minds of man, then you need a tactical set of tricks to get a confession that articulates that intention. Witchcraft then is and is not theatrical. It is not in the sense that there is a hidden and invisible part of it incapable of being demonstrated, but it is theatrical in the sense that it generates visible effects in the world.

Perhaps here the broader question of under what circumstances justice can see its affinities to the crime it examines will actually be of use. For what is suggested by Bodin's attack on German judges who use witches to make sieves jump is not only that it is easier to see the affinities between justice and the crime it prosecutes when it is another justice, preferably a German justice, you are watching, but that it is easier to see the affinities between justice and the crime it examines when the similarity between them takes the form of a bizarre spectacle than it is when it consists in an ideology, a mental outlook, like the belief that words can alter the universe simply by being uttered. It is easier to see the affinities between justice and the crime it examines when those affinities take a visibly theatrical form like jumping sieves and floating witches than it is when they take the form of a system of belief, a set of mental attitudes, an ideology. If we turn this around, then a judicial process that *utilizes* the power of words to constitute and make reality will be better able to conceal from itself its resemblance to the witchcraft it examines than one that resorts to greasing pigs' shoes in church or employing jumping sieves.

CHAPTER 3

# Our Mutual Fiend
Reginald Scot and the Exorcism of the Other

Early in book 12 of *The Discoverie of Witchcraft*, Reginald Scot says that the words of incantations and charms have no magical power: "For by the sound of . . . words nothing commeth, nothing goeth" (175).[1] Although he insists that charms and incantations have no magical power, Scot recites ad nauseam most of the charms and incantations he knows. Book 12 is made of up of some seventy-odd charms, and it is almost a critical cliche to say that if you want a magical formula for keeping thieves away or curing snakebite, Scot's *Discoverie*, despite its skepticism, is a better place to look than any of the mammoth treatises written during the period dedicated to the proposition that witches exist and that they should be exterminated.[2]

But if Scot doesn't believe the incantations he cites have any magical power, why does he recite them at such length? In this chapter, I argue that Scot's recitation of charms and incantations functions in part to exorcise from his own way of thinking habits of mind which have a potential grip on him and which share a fundamental similarity with those of the "witchmongers" he exposes. In this way he expels them as irrational. At stake in such a claim is the attendant one that "statemental" ideals of language—what J. L. Austin has called the ideal of constativity and what in Scot's terms is a commitment to the belief that words "mean"; they do not "do"—are often achieved by deeply performative means.[3] If I am right, then it follows that to understand how a "skeptic" like Scot achieved the distance he did from the positions of many of his contemporaries concerned with the problem of witchcraft, we need to pay as much attention to the verbal performance of the *Discoverie* as we do to the kinds of influences that have been seen as formative for Scot.[4]

## How Loud the Papists Lie

Scot's explicit and self-confessed reason for repeating the several dozen incantations he repeats is that he wants to expose "how lowd [the papists] lie." He says he means to set down "for a tast" the "charmes, conjurations, blessings, curssings &c" of "the pope himselfe, and others of that / holy crue," to show "how loud . . . they lie, and what they . . . ascribe to their charmes and conjurations" (185). Typical entries in book 12 include "a papisticall charme," "a charme found in the canon of the masse," "other papisticall charmes" (188–89), a set of verses written by Pope Urban V "conteined in a periapt or tablet," and a charme against the "falling evill," based on "a true copie of the holie writing, that was brought downe from heaven by an angell to S. Leo Pope of Rome" (187). Scot describes in laborious detail Agnus Dei (little cakes with Christ's head on one side, a lamb carrying a flag on the other, and the Gospel of John on fine paper slipped into a cavity inside) and "wastcote[s] for necessitie," holy garments worn as holy relics which Scot says are given to the wearer "by the pope, or some such archconjuror," who promises "all manner of immunitie" to the wearer (186). For Scot the "manufacturing" of holy water itself is part of the same "cousinage" as witchcraft, and he says he would tell us how to manufacture it but that doing so would take so much time we should read the pontifical instead. The Catholic church is as implicated in witchcraft as it is like it: Pope Nicolas V gave an indulgence to a Bishop Miratis to get help from a witch for being bewitched with impotence. There is no question, then, that part of Scot's project in the recitation of papist charms is what he says it is, an exposé of Catholicism as fraught with superstitious fraud and humbug.[5]

But for every "papistical" charm Scot cites, there is one that has nothing to do with papistry—"Against the biting of a scorpion . . . Saie to an asse secretlie, and as it were, whispering in his eare: I am bitten with a Scorpion" (196); "Against the biting of a mad dog . . . Put a silver ring on the finger, within the which these words are graven +Habay+habar+hebar+ & saie to the person bitten with a mad dog, I am thy saviour, loose not thy life: and then pricke him in the nose thrise" (196); to expedite childbirth for women in labor, "Throwe over the top of the house, where a woman in travell lieth, a stone or any other thing that hath killed three living creatures; namelie a man, a wild bore, and a she beare" (197). How will an exposé of how loud the papists lie help account for the *non*papistical charms Scot recites? Or for that matter account for the sheer number of charms he cites?

It is tempting to think that despite Scot's insistence to the contrary, he must really, on some level, believe in the magical power of those charms he "rehearses." It is primarily the specificity of his own analysis of the fantasies that other people have about words which creates the sense of some hidden affinity on Scot's part. He distinguishes, for instance, between those who believe that the power or efficacy is embedded in the word itself, those for whom in "certeine wordes, verses, or charmes, &c" there is thought to be "miraculous efficacie" (174) and those for whom the power is in the "form" of the utterance, whether in the belief that the word must be "secretlie uttered" (174) or in the injunction that a "speciall forme of wordes be alwaies used" (174). He distinguishes between those who believe it is the *intent* of the person uttering the words that makes them effective "so the charmer have a steddie intention to bring his desire about" (228) and those for whom it is the complicity or belief of the auditor that allows the words to work. It is primarily the care with which Scot identifies each of these various fantasies about words' magical power that makes one imagine they resonate in some way for him.

While it is tempting to posit such an affinity on Scot's part, he is quite explicit in his insistence that the words of charms have no power: language cannot create material change. Humans in general and word-users in particular cannot *make anything new*; "For we, neither all the conjurors, Cabalists, papists, soothsaiers, inchanters, witches, nor charmers in the world, neither anie other humane or yet diabolicall cunning can adde anie such strength to Gods worksmanship, as to make *anie thing anew*, or else to exchange one thing into another" (emphasis mine, 175). Scot acknowledges the value of things like blessings for food and sanctification, but the blessings don't materially change the substance of the meat: Neither the cunning of witches, nor the illusion of devils can create new matter. No new substances can be created by man (175). But most especially speech doesn't create material change: "For by the sound of the words nothing commeth, nothing goeth" (175).

If witches could create magical effects through words, they would be appropriating God's powers: "We ought not to take upon us to counterfet . . . [God who] with his word created all things" (175). The 58th Psalm alludes to an adder "stopp[ing] his eare, and hear[ing] not the voice of the charmer, charme he never so cunninglie" (202). Jeremiah says he will send "serpents and cockatrices among you, which cannot be charmed" (202). Both passages for Scot argue that the words of charms have no magical power. And both kinds of religious arguments (scriptural authority on charms and the fear of appropriating God's power) buttress a sense of language as descriptive rather than capable of creating material change in the universe.

If incantations and charms are not efficacious, what are they? In a trio of vignettes, Scot spells out the sense in which charms and conjuration in particular and witchcraft in general are (as others have noted) a form of theatricality, if by theatricality we mean an illusion for which there is a natural cause.[6] Scot says the kind of snake charmer he believes in is the kind who rips the snake's teeth out with a woolen rag:

> But they that take upon them to worke these mysteries and miracles, doo indeed (after rehearsall of these and such like words and charmes) take up even in their bare hands, those snakes and vipers, and sometimes put them about their necks, without receiving anie hurt thereby, to the terror and astonishment of the beholders, . . . But these charmers . . . dare not trust to their charmes, but use such an inchantment, as everie man maie lawfullie use . . . marie with a woollen rag they pull out their teeth before hand. (207)

The anecdote casts witchcraft as theatricality (the "rehearsall of these and such like words and charmes" leading to the "terror and astonishment of the beholders")—an illusion whose material or physical explanation is the pulling-out of the snake's teeth.

In a more extended anecdote, Scot develops the same kind of argument about the "witch" of Westwell, a local demoniac a few miles away from him. At 2 p.m. on October 13, 1574, two ministers, Newman of Westwell and Brainford of Kennington, came to examine Mildred Norrington, the "base daughter" of Alice Norrington, servant to William Sponer of Westwell in the county of Kent (101). They came to try to drive away the devil possessing her, to understand how she had become afflicted, and they signed a statement with a number of other witnesses, testifying to what they saw. Among other things, they testified to the fact that the voice that spoke out of Mildred was different from her own: "Sathans voice did differ much from the maids voice, and all that he spake, was in his owne name" (103). Thus the initial story Scot tells is of an agon with Satan, seemingly an authentic one—not a fraudulent impersonation.

Beyond that, it is a drama of *intelligibility*, a battle in which the ecclesiastical forces seek to compel Satan in the name of Christ "to speake with such a voice as they might understand" (101), a drama in which they meet first with silence ("and though we did command him . . . to speake; yet he would not" [102]), then a refusal to descend into language ("roring, crieng, striving, and gnashing of teeth" [102]), then a manner of speaking "but verie strangelie" [102]), then the use of comprehensible words, but stripped of a context that would make them meaningful ("He comes, he comes: and that oftentimes he repeated; and He goes, he goes" [102]), and finally a series of intelligible words which incriminate Mildred's mother ("Then we charged him as before, to tell . . . what his name was. . . . The divell, the divell. . . . Who sent thee? He said, Old *Alice*, old *Alice*" [102]). By the end, the forces of light have turned Satan into a model of intelligibility, not only identifying the precise spot Mother Alice hired him to possess her daughter, the precise crimes she committed in the past, and the various locales he came to her, but forcing Satan to match his own actions with his words ("Then he said he would go, he would go: but he went not. Then we commanded him as before with some more words. Then he said, I go I go; and so he departed" [103]). In this happy outcome, Satan has not only departed but has been forced to speak intelligibly, descriptively, even referentially. His words refer to visible things and actions and he can be made to demonstrate this correspondence. The power of the gnashing teeth, the roaring, and various other kinds of physical symptomatology has been banished, even revealed as a front for an ideal of plain (which is to say, referential) speech. Satan is now, like everybody else, an utterer of words which describe, not a wielder of words which create material changes and symptoms out in the universe.

But if the drama enacted is that of the demonic made intelligible, then Scot frames that drama by making clear it is not only a drama but a fraud, a performance. However cunningly the certificate the ministers produced was penned and whatever show of truth it had, a second set of examiners, Thomas Wotten and George Darrell, were quick to detect knavery: "the fraud was found, the coosenage confessed, and she received condigne punishment" (105). Scot goes to great lengths to differentiate their method from that of inquisitors and witch-hunters like Bodin.[7] The examination utilized no torture, no presumptions, no "extorted confessions, contrarie to sense and possibilitie," no tricks. "But through wise and perfect triall of everie circumstance the illusion was manifestlie disclosed" (105). The witch of Westwell reveals her possession as a piece of theatricality, shows "hir feats, illusions, and transes, with the residue of all hir miraculous works" in the presence of her examiners (105). Like the snake charmer who duped his audience by pulling the snake's teeth out, her performance has a natural explanation: she is a ventriloquist, a word derived, Scot says, from "Ob" which "signifieth most properlie a bottle . . . bicause the Pythonists spake hollowe; as in the bottome of their bellies, whereby they are aptlie in Latin called Ventriloqui" (101).

Scot's reading of the witch of Westwell is consistent with his position that speech doesn't create material change because it was all the "witch" of Westwell speaking in the first place. The fantasy within the performance—that the devil's power can be domesticated by being turned into intelligible, even referential speech—is regulated and contained by Scot's exposé of the performance *as* performance, as impersonation, fraud, an image or imitation of a thing, rather than the creation of something new. We tend to think of "reference" and "theatrical," words which denote, and theatrical illusions, which connote, as opposites—and in one sense they are. But in another way, both words and illusions, signifying accurately or inaccurately, are, in their signifying capacity, more like each other than they are like things that in performing generate new matter or material change in the universe.

Scot's most sustained insistence on a natural explanation and one of the positions that differentiated him from his most famous detractor, King James, is his reading of the witch of Endor story, the story of Saul seeking the witch or woman of Endor, to raise the dead Samuel. What really happened at Endor? Scot asks.[8]

He reviews three possible alternatives, each with an implication for language. The first is that the witch really did raise Samuel, but this cannot be, says Scot, because the souls of the righteous are in a fixed place and can't be moved. What sleep would the elect have in the bosom of Abraham if they could be woken by every passing witch? The living are not taught by the dead but by the testament, and moreover Samuel was forbidden to answer Saul in life, so why would he be permitted in death? Scot's dismissal of this possibility—that Samuel was really raised—is compatible with his insistence that words don't create material change. It isn't, for instance, as if the witch's words infuse dead clay with the spirits of the patriarchs.

The second possibility and the one that James ultimately adopted in opposition to Scot is that the witch didn't raise Samuel at all, but the devil.[9] But this, for Scot, is also unthinkable, first, because Jehovah's name was invoked (115), and second, because even if witches could raise devils, they wouldn't be able to work miracles like this one. Finally, and most importantly from Scot's point of view, it is ridiculous to turn to the unknown and supernatural, to "fetch up a devil from hell," when a *natural* means may explain the situation. This reading is also compatible with the view that words don't bring about material change: the witch's words summoned no one, wrought nothing supernatural, let alone anything miraculous.

But if the witch of Endor didn't raise Samuel or a devil, what did she do? Though Scot acknowledges that it is written in Samuel that the witch of Endor raised Samuel and that elsewhere the words of the text are "placed" strongly to imply that, if you weigh the text well, he says, you'll see Samuel wasn't raised at all; it was all "an illusion or cousenage practised by the witch" (112), an "illusion . . . contrived by the art and cunning of the woman, without anie of these supernaturall devices" (114). The witch of Endor is both a stage manager (modulating the feigned voice of Samuel to play to Saul's anxieties about the Philistines) and a ventriloquist literally playing all the parts, her own, that of her "familiar," and that of Samuel: "Now commeth in Samuel to plaie his part," Scot says, "but I am persuaded it was performed in the person of the witch hir selfe, or of hir confederate" (119). Though occasionally Scot pictures the witch's familiar as some "lewd craftie priest" (117), much more frequently he pictures her as playing all the parts herself (herself, Samuel's, and the familiar's): "She finished hir conjuration, so as both Saules part, the witches part, and also Samuels part was plaied" (116). It is in fact the way the ghost of Samuel talks, prophesying and predicting that God will rend Saul's kingdom, that characterizes the voice for Scot as a human voice, not a devil's. Devils don't offer such constructive warnings: "This (I say) is no phrase of a divell, but of a cousener" (119).

There are two assumptions implicit here, one that theatricality itself is not constitutive—she doesn't raise Samuel from the grave—but is an imitation, a copy, an illusion. The second that the reality behind such an illusion is a physical, material, and observable one which can be used to expose the illusion as illusion.

That theatricality is simply or merely illusion is a regular feature of Scot's *narrative* of the witch of Endor, of her capacity in particular to manipulate Saul's expectations by presenting him with things that look like what he most fears and expects: He asks what she sees. She says angels and Gods ascending. He assumes she must mean Samuel and asks, "What fashion is he of?" (118). A shrewder man would have seen through her knavery, says Scot, but Saul was too busy being out of his wits.

Equally important for Scot is the way that the witch's theatricality is always explainable by natural facts: Saul's diseased state of mind is a natural fact which allows him to accept the witch's fiction. The fact that he only heard not saw what she did in her closet is another "natural" fact explaining both his gullibility and her stage technique. (From the question "Of what manner of man was he?" we know that he "sawe nothing," but stood outside like a "mome" [a blockhead] (118), able to "heare the cousening answers, but not to see the cousening handling . . . and the counterfetting of the matter" [117–18].) And the witch's ventriloquism is the ultimate natural fact, a physical set of tricks that account for the illusion of conjuration.

So far, then, a worldview that imagines the reality behind illusion as physical and material and natural and a view of language as descriptive, not performative, are compatible with each other. But how will any of this help us to understand Scot's own recitation of the charms which he insists have no power, the endless anatomization and distinctions, the reiteration of variants (if "habay, habar, hebar" doesn't work for mad dog bites, try pills made of the skull of a dead person)?

At the center of Scot's argument against the persecution of witches *and* at the center of his belief system about language itself is the claim that there are no witches as the period understood the term because the Bible admits none. As far as Scot is concerned, much of the confusion about whether witches exist comes from a mistranslation of Exodus 22, "thou shalt not suffer a witch to live." He begins book 6: "*Chasaph*, being an Hebrue word, is Latined *Veneficium*, and is in English, poisoning, or witchcraft; if you will have it. The Hebrue sentence written in Exodus, 22 is . . . in English, You shall not suffer anie poisoners, or (as it is translated) witches to live" (89).

There are poisoners in the Bible, he says, and there are certainly couseners. When Paul says to the Galatians "O ye foolish Galathians . . . who hath bewitched you?" (90), he shows plainly "that the true signification of witchcraft is cousinage" (89), "to wit, cousened . . . [made to] beleeve a thing which is neither so nor so" (90).

Much of the misunderstanding that surrounds the issue of witchcraft can be traced in Scot's view to *mistranslation*. Whatever *Malleus* and Bodin say, Moses spoke only of four kinds of "impious couseners or witches" (87): 1) "*Praestigiatores Pharoanis*," which all divines, both Hebrews and others, conclude were but "couseners and jugglers, deceiving the Kings eies with illusions and sleights; and making false things to appear as true: which nevertheless our witches cannot do" (87); 2) *Mecasapha* (or poisoners) (87); 3) those who use "sundrie kinds of divinations," and go under names like *Kasam, Onen, Ob, Idoni* (87); and 4) "*Habar*: to wit: when magicians, or rather such, as would be reputed cunning therein, mumble certeine secret words, wherein is thought to be great efficacie" (87).

All of these abuse people ("These are all couseners and abusers of the people in their severall kinds" [87]), but because they were all translated—or implicitly *mistranslated*—by the word "witch," the stories of *Malleus Maleficarum* and Bodin get applied to them: "But bicause they are all termed of our translators by the name of witches in the Bible: therefore the lies of M. Mal and Bodin, and all our old wives tales are applied unto these names and easilie beleeved of the common people *who have never hitherto been instructed in the understanding of these words*" (emphasis mine, 87). Scot is going to set the record (and the reader) straight: "In which respect, I will (by Gods grace) shew you . . . the opinion of the most learned in our age" (87), which turns out to be Weyer, aided by the Hebrician, Andreas Massius.

My interest in this is not in whether or not the word "witch" is actually a mistranslation but rather in the assumptions about language itself built into this notion of mistranslation. Scot believes there is an original and true meaning in a word that can be found in the Bible. The biblical text is both the apparent referee about whether things exist and the locale in which the true and essential and real meanings of words reside. These meanings can be correctly translated and made to live in a new language years later. But unfortunately they have not always been correctly translated. Scot tends toward essentialism in at least two senses then: First, in contrast to those who believe in language as a set of acts, he believes in words as the repository of meanings or truths. Second, within that belief in words as repositories of meanings, he believes that meanings are not arbitrarily bestowed by situation or circumstance but rooted in the word itself. Finally, he believes that the biblical text is the place in which we can find those meanings rooted and hence the ultimate authority for what those meanings are.

All of these beliefs are potentially compatible with each other, and they are all compatible with what Scot has said so far about charms, which is that they create no material change, that from them nothing comes or goes. But a belief in the Bible as the place where the essential meanings of words are stored is not compatible with his method of arriving at his reading, or at least not his reading of the witch of Endor story. Nor, in a broader way, as we shall see, is his sense of words as meaning-bearers rather than actors or behavers compatible with what he has to say about language elsewhere in the book.

One of Scot's strongest reasons for insisting that the witch of Endor did not conjure up a devil is that if she had, the biblical text would have said so: "And it is to be surelie thought, if it had beene a divell, the text would have noted it in some place of the storie: as it dooth not" (114). In this instance, Scot's respect for the literal level of the biblical text and his sense that the common-sense, *natural* explanation is superior to a supernatural one happen to coincide: "But in truth we may gather, that it was neither the divell in person, nor Samuell. . . . But we shall not need . . . to descend so lowe as hell, to fetch up a divell to expound this place. For it is ridiculous (as Pompanacius saith) to leave manifest things, and such as by naturall reason may be prooved, to seek unknowne things, which by no likeliehood can be conceived, nor tried by any rule of reason" (114). In general Scot's attitude toward explanations which rely on the supernatural can be summed up as "what need so farre fetches, as to fetch a divell supernaturallie out of hell when the illusion may be here by naturall means deciphered?" (119).[10]

But, as Scot's reading of the witch of Endor continues, he is forced by his own admission to deviate more and more from the literal level of the text. From the very beginning, he has admitted that "it is written in 2. Sam. cap 28 that she raised up Samuel from death" (111) and that "other words of the text are stronglie placed, to inforce his verie resurrection" (111). But, says Scot, "He that weigheth well that place, and looketh into it avisedlie, shall see that Samuel was not raised from the dead, but that it was an illusion or cousenage" (112). Weighing the text well, then, comes to mean going against its literal claims. This gets more and more pronounced as Scot's reading continues. Though he differs from the *content* of Augustine's reading (that "the divell was fetcht up in [Samuel's] likenesse" [114]), what he values about Augustine is the "libertie" he provides biblical readers to deviate from the literal level of the text:

> But in so much as we have libertie by S. Augustine's rule, in such places of scripture as seeme to conteine either contrarietie or absurditie to varie from the letter, and to make a godlie construction agreeable to the word; let us confesse that Samuell was not raised (for that were repugnant to the word) and see whether this illusion may not be contrived by the art and cunning of the woman, without anie of these supernaturall devices. (114)

Thus much of what follows is not Scot's "reading" of the biblical text in a literal sense but his conjecture about the causality or sequence which lies behind the biblical text—not stated, but for Scot surely meant. Nowhere is this as true as when he gets to the witch's actual conjuration: "The manner and circumstance of their communication, or of hir conjuration, is not verbatim set downe and expressed in the text; but the effect thereof breeflie touched, *yet will I shew you the common order of their conjuration, and speciallie of hirs at this time used*" (emphasis mine, 117). What Scot is showing us under the name of biblical interpretation is the custom of conjuration as he understands it:

> And so goeth she to worke, using ordinarie words of conjuration, of which there are sundrie varieties and formes (whereof I shall have occasion to repeat some in another place) as you see the juglers (which be inferior conjurors) speake certeine strange words of course to lead awaie the eie from espieng the maner of their conveieance, whilest they may induce the mind to conceive and suppose that he dealeth with spirits; saieng, *Hay, fortune furie, nunq; credo, passe, passe, when come you sirra.* (118)

Scot is as much reading the witch of Endor by the witch of Westwell as he is reading the witch of Westwell by her biblical precedent, the witch of Endor: "Well, I perceive the woman of Endors spirit was a counterfeit and kept belike in hir closet at Endor, or in the bottle, with Mother Alices divell at Westwell, and are now bewraied and fled togither in *Limbo patrum* &c" (116).

Not only is the "common order of their conjuration" not supplied by the biblical text, but much of the causality of the witch of Endor's contact with

Saul is supplied by Scot. In fact, everything he labels as cousenage and illusion is supplied, his conjecture that she must have known Saul, his conjecture that Saul heard but didn't see what happened, his conjecture that she said she was afraid of a snare as part of her own snare because couseners always say they're afraid of being trapped when they're trying to gull you, everything that is for Scot the hallmark of her cheap theatricality. By the time he's concluded his reading, Scot has said that it is a "great offense for a man to beleeve the bare words of the storie" (120).

My point here is not just to suggest that Scot (like myriad biblical commentators of his time) ignores the literal level of the text when he needs to do so, but to suggest that when he does so he not only leaves behind the text, he leaves behind the ideal of language he so insistently articulates, the ideal at the root of his view of translation. In theory he believes that the literal words of the sacred text are the absolute referees for contradictions, but in practice he is drawn to a sense of the custom of the time, the natural and probable explanation. In theory he believes that words are not actors or behavers but things which have meanings literally embedded in them, and that the meanings embedded in the words of the sacred text are so deeply embedded as to be undislodgeable, but in practice he cannot live up to his ideal.

It is also the case that while in theory he believes that words are meaning-bearers, not actors or behavers, in practice he knows language often fails to work that way. This is true not only in his discussion of conjuration, where words like *"Hay, fortune furie nunq"* work to distract the eye from sleight of hand, but in his treatment of confessions and why confessions, even voluntary ones, cannot be regarded as the truth. For nowhere else is language more clearly behavior, action, susceptible to being looked at as a set of acts or performances, rather than being looked at as a series of meanings, true or false. "If their confession be made by compulsion, of force or authoritie," Scot says, "or by persuasion, and under colour of freendship, it is not to be regarded; bicause the extremitie of threts and tortures provokes it; or the qualitie of faire words and allurements constraines it" (38). But even if confessions are voluntary, they are not to be trusted, but rather likely to be acts (that is, acts of suicide) that are the product of melancholy. Judges, he says, should not accept confessions of impossible things ("impossibilities, as that they flie in the aire, transubstantiate themselves, raise tempests, transfer or remoove corne, &c" [38]), for the *legally* possible is the naturally possible. "There is nothing possible in lawe, that in nature is impossible" (11), says Scot, in direct opposition to Bodin, for whom legal confessions need not be bound by natural truth because there are, in effect, more things in the universe than there are in nature.[11] One woman confessed to causing all the frosts in the winter of 1565. Such confessions are the product of: an unsound mind, often bred of melancholy, and "his word is not to be credited that is desirous to die" (38). Neither extorted nor voluntary confessions should be accepted or even approached on a true-false axis, because both are tactical acts, strategies, and behaviors. The first are tactical maneuvers to avoid death, the second are tactical maneuvers to bring it about.

If Scot believes in an ideal of language in which words mean rather than do, but he knows that in the world words do rather than mean, and if his own interpretive practice is unable to live up to the ideal he articulates, perhaps his own text, his recitation of charms in the face of his claims that they're meaningless, is best understood as a series of speech acts. But what acts would those be? If we look at a set of analogies between Scot's habits of mind and those he attacks, a parallel emerges: Scot's recitation of the charms he says are meaningless ultimately functions to exorcise those forms of irrationality which his own thinking occasionally approaches. The recitation and performance are his method of achieving the rationality of skepticism or empiricism about the subject he rehearses.

## Exorcism of Analogies

One of the stylistic habits that characterizes Scot's discussion of incantation and charms is the attempt to include all possible variants of a thing, to anticipate all possible contingencies, identify every possible case. Typical but discrete (and different) entries in book 12, for instance, include: "Charmes to find out a theefe" (211), "Another waie to find out a theefe that hath stolen anie thing from you" (212), "To put out the theeves eie" (213), "Another waie to find out a theefe" (213), "A charme to find out or spoile a theefe" (213), and "Saint Adelbert's curse or charme against theeves" (214). Scot never allows the part to stand for the whole. An exposé of one kind of foolishness is never sufficient to expose all the other things in the same class.

But one of the properties of these curses themselves is the same tendency to try to anticipate every possible version of a situation, and in so doing control every possible outcome. They exhibit a kind of obsessive-compulsive approach to language. St. Adelbert's curse or charm against thieves, for instance, curses thieves in "the field, in the grove, in the woods, in their houses, barnes, chambers and beds; . . . in the court, in the waie, in the towne, in the castell, in the water, in the church, in the churchyard" (214). This same need for comprehensiveness that curses in both church and churchyard, wood and grove, also curses thieves in all possible physical positions and activities ("in their talke, in silence, in eating, in watching, in sleeping, in drinking, in feeling, in sitting, in kneeling . . . in lieng, in idlenes, in all their worke" [214]) and, even more exhaustively, curses each individual body part: "Curssed be their heads, their mouthes, their nostrels, their noses, their lips, their jawes, their teeth, their eies and eielids, their braines, the roofe of their mouthes, their toongs, their throtes, their breasts, their harts, their bellies, their livers, all their bowels, and their stomach" (214). Not content with eyes and eyelids, tongue and roof of mouth, the curse continues:

> Curssed be their navels, their spleens, their bladder. Curssed be their thighs, their legs, their feete, their toes, their necks, their shoulders. Curssed be their backs, curssed be their armes, curssed be their elbowes, curssed be their hands, and their fingers, curssed be both the nails of their handes and feete; curssed be their ribbes and their genitals, and their knees, curssed be their flesh, curssed be their bones, curssed be their bloud, curssed be the skin of their bodies, curssed be the marrowe in their bones, curssed be they from the crowne of the head, to the sole of the foote; and whatsoever is betwixt the same. (214–15)

We could say then that Scot shares a *habit of mind* with those he ridicules, a tendency toward comprehensiveness, or all-inclusiveness, that at least in those he attacks has something to do with the need to control all future possible outcomes.

But this tendency is not just characteristic of curses Scot cites; it is a feature of the office of conjuration of exorcism itself. Among charms for dispossession, Scot includes an "office or conjuration . . . first authorised and printed at Rome, and afterwards at Avenion, Anno 1515." Lest the devil should lie in some secret part of the body, each part is named:

> I beseech thee, O Lord Jesus Christ, that thou pull out of everie member of this man all infirmities, from his head, from his haire, from his braine, from his forhead, from his eies, from his nose, from his eares, from his mouth, from his toong, from his teeth, from his jawes, from his throte, from his necke, from his backe, from his brest, from his paps, from his heart, from his stomach, from his sides, from his flesh, from his bloud, from his bones, from his legs, from his feete, from his fingers, from the soles of his feete, from his marrowe, from his sinnewes, from his skin, and from everie joint and members, &c. (200)

Doubtless, Scot says, Christ could have no "starting hole" (hiding place) since it was insufficient for him to have said, "Depart out of this man thou unclean spirit" (200).[12] We could say that Scot both exhibits and yet stands aware and outside of the relentless tendency to anatomize and itemize.

If the office of conjuration seeks to exorcise a devil, what particular irrationality or wicked thing is it that Scot's repetitions and strings of alternatives are in the service of exorcising? One of the ugliest passages Scot summarizes among those he exposes is a passage by Leonard Vairus (Leonardo Vairo) on the way bodies of women bewitch: by means of hate, "fierie inflammation[s]" enter the eye which, being violently sent out by "beams and streames," infect and bewitch the body exposed to it. Women have such "an unbrideled force of furie and concupiscence naturallie" that they like "brute beasts" fix their eyes on those whom they want to bewitch. But it is not just that women's emotions are (literally) toxic, but that their bodies exhale infectious and poisonous fumes and toxic excrescences: "They are so troubled with evill humors . . . that out go their venomous exhalations, ingendered through their illfavored diet, and increased by means of their pernicious excrements which they expel" (227). After describing menstruation as the filling up of "superfluous humors" with which melancholy blood boils, Vairus is characterized as saying that "they belch up a certeine breath, wherewith they bewitch whomsoever they list" (227). The passage encapsulates all the horror at the female body implicit in the period's witch hunts.

Scot is clearly disgusted by this antifeminism, and his conclusion is that if Vairus is right, no woman can avoid being a witch except by locking herself in solitary confinement. But despite his explicit disgust at such attitudes, a seed of the same antifeminist bias informs the way that Scot thinks about these very women scapegoated as witches. Thus, even as Scot is at pains to show that old, helpless women are labeled witches because those that scapegoat them cannot take responsibility for their own role in misfortunes or punishments, he thinks of the old women who are scapegoated as: "lame, bleare-eied, pale, fowle and full of wrinkles" (5); "Poore, sullen, superstitious and papists; or such as knowe no religion: in whose drousie minds the divell hath goten a fine seat" (5); "leane and deformed, shewing melancholie in thir faces" (5), evoking horror, doting mad scolds.

It is melancholy that has allowed the devil to get a "seat" in the minds of these women accused of witchcraft in the first place and melancholy that allows them to believe the accusations against them. They go begging, house to house, and when inevitably they are turned away and curse their neighbors and some misfortune occurs, they think they are responsible. "Being called before a Justice . . . [they are] driven to see [their] imprecations and desires, and [their] neighbors harmes and losses to concurre" (6). Clouded by melancholy, such a woman concludes that she "as a goddes" has brought the misfortune about.[13] Throughout history melancholics have distorted reality, ascribing strange and impossible causes to all sorts of phenomena. Some are convinced that they are urinals or earthen pots and terrified that they will be broken (41). Others suffer from the conviction that everyone is trying to kill them, and kill themselves instead. Scot's most extended anecdote involves a man who thought his nose was as big as a house. To be "cured," the surgeon inched around the room as if afraid of bumping into it, then blindfolded the man, caught his nose in a pair of pincers, went off and sacrificed a bullock, and then brought the bloody remains into the room, untied the nose, and told the man he was cured. If "normal" melancholics can suffer from bodily distortions though their bodies "neverthelesse remaineth in the former shape" (42), says Scot, how much more must accused women suffering from the same melancholy "falselie suppose they can hurt and infeeble other mens bodies" (42).

Scot's use of the notion of melancholy, then, is in the service of defending accused women from the charges made against them. But the concept of melancholy itself (a disease which seems to afflict the mind, but which really springs from the body) contains, at its core, some of the same antifeminism that Vairus articulates, for this melancholy is most deeply associated with (or at least exacerbated by) "the stopping of their monethlie melancholike flux or issue of bloud" which menopause brings on (42).[14] An analogy exists between Scot and those whom he repudiates.

Oddly enough, it is also possible to find the seeds of a skepticism like Scot's in the beliefs of those he ridicules. When Ferarrius distinguishes between the learned and unlearned attitudes toward incantations—the unlearned believing the force of the spell lies solely in the words of the incantation, the learned believing that the force lies at least in part in the bewitched person's capacity to lend the symbols and characters credence—he is, in effect, arguing that the force of bewitchment lies in part in the eye of the beholder, in the mind's ability to endow the charms with power. Scot himself implies the same thing when he tells various stories of "cures" that worked on melancholics: for the patient who thought he had no head, a cap of lead was put on him; for the woman fearful her entrails were consumed with serpents, a purge and serpents were slipped into her vomit so she believed she'd been cured; for the one who thinks he's lame, yell fire and watch him run out of the room. In all of these stories, belief is constitutive. Scot attributes to Plato the notion that "if a mans fansie or mind give him assurance that a hurtfull thing shall doo him good, it may doo so, &c." as a gloss on a story of a fraudulent charm which allowed a woman with "sore eyes" to improve her vision: the woman "made . . . mone to one" [a charlatan], who instructs her to put a scroll around her neck, but never to look inside it (198). She stops weeping and her eyes improve. She loses the scroll, starts weeping again, and her eyes become newly sore. When friends find the scroll and open it they find the words "The divell pull out both thine eies" (199). The story suggests, among other things, how close the worldview of skepticism comes at times to the worldview of the dogmatist witch-monger. Scot tells the story to show the fraudulence of the charms, the way the words *can't* have a magical power. But the story also shows the curative power belief can have for the afflicted. Scot and his opponents hold precariously similar beliefs but in vastly differing proportions and assembled in different ways. For the witch-mongers Scot anatomizes, the belief in the female body as toxic and malevolently magical is real and the sense that the mind has the ability to endow it with these qualities is provisional and speculative. For Scot, the sense of the mind's power to distort or alter reality is real and the horror at the female body latent and held at arm's length.

We could say, then, that where for those who believe in the reality of witchcraft, those Scot attacks, the antifeminist physiology is essential and real and the ability to glimpse the mind's role in predicating its reality conditional and speculative and fragmentary; for Scot, the ability to see the mind's role in constructing reality is central and basic, but the physiological bias against women, the physiological antifeminism, lingers in the concept of the source of melancholy. If those Scot attacks use recitation or repetition, the endless anatomizing of places and body parts to expel toxins and devils they imagine to be material and real, in *The Discoverie* Scot's recitation of charms and invocations, his endless anatomizing of illogical incantations, ultimately seeks to purge a similar kind of thinking, to purge the potential analogies that exist between himself and those he repudiates.

CHAPTER 4

# Strategies for Doubt
## Curiosity and Violence in King James VI and I's *Daemonologie*

Midway through book 1 of King James VI and I's 1597 *Daemonologie*, Epistemon, the spokesman for James in the book, describes the magician's perilous journey up what he calls the "slipperie and vncertaine scale of curiositie" (10). Learned men, he says, spiritually deficient and finding that they share too much in common with the "stupide pedants," become unsatisfied with knowing just the course of the stars and begin to try to make predictions from them. Finding that their predictions occasionally come true, they study to know the cause why this should be and "so mounting from degree to degree, vpon the slipperie and vncertaine scale of curiositie; they are at last entised, that where lawfull artes or sciences failes, to satisfie their restles mindes, even to seeke to that black and vnlawfull science of *Magie*." The moment is one of several in the book which criminalize curiosity.

At the same time, even as the book stigmatizes curiosity, it appears to seek to titillate it in its reader. James's preface tells us at length about the kinds of things he won't be telling us. We should forgive him, James says, for not telling us "the whole particular rites and secretes of these unlawfull artes" of magic, but if we are curious we can consult Bodin, "collected with greater diligence then written with judgment" (xiv–xv). If curiosity is so dangerous, why evoke it in the reader, first by calling attention to what the book won't be telling us, and second by pointing us to where we can go to find out?

Studies of *Daemonologie* don't typically pose this kind of question, but its importance lies at least in part in the light it sheds on the epistemological problems at the heart of the book. The creation of the desire for forbidden knowledge in a reader is one facet of the anxiety in *Daemonologie* about whether anything is knowable. To say this is to grant on the one hand what others have said—that the book is an exploration of epistemological problems, a conscious inquiry into what is knowable and an attempt to understand puzzling phenomena—and at the same time to suggest *Daemonologie* is an *example* of an epistemological problem, a portrait of a response to a set of contradictions and paradoxes.[1]

In this respect, the book's verbal strategies for handling a reader are also reflective of *Daemonologie*'s construction of its imagined "other." Where Reginald Scot, as the last chapter has argued, purges those analogies he shares with the witch-mongers he excoriates through the rehearsal and compulsive repetition of their charms and curses, in a very different way *Daemonologie* seeks to purge itself of doubt by passing that doubt onto the reader through the stimulation of curiosity. For both this pattern and its function to become visible, we need to examine the way the book's polemical claims strain against and are actually undermined by the phenomena it describes. Those phenomena, looked at sequentially, unfold to reveal a narrative.[2]

## The Slipperie Scale of Curiosity

Early in *Daemonologie*, Epistemon identifies the three passions by which those who are enticed to the dark arts are seduced: "Curiositie in great ingines: thirst of revenge, for some tortes deeply [suffered] or greedie appetite of [wealth] caused through great pouerty" (8). Witches, who are nearly always women and prone mostly to minor personal acts against those they know, are seduced by either greed or the need for revenge. Magicians, in contrast, who often work on a state level and predict the downfall of whole nations, are enticed by curiosity: "Curiosity, it is onelie the inticement of *Magiciens* or *Necromanciers*," Epistemon says (8). The journey up the slippery scale of curiosity before falling into the depths of hell is the most vivid and detailed rendition of the dangers of curiosity in the book, but there are other ways in which the book stigmatizes curiosity as well. Thus, book 1 makes a distinction between "baser" sorts of magicians and more "curious" sorts, with "baser" meaning cruder and less skilled and "curious" meaning more learned or advanced in the dark arts and thus more skilled. More typically, James uses the word "curious" to describe people—whether they're writers or magicians—who waste their time on things better not known: "But to speake of the diuerse formes of the circles, of the innumerable characters and crosses that are within and without . . . I remit it to ouer-manie that haue busied their heades . . . as being but *curious*, and altogether unprofitable" (emphasis mine, 17–18).

But even as the book demonizes curiosity, James has a way of titillating the very curiosity he seems to condemn. In the preface to his book, for instance, he explains that he's going to give us genus, not species. If he tells us, for example, that magicians can have all sorts of "daintie disshes" (xiii) brought to them by a familiar spirit, he's not going to dwell on the particular dainty dish or the way that these magicians can cause wine in particular to be brought out of a wall. If he proves by "diuerse arguments" that witches can "cure or cast on disseases," he's not going to explain how they can make men impotent or sex-crazed, "weakening the nature of some men, to make them vnable for women: and making it to abound in others, more then the ordinary course of nature would permit" (xiii). By calling attention to the aspects of the dark arts he won't be talking about, by telling us what he won't tell us, James immediately excites an interest in this material. And by telling us to consult Agrippa, book 4, for more detail, he sharpens our curiosity. If curiosity is such a dangerous passion, why stimulate it in the reader? Why titillate us to go to forbidden texts to satisfy it?

It is tempting to answer this question by arguing that the book stimulates curiosity in the reader because it is much more interested in, even identified with, the dark arts than it would care to admit. There is support for this idea in the uneasy identification which exists between Epistemon and witchcraft itself. Thus, when Philomathes, the questioner in the dialogue, implores him, "discourse me some-what of [the Magician's] circkles and conjurationes," Epistemon rebuffs him by saying, "I thinke ye take me to be a Witch my selfe" (16). But even as he seeks to distance himself from witchcraft, Epistemon metaphorically reinscribes himself in the imagery and language of the dark arts again when he compares the premises of his own argument to the circles that conjurors draw: "Ye must first remember to laye the ground, that I tould you before," he tells Philomathes. The "ground" that must be laid is that there is "no power inherent in the circles" (16–17), or any of the rites or words magicians use, but the language Epistemon uses, the fact that he draws on the imagery of conjuring ("lay[ing] the ground") to describe his own argument, suggests the way the book hovers precariously toward an identification with that which it officially eschews. It is tempting to say that James titillates our curiosity because he is much more interested in witchcraft than he would admit and that one method for distancing himself from this interest is to pass it on to us.

But though tempting, such a position is problematic. One problem is that the moments of identification with witchcraft in the book are occasional and sporadic, whereas the condemnation of the dark arts and curiosity in particular is consistent and repetitious. But a more significant problem lies in what the explanation won't account for: an escalation of unacknowledged doubt in the book. Over and over, assertions of certainty in *Daemonologie* are punctuated by moments of unacknowledged doubt. If we were to find a correlation between these moments of rising doubt and the book's tendency to titillate curiosity in the reader, we might hypothesize that this titillation was a response to the anxiety caused by doubt, that the creation of the desire to know in another person was a method for combating the desire to know—the desire for certainty—in the self. From this point of view, the titillation of curiosity becomes a method for managing anxiety, an attempt to quell doubt by passing it on to another person so it seems to exist outside rather than inside the self.

From the very beginning the text articulates the wish to be resolved of doubt. He is glad to have met Epistemon, says Philomathes, "for I am of opinion, that ye can better resolue me of some thing, wherof I stand in great doubt" (1). Doubt about what? About the existence of witches. "What part of it doubt ye of?" Epistemon asks. All of it, says Philomathes, "that there is such a thing as Witchcraft or Witches" (2). Epistemon's first response to the doubt Philomathes expresses is a dogmatic one—dogmatic in the sense that he expresses a faith in the possibility of moving from evidence to knowledge: "so cleare and plaine confessions . . . haue neuer fallen out in anie age or cuntrey," he says.[3] "No question if they be true," says Philomathes, "but thereof the Doctours doubtes" (2). This pattern—doubt, dogmatism, residual doubt—sets the stage for the central battle of the book, a battle between the assertion that knowledge is possible and the anxiety that it is not.

The first skirmish of this battle is fought over the witch of Endor story, in 1 Samuel 28, in which Saul consults the witch of Endor to raise the dead Samuel. Anticipating that Epistemon will cite the woman of Endor as proof that witches exist, Philomathes says it won't prove much and repeats the skeptical arguments on the subject we have just been examining made by Reginald Scot, whom James attacks (along with Weyer) in his preface and whom he ostensibly writes his book to disprove.[4] The witch of Endor story couldn't possibly prove the existence of witchcraft, Philomathes, like Scot, says, because what is it the witch of Endor could have raised up for Saul to see? Not Samuel, certainly, because it would be "profane" and "against all theology," and not the devil impersonating Samuel because then the prophets "in those daies [would never] haue bene sure, what Spirit spake to them in their visiones" (3). If witches could summon up the devil in the forms of the patriarchs, how would

God's prophets ever know the difference between a true voice sent by God and a false one from the devil? Rather, Saul, delusional from both fasting and guilt, must have only imagined he saw Samuel.

The devil could take the form of Samuel, Epistemon says in response. More to the point, his doing so wouldn't bring "any inconvenient with the visiones of the Prophets, since it is most certaine, that God will not permit [the devil] so to deceiue his own: but only such, as first wilfully deceiues them-selves" (4). In effect, Epistemon argues that knowledge is an index to one's spiritual state. The claim, at least here, is that delusion is possible only to those who first deceive themselves.

In one way, the premise that knowledge is possible is embedded in *Daemonologie*. It is a tenet fundamental to the prosecution of witches. For without the ability to know one person from another, a witch from a non-witch, how could one tell the guilty from the innocent? How could one prosecute? Applications of this premise to individual situations recur throughout the book.

Thus at the beginning of book 2, in response to Philomathes asking how to tell a melancholic from a witch, Epistemon provides visible signs that he argues will lead to knowledge. Melancholics are lean, pale, and constantly seek solitude, where witches are "rich . . . worldy-wise, some of them fatte or corpulent in their bodies, and most part of them . . . given over to the pleasures of the flesh . . . and all kind of merrines, both lawfull and vnlawfull" (30). More importantly, melancholics voluntarily turn themselves in, confessing to witchcraft, whereas witches have to be tortured before you can get a confession out of them.

But a few chapters later, Epistemon presents a problem that calls into question the possibility of knowledge. Witches confess to three modes of travel. Two of these—natural "going" and being blown through the air—are possible, but the third is not: "for some of them sayeth, that being transformed in the likenesse of a little beast or foule, they will come and pearce through whatsoeuer house or Church, though all ordinarie passages be closed" (39). This mode of traveling is not possible. It's not possible because it is as proper for a natural body to have "quantity" as it is to a spiritual body to lack it. It's not possible because it would hurt. It's not possible because it would be too much like transubstantiation. And it's not possible because when Peter got out of prison he didn't pass through a solid wall; he opened the door. And the devil can't orchestrate anything God can't do. How is it, then, that if such transport is not possible, witches confess to travelling this way? The devil "rauishe[s] their . . . sences" and presents to their spirits "as it were in a dreame" the idea that they've engaged in out-of-body travel (41). He can even get his "fellow angelles" to delude other persons at the same time, leaving false tokens so that they imagine they have witnessed what the witches confess to. The witches are not lying, but they nonetheless give confessions that aren't true.

But if witches can confess to things which, though not a lie, are also not true, then confessions are, by definition, unreliable. Surrounding and undermining the premise that it is possible to know a witch from a non-witch is the problem of unreliable confession.

The same pattern repeats itself in book 3, when Philomathes asks how it's possible to tell a demoniac from a person merely manic or frantic, and Epistemon provides him with three "signs": "incredible strength" (70), an iron-hard chest, and the ability to speak in languages previously unknown. By these signs it is possible to discern the devil's work from natural illness.

But a chapter later, the problem of unreliable confessions resurfaces: How is it, Philomathes asks, that witches go to their death confessing to have seen fairies when Epistemon insists fairies don't exist? Numerous witches insist they've been transported "with the *Phairie* to such a hill" (74), with a house in it and a glittering court, and they come back with a stone or some other token in their hands. How can it be that witches go to death confessing that they've been transported this way? The answer is the same as with out-of-body travel. The devil "object[s] to their fantasie, their senses being dulled, and as it were a sleepe, such hilles and houses . . . such glistering courts and traines, and whatsoeuer such like . . . he pleaseth to delude them" (74). As further evidence, he leaves a stone or some other token in their hands. The belief that it's possible to tell a witch from a non-witch is central to the project of prosecution. But punctuating each assertion that knowledge is possible is a rising doubt that it is not.

Stuart Clark has rightly pointed out the interconnectedness of doubt and belief in demonological treatises. "Demonology presupposed doubt," Clark says. In the service of demonstrating the way that the arguments of skeptics and "believers" in witchcraft bleed into each other, Clark has argued that both groups allowed for "an important measure of delusion in witchcraft matters," that confessions could "contain impossible feats," and that "all contributors to the field of demonology . . . had to differentiate demonic from non-demonic, true from illusory phenomena."[5] But it is one thing to entertain doubt as a form of skepticism and another, perhaps more difficult thing to make peace with the anxiety born of uncertainty. What do demonologists do with the affects that contradictions in knowledge cause? What mechanisms and strategies, rhetorical and otherwise, are available to them?

One mechanism (as *Daemonologie*'s preoccupation with the outer signs of melancholy and the signs of demonic possession suggests) might be the book's dogmatism itself. The insistence that knowledge is possible seeks to suffocate the doubt which permeates the book even as it is undermined by that very doubt itself. But another mechanism might consist of locating the doubt outside of the self by passing it on to another person. Where Reginald Scot rids himself of those patterns of thought he shares with the witch-mongers through compulsive repetition of the formulas and spells he disdains, thus expelling them outside the self, James seeks to locate outside of the self the doubt that haunts the book by passing it onto the reader. In this sense, the creation of curiosity in the reader, a curiosity which cannot be satisfied without turning to the very texts that James condemns, can be seen as a method of managing the sensation of uncertainty and the anxiety that sensation causes.

What would determine the use of one strategy as opposed to another to quell doubt? When would a new strategy become necessary or even possible? *Daemonologie* tells more than one "story," if by story we mean not a local anecdote like the one the inquisitors tell about the man who lost his virile member but a chronological sequence of moments that reveals a conflict. For this story to become visible, though, we need to look at the order in which what might be dismissed as set pieces or conventional tropes unfolds in the text—tropes typically regarded as so purely conventional that the order or sequence they occur in is deemed irrelevant. To do this is to depart from looking at a trope like the devil's mark or the anal kiss for its typicality but rather to look at it as part of an unfolding narrative.[6]

## Entresse

Just as book 1 begins with Epistemon's claim that only those who first deceive themselves can be deceived, a claim which ultimately gives way to a pattern of rising doubt, so book 2 begins with the claim that "it is to be noted now, that that olde and craftie enemie of ours, assailes none . . . except he first finde an entresse reddy for him" (32). The devil cannot get "entresse" unless we allow him in.

But this polemical claim is at odds with the narrative that unfolds in the last two books of *Daemonologie*. For if book 2 begins by insisting that entresse is voluntary, a matter of consent, it increasingly tells the story of a forced entrance or rape.[7] As I've argued elsewhere, this story begins as a seduction narrative, for the most part a heterosexual seduction narrative, since, as the text tells us, twenty out of every twenty-one witches are women. Even before the devil meets the prospective witch he plans to seduce, he prepares the way for himself by manipulating the witch's despair by "feeding [her] craftely in [her] humour" while waiting for the right moment to "discover" himself.

He then finds her alone walking in a field or "pansing" [ruminating] in her bed and appears to her in the form of a man or disembodied voice and sets a second "tryist."

At the time of this next appointment he gets the witch to "addict" herself to his service by getting her to renounce God and baptism and marks her on some "secreit place" on her body which remains "soare unhealed" (33). The mark is an eroticized place made by the devil's lick or touch which leaves an "intollerable dolour" which serves to "waken" the witch and will not let her rest. What is of interest here is the moment at which the devil's mark occurs in *Daemonologie*, the way it functions not just as an isolated trope but as a stage in an unfolding narrative or story.

So far this story is one of heterosexual seduction, a story which falls into separable stages of foreplay: a meeting, a lick, an eroticized part of the body. In the next stage, witches convene en masse to kiss the devil's "hinder partes." The text creates the expectation that this foreplay will culminate in the act of heterosexual penetration that characterizes so much European demonology: the devil, the male, penetrating the witch.

But even as it creates this expectation, the book switches to a weird preoccupation with what acts of penetration witches can accomplish. "For some of them sayeth," Epistemon says as we have noted, "that being transformed in the likenesse of a little beast or foule, they will come and pearce through whatsoeuer house or Church, though all ordinarie passages be closed, by whatsoeuer open, the aire may enter in at" (39). The witches must be deluded to make such a claim, Epistemon says, and in so saying he seems to neutralize the threat that witches can penetrate solid walls. But no sooner has he done so than the fear of penetration comes back in another form.

Philomathes asks whether spirits can penetrate the same solid walls, "Doore and Window being steiked," and Epistemon says that they can. If they've assumed dead bodies, they can "easely inough open . . . anie Doore or Window" and enter that way, or they can enter as "spirite[s]," . . . "anie place where the aire may come in at, is large inough" for them to get in (59). Nor is it simply that they can penetrate the walls of houses. They can penetrate the human body. Is it true that there's a spirit "more monstrous" than all the rest, Philomathes asks, one that can "converse naturally [have sex with] them whom they trouble and hauntes with (66). Epistemon answers that it's true. Such spirits are called incubi and succubi, and they get into the human body the same way spirits get into houses. They can "borrow" a dead body "and so visiblie" converse with those they have sex with. Or, as spirits, they can steal "out the sperm" of a dead person, abusing their victims that way, the victims "not graithlie seeing anie shape or feeling anie thing" (67).

But it is not just that they can get into the body but what the spirits do when they get there that matters. What they do when they get into the male body is to take out its sperm, what the text calls its "nature."[8] Thus what begins as a narrative of heterosexual seduction ends with the possibility of male rape. The text rehearses over and over again the fear of what acts of penetration are possible and who or what it is possible to penetrate. No sooner has one version of entresse been put to rest than another replaces it.

Just as the polemical claims *Daemonologie* makes that knowledge is possible are undermined by the pattern of rising doubt that punctuates the book, so the claim that the devil can only gain entresse with consent is undermined by the fear of things getting into the human body, a fear that coalesces as a narrative of rape. What strategies might exist to cope with this fear? A look at the last moments of *Daemonologie* suggests a possible answer.

James devotes the last chapter of *Daemonologie* to the trial and punishment of witches and offers an accumulation of rationales for killing a witch. Book 2 has already argued that the magistrate's power over a witch depends on how rigorously a magistrate punishes. If the magistrate is slothful, God will make the witch an instrument to punish that sloth, but if the magistrate is "diligent in examining and punishing of them" (50), God will not permit the devil, the witches' master, to trouble the magistrate. Further, Epistemon has argued, the witch's power depends not only on how rigorously punishment is meted out but who it is that does the punishing. "If they be but apprehended and deteined by anie private person," witches retain the power to escape and do harm. But if the lawful magistrate apprehends and imprisons them "vpon the iust respectes of their guiltinesse in that craft," they have no more power than they did before they turned to the devil. Clark calls this power the "inviolability" of the magistrate. But the narrative of entresse which unfolds throughout the book suggests that an equally powerful fear of violability informs *Daemonologie*.[9] Now, in the last chapter of the book, invoking the laws of God, civil and imperial law, and the municipal law of Christian nations, Epistemon insists on the necessity of never sparing a witch's life ("They ought to be put to death according to the law of God, the civill and imperial law, and municipall law of all Christian nations" [77]). Is there any "sexe, age or ranck to be exempted?" No. Should anyone's evidence count as evidence? Yes. Should even the evidence of a witch, ravished in mind and deluded by the devil, count as legitimate evidence? Yes. ("What if [the witches] accuse folke to haue bene present at their Imaginar conuentiones in the spirite, when their bodies lyes sencelesse, as ye haue said" [79].) Should the accused still be held guilty and killed even if the accuser accuses them out of a delusion? Yes. "They are not a haire the less guiltie," Epistemon says, because God would never have allowed the devil to have borrowed the "shadow" or "similitude" of the accused person for such a purpose if the "consent" of the person whose similitude is borrowed had not been operative in some way.[10] At the very least, this person must have led an evil life. Can a magistrate ever spare a witch? Can he ever spare "anie that are guiltie of that crafte?" Philomathes asks (78). He can delay for more information ("for further tryals cause"), Epistemon says, but in the end, "to spare the life, and not to strike when God bids strike" is not only unlawful but analogous to Saul sparing Agag against God's instruction and therefore "comparable to the sin of Witch-craft it selfe."

Having imagined and authorized the magistrate's violence against witches, the sensation of doubt and the attendant need to pass it onto another person recedes. At the very end of the book the text reverts to an even more naïve faith in signs than it began with. Epistemon reassures Philomathes that if all other evidence fails, God has appointed at least one "secret super-naturall signe" that will reveal the crime of witchcraft to a judge: witches can float because the water "shal refuse to receiue them in her bosom," the witches having "shaken off . . . the sacred Water of Baptisme." Similarly, it's a sign of witchcraft if a woman can't cry (especially if she tries to dissemble like a crocodile). It's another "good helpe" at a trial to find "the [devil's] marke" on the accused's body, as such a mark is likely to be insensible to pain. (We see the court turning to this mark in *Newes from Scotland*, the pamphlet that describes James's role as an examiner of witches before he became, as James I, king of England.)

To return to the question of when a new strategy for managing doubt might become necessary, it might become necessary when an old strategy failed. Ultimately passing doubt on to the reader is insufficient to contain the anxiety caused by the story of entresse told in the latter parts of the book. Only when this anxiety has been neutralized by a vision of violence can the speakers return to the faith in signs and certainty with which the book began. What happens when such signs are not available and the rotating strategies James and his examiners turn to in *Newes from Scotland* is the subject of the next chapter.

# Chapter 5

# *Newes from Scotland* and the Theaters of Evidence

Toward the middle of *Newes from Scotland*, the 1591 pamphlet describing King James VI and I's interrogation of a set of witches, the king has one of the defendants reenact for him the actions she is accused of having committed.[1] Geillis Duncane, maidservant to a local deputy bailiff, David Seaton, is brought in to play upon a "Iewes trump" the "reill" or song she is supposed to have played at a nocturnal sabbath on Halloween. In a progression of affects similar to that of the bailiff who initially examines Duncane, King James moves through the course of her performance from "wonder" at the doings reported to him to "great delight" at their reenactments. The performance itself seems to calm him and to deflect violence. This, despite the fact that in his own book, *Daemonologie*, James repeatedly presents witchcraft itself as a kind of theater in which Satan, the supreme illusionist, impersonates everyone from the ghost of Samuel to the fairies who accompany Diana.

If witchcraft is the devil's performance, what need is served on the part of the court by having it reenacted? In one sense the answer to this is obvious: such performances serve as evidentiary procedures, confirming to king and court that the crimes for which the defendants are being tried have actually taken place. But not all the actions defendants are accused of are susceptible to being acted out. At these moments, what kinds of evidentiary procedures does the court turn to?[2]

In the section dedicated to evidence in his mammoth *Demonomanie*, Jean Bodin offers an explicit hierarchy of the kinds of evidence that can be used in a courtroom. The first is the truth of the acknowledged and concrete fact. (Witnesses swear Pierre is dead, but Pierre shows up very much alive in the courtroom as a concrete fact.) The second is voluntary confession. The third is the testimony of several sound witnesses. Like lesser pieces of evidence such as forced confession and reputation, each piece of evidence has an equivalence and a distinct place in a hierarchy. In *Discipline and Punish*, Foucault describes similar hierarchies of evidence as part of what he calls the "penal arithmetic" (37) of the Middle Ages and Renaissance (36).[3] But no such penal "arithmetic" appears to operate in *Newes from Scotland*, where the court seems to lurch back and forth from one standard of evidence to another without any articulated rationale. Is there some kind of invisible hierarchy of evidence operative in the pamphlet?

Writing about the way Roman canon law replaced the ordeal after 1215 as a means of determining guilt or innocence, John H. Langbein says of the new standard of evidence—two eyewitnesses or confession—that "no one would be concerned that God was no longer being asked to resolve the doubts. There could be no doubts."[4] This chapter suggests that what *Newes from Scotland* exhibits is precisely the longing for certainty and a recidivism to methods of trying to attain it characteristic of the old ordeals. In the absence of such certainty, what prevails is obsessive doubt—doubt not in the sense of an act of skepticism but in the sense of a fundamental and unresolvable uncertainty. I chart the existence of that doubt and the increasingly ineffective strategies both the pamphleteer and the court he describes turn to in order to contain it, strategies which imply a hierarchy of evidence but which never stay fixed long enough to amount to a coherent system.

In its attention to this doubt my account differs in at least one significant way from the one Foucault offers of judicial torture in the period. Built into his claim that torture is a technique is a series of subsidiary claims that cast judicial torture during the period as being "regulated" in such a way as to suggest it exists almost independently from the affects of the examiners who order it.[5] But *Newes from Scotland* devotes considerable attention to the responses and affects of the examiners, including the sovereign himself, suggesting that these play a significant role in the torture the pamphlet describes. My argument focuses on those particular affects that seem to coalesce around the experience of uncertainty. I argue not only that in comparison to the trial records and indictments he draws on, the pamphleteer dwells on these affects, transferring his attention and emphasis from the deeds of the accused to the responses of the examiners, but that these responses fall into a specific progression with recognizable stages. I consider the cases of the defendants who receive the most sustained attention in the pamphlet—Geillis Duncane, Agnes [Agnis] Sampson (who appears first under that name but becomes increasingly merged with an Agnes Tompson), and Doctor Fian—against the background of examination records and indictments we have for them, not because these records themselves constitute "truth" but because the liberties the pamphleteer takes in embellishing them suggest the values of the pamphlet.[6] *Newes From Scotland* draws selectively from these records, suppressing some details and expanding and improvising on others. My focus accordingly is less on "what happened" than on the values the pamphlet itself exhibits, though the comparison of pamphlet to trial and indictment records illuminates the needs of both those participating in and those shaping the narrative. This is ultimately an essay about the pamphlet, not the events which may have preceded it.

## Matters Miraculous

Geillis Duncane is the first defendant examined in *Newes from Scotland*. Maidservant to David Seaton, she takes to disappearing from her master's house every other night and additionally develops mysterious healing powers for "all such as were troubled or greeued with any kinde of sicknes or infirmitie" (8). Moreover, the pamphleteer tells us, these gifts come upon her suddenly. In a "short space [she] did perfourme manye matters most miraculous . . . Upon a sodaine, having never doon the like before" (8–9). Seaton, her master, suspects witchcraft and torments Duncane with a thumbscrew torture called the "Pilliwinckes" and binds her head with a rope. When she still will not confess, Seaton makes a "dilligent search about her," suspecting she has "beene marked by the Diuell (as commonly witches are)" and finds the "enemies marke to be in her fore crag or forepart of her throate." Once it is found, she confesses that all her doings were "doone by the wicked allurements and inticements of the Diuell, and that she did them by witchcraft" (9).

What counts as "proof" in Duncane's case is the devil's mark. It has "latelye beene found," the pamphleteer tells us, "that the Deuill dooth generallye marke [witches] with a priuie marke," and "so long as the marke is not seene to those which search them," so long will the witches never confess (12–13). Writing about the ordeals abolished in 1215 by the Lateran Council, Langbein writes, "God revealed the innocence of an accused whose hand withstood infection from the hot iron; God pronounced the guilt of one who floated when subjected to the water ordeal" (6). Like the old ordeals—the hand that failed to infect or the body that floated—the devil's mark functions as a sign both to the pamphleteer and the examiners that the accused is a witch.[7] Similarly it is a sign to the witch herself that she had better confess. But it functions in another, almost transformative way as well. This function becomes apparent if we look at the sequence of affects Seaton goes through.

Seaton first exhibits admiration. Duncane, we are told, initially makes "her Maister and others to be in great admiracion"; they "wondred thereat" (8). But Seaton then comes to hold his maid "in some great suspition." He fears "that she did not those things by naturall and lawfull wayes, but rather supposed it to be doone by some extraordinary and vnlawfull meanes" (10). Seaton begins to "growe very inquisitiue" and examines Duncane about "which way and by what meanes she were able to perfourme matters of so great importance." It is when she gives him no answer and he cannot satisfy that "inquisitive[ness]" that he seeks to "better trye and finde out the trueth of the same" and torments her with the torture of the Pilliwinckes and rope, suspecting and finding the mark, which restores certainty. From admiration or "wonder" to suspicion and inquisitiveness, to trying to find out the truth, to violence, to a resting point in certainty, Seaton finds a way to quell his own doubt. The violence ends when the *sensation* of certainty comes about.

Here, then, judicial certainty and the sensation of certainty seem to coincide. What counts as evidence in court coincides with the sensation which relieves doubt. But what if the two failed to align? What if Seaton or any examiner were unable to complete such a progression of affects and remained stuck at suspicion or inquisitiveness? What would the consequences be in terms of the violence directed at the defendant? The recurrent references the pamphlet makes to the reactions of the examiners suggest the need to take these into account in defining the function of spectacle. As we shall see, doubt and the various sensations that accompany it are in fact operative forces behind much of the violence the pamphleteer describes.

No equivalent portrait of David Seaton's reactions to her emerges in Geillis Duncane's examination records in late 1590 or in the dittay (the formal indictment) that ultimately followed. But both Duncane's and other defendants' confessions and dittays do reveal a plot against Seaton which is notably absent in *Newes from Scotland*. In these records, a group of persons accused of witchcraft—Duncane among them but certainly not chief among them—conspires to find a way to "wrack" David Seaton and his goods.[8] The plot, which involves littering the moor with something like ground glass and cord, eventually goes awry. But the author of *Newes from Scotland* mentions none of this, focusing instead on the progress of Seaton's responses as he examines Duncane. This shift from maleficium on the part of the defendant to response on the part of the examiner typifies the pamphleteer's interest in the reaction and affect of the examiner and the measures necessary to calm the examiner down.

James has Duncane recalled to him, because one of the defendants she incriminates describes a nocturnal Sabbath at which she claims Duncane provided musical accompaniment. With a great many other witches, the defendant says, "to the number of two hundredth," they sailed to sea in sieves on the night of Allhollon Eve "with Flaggons of wine making merrie and drinking by the waye" (13). There, after landing and arriving at the church of North Berwick in Lothian, they all "tooke handes on the land and daunced this reill or short daunce, singing all with one voice:

*Commer goe ye before, commer goe ye.*
*Gif ye will not goe before, commer let me.*[9]

The defendant claims that at this time Geillis Duncane "did goe before them playing this reill or daunce vpon a small Trump, called a Iewes Trump, vntill they entred into the Kerk of north Barrick" (14). This confession puts the king in such a "wonderful admiration" that he sends for Geillis Duncane to get her to reenact her performance, "who vpon the like Trump did playe the said daunce before the Kings Maiestie, who in respect of the strangenes of these matters, took *great delight* to bee present at their examinations" (emphasis mine, 14).

Again, the pamphleteer dwells on the king's reaction. But here, in contrast to Seaton's experience, the king's "wonderful admiration" does not progress to suspicion or rage but instead turns to "great delight." The performance itself seems to be what accomplishes this transformation. Two different authenticating procedures are employed by two different examiners at two different times to verify Duncane's guilt: one (the "discovery" of the devil's mark) by her master, a "sign," reminiscent of the signs God provided at the old ordeals; the other a competing strategy (the reenactment of secret doings) in the form of a performance before the king. Each satisfies its respective examiner, through the first requires more violence. What determines which of the procedures an examiner turns to?

Duncane can only make a piece of the invisible visible, can only reenact part of the charge against her, the visible—or in this case, audible or musical—part, not the sailing to sea in sieves or kissing of the devil's buttocks. What happens, then, when none of a confession can be reenacted? The next defendant accused of witchcraft, Agnes Sampson, would seem to provide a possible answer to this question. None of what she confesses to can be reenacted. Instead she turns to narrative.

A word is in order about Agnes Sampson and Agnes Tompson. The pamphlet starts with a very clear distinction between the two, differentiating between "Agnis Sampson the eldest witch of them al, dwelling in Haddington" and "Agnes Tompson of Edinburgh." As it progresses, however, the narration becomes increasingly confused ("Item the said Agnes Tompson," the pamphleteer says in the middle of Agnes Sampson's story; "touching this Agnes Tompson," the pamphleteer continues, talking about Agnes Sampson). Many scholars see "Tompson" as a mistake for Sampson, including Normand and Roberts, who say Tompson is "likely to be an error," presumably because there is no mention of an Agnes Tompson in the "extant dittays and depositions" (312). James Craigie treats the two as different witches but attributes actions of "Tompson" to Sampson. Pitcairn's *Criminal Trials* (one of Craigie's sources) glosses "Tompson" by putting "Sampson" in parentheses every time Tompson's name appears. Tompson may well have been Sampson. Although a Bessie Tompson and a Margaret Tompson appear in the examination records and dittays, no independent record of an Agnes Tompson exists. In keeping with the quartos which are the source of the Bodleian Library edition I have tried to preserve the ambiguity in the text where it occurs.[10]

Agnes Sampson, "the eldest witch, dwelling in Haddington," is one of the defendants Geillis Duncane incriminates. She is taken directly before the king and other nobility to be "straitly examined." Like Duncane, she resists various "perswasions," and like Duncane, she refuses to confess and is taken to prison (12). Like Duncane, Sampson is searched for a devil's mark. But unlike Duncane, Sampson has to be shaved before the devil's mark is found, and when it is found, it is not on her throat but on her genitals. (She is ordered "by special commaundement" to have "all her haire shauen off, in each parte of her bodie, and her head thrawen with a rope according to the custome of that Countrye" until "the Diuel's marke [is] found upon her priuities," at which point she "immediatlye confesse[s] whatsoeuer was demaunded of her" [13].) Implicitly, the court's treatment of Sampson raises the issue of why she receives more torture and more explicitly sexual torture than Duncane.[11]

Unlike Duncane's confession, Sampson's doesn't initially dispel her examiner's doubt. Here, evidentiary procedures and affective states don't seem to coincide. The things Sampson confesses to strike the king as so "miraculous and strange" that he claims the witches are "all extreame lyars." In addition to all her other problems, then, Sampson finds herself in the difficult position of having to compel belief: "She answered, she would not wishe his Maiestie to suppose her woords to be false, but rather to beleeue them" and promises to "discouer such matter vnto him as his maiestie should not any way doubt off" (15). Sampson solves the problem of how to ease the growing frustration her examiner's doubt generates not with a theatrical performance but with a narrative. She tells the king what he said to his wife on his wedding night: "She declared vnto him the verye woordes which passed betweene the Kings Maiestie and his Queene at Vpslo in Norway the first night of their mariage, with their answere eache to other" (15). At this, the king "wonder[s] greatlye." He swears "by the liuing God, that he beleeued that all the Diuels in hell could not haue discouered the same: acknowledging her woords to be most true" and therefore gives "the more credit to the rest which [she] before declared." In this instance, then, it is a narrative which accomplishes the transition from doubt to wonder and eventual belief.

Here again, if we consult the record of Sampson's examinations and indictments and compare them to *Newes from Scotland*, we see a shift on the pamphleteer's part from the doings or maleficia of the witch to the reactions, the affect, of the king. There, in the court records, on December 4, 1590, in response to a long, garbled story about her confrontation with the devil in the form of a dog, King James reproaches Sampson with the contradictions in her account. (On the one hand, says the king, Sampson has intimated that she and the group of gentlewomen she was with all saw the dog at the same time; on the other that she was summoned after the dog appeared. On the one hand, he says, Sampson claims she and her companions slew the dog; on the other that the dog fled.) The king charges her to confess the truth, and she thanks him, praising God for the repentance thus "wrought" in her.[12] All this, that is, the content of her contradictions, *Newes from Scotland* leaves out. More importantly, where in the examination record the king's rebuke serves as a stimulus to Sampson's conversion from defiance to repentance, *Newes from Scotland* uses the incident to dramatize the *king's* movement from doubt to belief, his willingness to give "more credit to the rest which [she] before declared" (15). Here again the emphasis is on the response of the person conducting the examination, the transformation from the sensation of doubt to that of belief.

The very beginnings of a hierarchy seem to emerge if we compare Sampson's case to Duncane's, but what emerges is not a hierarchy of evidence like the kind Bodin enumerates or Foucault alludes to in his description of penal arithmetic but rather a hierarchy of undemonstrability. Duncane can reenact part of the crime she is accused of, but Sampson, able to reenact none, is forced to resort to narrative. The "narrative line" or progression of the pamphlet itself seems to be one in which the crimes confessed to increasingly elude reenactment, escape the parameters of what is available for demonstration. But we are also seeing in action three competing forms of authenticating guilt: the "signs" that the devil's marks, reminiscent of the old ordeals, provide (the mark Seaton "discovers" on Duncane's throat); the performance which seeks to but only partially succeeds in replicating the crime the defendant confesses to (Duncane on the Jew's trump); and the narrative which doesn't reproduce but seeks to bear witness to the crime (Sampson on what the king said on his wedding night).

We might theorize, then, that either of two conditions could account for the intensifying violence—and specifically sexual violence—directed at Sampson. Where only parts of Duncane's confession are not susceptible to being reenacted, none of Sampson's confession is susceptible to reenactment. In this scenario, the less a confession lends itself to theatrical demonstration, the more torture a given defendant receives. Implicitly, this would suggest a partial hierarchy of authenticating procedures: narratives rank lower than performances, offering a less *satisfying* means of relieving doubt. Alternatively, the more of a threat a given defendant offers, the more violence she or he receives. Where Duncane merely exhibits mysterious healing powers, Sampson, hovering around the king's bedchamber on his wedding night, conjures up fears of impotence.

The problem lies in what it means to constitute a threat. One would think that few threats would outstrip attempts to kill the king. But it isn't the woman accused of attempted regicide who receives the most intense torture in the pamphlet, but rather the male conjuror John Fian, who through amatory magic seeks to seduce a village girl and whose story occupies the last half of the pamphlet.

The pamphleteer tells us that "Tompson" (by whom he seems to mean Sampson) confesses to two attempts on the king's life, most famously to christening a cat and binding to it "the cheefest partes of a dead man" in order to raise winds to sink the king's ship on its way back to Scotland. She also confesses to taking a "blacke Toade" which she "did hang . . . vp by the heeles three daies, and collected and gathered the venom as it dropped . . . in an Oister shell." She is the only woman, the pamphleteer says, "who by the Diuels perswasion should haue entended and put in execution the Kings Maiesties death in this manner" (15–16).

She kept the venom "close couered," she says, waiting until "she should obtaine any parte or peece of foule linnen cloth, that had appertained to the Kings Maiestie, as shirt, handkercher, napkin or any other thing." She approaches "one John Kers," an attendant in his majesty's chamber, for the linen cloth, asking him "for olde acquaintance betweene them, to helpe her to one or a peece of such a cloth," which he refuses to give her. She says "that if she had obtained any one peece of linnen cloth which the King had worne and fouled, she had bewitched him to death, and put him to such extraordinary paines, as if he had beene lying vpon sharp thornes and endes of Needles" (16).

It is important to keep in mind the principle at work here, which, as far as the pamphleteer is concerned, has nothing to do with attempted poisoning. The venom need not ever touch the king.[13] It needs only to touch some "peece of foule linnen cloth" that has "appertained" to the king. There are two overlapping notions of magic here. What has touched the king, in being altered, can alter the king (what is often called contagious magic) and what refers to or stands for the king, in being altered, can alter the king (what is often called sympathetic magic).[14] This second notion is deeply theatrical, but not in the sense that Duncane's performance is—it does not reenact what has already taken place. Rather, it construes images as having the power to alter the things they should only represent, and in that way resembles the fear of those who attacked the stage during the period—the fear that costumes would alter the gender of the boy actors who wore them and performances would change the spectators who watched.

Codifying his beliefs about image magic in his own book, *Daemonologie*, James denied that either images or objects like the "piece of [fouled] linnen cloth" had any constitutive power. Rather, they were all part of a theatrical performance orchestrated by the devil. Epistemon, James's spokesman, says that though the devil can teach witches "how to make Pictures of waxe or clay: That by the rosting thereof, the persones; that they beare the name of, may be . . . melted or dryed awaie by . . . sicknesse," the images only *seem* to do the roasting because "that instrumente of waxe haue no vertue in that turne doing" (45–46). To create the belief that the images have the power, the devil *times* his own assaults on victims to coincide with the witches melting wax but actually injures the victims himself. ("May he not I say at these same times [that the witches melt wax pictures] subtilie as a spirite so weaken and scatter the spirites of life of the patient" so that he, the devil, "sweate[s] out the humour of [the patient's] bodie: [so that] . . . hee [the patient] at last shall vanish awaie, euen as his picture will doe at the fire," Epistemon says [46].) The devil schedules his assaults in such a way that they coincide with the witches melting wax images so that the images appear to be what are destroying the victims (46). Thus Satan stages elaborate scenes of theater, deceptions built around coincidence, in order to create the belief that the images the witches carve are efficacious.

In one way, then, the king's apparent "delight" in the various performances and reenactments like Duncane's, which he demands throughout the pamphlet, makes sense from the standpoint of rival theaters, performance, and counterperformance, and the kind of mastery such a counterperformance implies. No longer is it Satan who orchestrates the performance to dupe his victims into false belief, but the king, who through those victims is in control.

## CHAPTER 5

But there is another, more curious way in which the performances depicted in *Newes from Scotland* might give James "delight." Among the items in Agnes Sampson's January 1591 confession is an entry whose details never make their way into *Newes from Scotland*. We are told that Sampson conjures a "picture of wax concerning Mr. John Moscrop,"[15] a picture which offers a "similitude of Mr. John Moscrop, father-in-law to Euphame MacCalzean," in order to help Euphame destroy "the said Mr. John," and that after passing over a steep bank Sampson raises a spirit to help prepare the image for Moscrop's destruction (240).[16] Similarly, she prepares a "small picture of yellow wax" to endanger the life of a goodman named Archie (245).[17] Regardless of the way James subsequently relegates image magic to the status of coincidence in *Daemonologie*, the examination records and indictments seem to treat such images themselves as dangerous.

One way of understanding the court's need to script the performances it does in *Newes from Scotland*, then, and the "delight" these seem to bring on, is as attempts to strip representations of their performative power by making them strictly evidentiary procedures, and thus reducing them from things that "behave" to things that "refer." Sampson (who is still being called "Tompson") is threatening not only because she confesses to two attempts to kill the king but because she draws on the fear that images do have an autonomous power—that had she gotten the linen that "appertained" to the king she might have effectively bewitched his majesty to death and put him to "extraordinary paines." By staging through the bodies of those who come before them a theater of evidence, one which indicates events that have actually happened, the court seeks to neutralize the fear of sympathetic magic.[18] These performances, then, serve multiple purposes, not only seeking to restore the sensation of certainty but seeking to undo the very mechanism by which sympathetic magic is imagined to work.

For all this, *Newes from Scotland* leaves Sampson in prison still waiting for judgment after Fian has been executed.[19] (And if the two women named Agnes are really different people, it tells us nothing about the ultimate punishment of a person named "Agnes Tompson of Edenbrough." The pamphleteer leaves her fate hanging.) In comparison, the last part of the pamphlet relentlessly details the torture and execution of Doctor Fian, alias John Cunningham, notable primarily for trying to seduce a local village girl. Foucault claims that torture "correlates" the "corporal effect"—the "quality, intensity, duration of pain, with the gravity of the crime, the person of the criminal [and] the rank of his victims" (34). Under what circumstances is an attempt to seduce a village girl comprehensible as more threatening than an attempt to kill a king?

## Again Newly Marked?

Fian's story dominates the last half of *Newes from Scotland*, occupying as much space as that of all the other defendants together. The pamphleteer improvises more of its events than he does in the case of other defendants. In part this may be due to the fact that we have no examination records for Fian, just a brief indictment. But the pamphleteer's additions are so outlandish that scarcity of records by itself cannot account for them. In the course of the pamphlet, Fian offers a reenactment of one of the events he confesses to, an extended narrative about another, and is searched for a devil's mark, though none is ever found. As such, his case offers not only an opportunity to compare evidentiary procedures but a chance to try to understand what determines the use of one rather than another.

Fian is a schoolmaster from Saltpans enamored of a local village girl, and he confesses to throwing a rival, a gentleman also enamored of the girl, into something like a possession every twenty-four hours. By means of "Sorcerye, witchcraft and diuelish practices," he says, "he caused the said Gentleman that once in xxiiij howres he fell into a lunacie and madnes, and so continued one whole hower together" (19–20). Parts of this story appear in Fian's dittay. Two counts of his indictment charge him with the "bewitching and possessing of William Hutson in Windygoul with an evil sprite," though no mention is made of Hutson as a rival, or indeed of any love rival, and instead of the fits coming on once in twenty-four hours we hear that Hutson is affected for twenty-six weeks.[20]

In *Newes from Scotland*, Fian actually brings the rival into court and stages a reenactment of the possession "for the veritie of the same." No such reenactment occurs in the records we have of Fian's indictment, but in *Newes from Scotland*, the performance takes place to the "great admiracion" of his majesty. The gentleman exhibits the signs of demonic possession ("suddenly he gave a great scritch and fell into a madness, sometime bending himselfe, and sometime capring so directly vp, that his head did touch the seeling of the Chamber" [21]). When he awakes after "his furye were past," he says he has been sound asleep.

So far, the performance conforms roughly to the pattern Geillis Duncane's performance on a Jew's trump establishes. Like Duncane's, it creates "great admiration." Like Duncane's, it makes visible what could otherwise not be made so. If we had nothing more of Fian's case, it would seem to imply that he who can best stage what cannot be seen can best avert violence. (He who can channel and give shape to the anxiety in the court generated by things unseen can avoid the consequences of that anxiety.) Fian's reenactment of the gentleman's possession takes place on Christmas Eve and has the feel of a revel or holiday gambol. The pamphleteer's affect, like the king's, is upbeat, admiring.

But when the pamphleteer gets to the part of Fian's confession that cannot be reenacted, the mood changes. Fian confesses to trying to seduce the girl by "coniuring, witchcraft and Sorcery." To accomplish this feat, he promises to teach her brother, a student of his, "without stripes" (lashes) if he will steal from his sister three pubic hairs, "three haires of his sisters privities." The boy takes the conjured paper and attempts to "lappe the haires" in them while his sister sleeps (22). The principle at work here is the same principle at work in the attempt to steal the king's linen; what "appertains" to the girl, the sign or representation of her sexuality, governs that sexuality. We come to understand this by what happens next in the story.

The girl cries out in the night, and her mother suspects Fian's intention. Why? "By reson she [is] a witche" herself. She substitutes for the girl's hairs three hairs from the udder of a "young Heyfer which neuer had borne Calfe nor gone to the Bull," and puts them in the conjured paper. Fian goes to work conjuring the "haires," "thinking them indeede to bee the Maides haires," and wreaks his art upon them. But no sooner has he done so than the "Hayfer or Cow whose haires they were indeed" comes into the church and makes toward Fian, "leaping and dauncing vpon him," "following him foorth of the church and to what place so ever he went" (23). Needless to say this material is totally absent from Fian's indictment—Normand and Roberts suggest the possibility of Apuleius's *Golden Ass* as a source—but we see in it, in its clearest form, the principle so rigorously denied by *Daemonologie*, the principle of sympathetic magic: when the cow's hairs (both part of the cow and what stands for the cow) lead the cow to do what Fian wanted the girl to do.[21]

For the pamphleteer, the threat of Fian's magic is neutralized by a larger spectacle which belongs to God. The mother is God's instrument, His means of revealing hidden things. The spectacle of the cow amorously embracing Fian is God's "declaration" of Fian's doings, the means by which the people of Scotland come to know Fian as a "notable Coniurer." From then on "the name of the said Doctor Fien (who was but a very yong man) began to grow so common among the people of Scotland, that he was secretlye nominated for a notable Cuniurer" (24). This revelation of Fian's identity is the consummate example of the ability to reverse the process of sympathetic magic: the spectacle of the cow following him into the church makes into a "sign," or piece of evidence, the man who had the potential to make a representation become performative, who sought to make an image alter what it should only represent. As such, the spectacle is the model for what the court seeks to make happen through the examination of all those on trial.

But how can the court bring about such a spectacle? Even if Fian were to strike a pose of appeasement, he lacks the requisite theatrical power: he cannot stage as evidence most of what he has confessed. Like Duncane, who can play the song the witches sang when they danced a reel but who cannot reproduce the sailing to sea in sieves, his subject matter eludes his medium. And yet, as a teller of stories like the narrator himself, as the "Regester," the "one man suffered to come to the Diuels readinges," "alwayes preasent" at general meetings of witches, "Clarke to all those that were in subiection to the Diuels service," the one who takes "their othes for their true seruice to the Diuell," writing "for them such matters as the Diuell still pleased to commaund him" (18–19), Fian has the same capacity to do for king and God what he did for the devil: authenticate and seal as truth what has happened. He can authorize through the written record that which cannot be performed or reenacted, serving the king instead of the devil as clerk or registrar or witness. Initially, after his signed confession, the court has high hopes for him.

Fian is committed to prison, "to a chamber by himselfe" (25), and seems to forsake his wicked ways, admitting that he had "too much folowed the allurements and entisements of sathan" (25). He renounces the devil and vows to lead the life of a Christian, seeming "newly connected towards God." The next morning, he says the devil has appeared to him dressed in black, carrying a white wand, demanding faithful service, but that he "utterly renounced [the devil] to his face, and sayde vnto him in this manner, Auoide Satan, auoide, for I have listned too much vnto thee" (26). Whether Fian is sincere in his penitence or playing the part of the penitent, the court has not only the signed document but precisely the scene before them they need to see. But that night he breaks out of prison and flees back to Saltpans, where he's apprehended, recaptured, and reexamined. Now the doctor denies everything he's said before, "notwithstanding that his owne confession appeareth remaining in recorde vnder his own hande writing" (27). In protesting his innocence, Fian not only denies the authenticity of his own previous testimony but reveals as mere theater the penitence that has appeased the court and that has seemed to authenticate the invisible world he confesses to.

Now the court cannot get Fian's actions to match his written record. The gap between the two widens, and in the gap the king is able to "imagine." What he imagines is "that in the time of his absence [Fian] had entred into newe conference and league with the deuill his master, and that hee had been agayne newly marked" (27). But now what the king "imagines" and "conceives" cannot be made visible. In contrast to Fian's dittay, which begins with the charge that Fian has "suffer[ed] . . . himself to be marked by the devil with a rod,"[22] when Fian is "narrowly searched" no devil's mark can be found ("it [the devil's mark] coulde not in anie wise bee founde").

What was "admiration" turns to "strange torment" in the service of "more tryall of him to make him confesse." It is as if the satisfaction born of certainty, the satisfaction generated by Fian's dramatic reenactment of the demonic possession, has begun to dissolve and the progression of affects he has been able to orchestrate in others has begun to slide backwards, from admiration to torment to rising violence; king and court are unable to sustain certainty. It is not now Fian's attempt to seduce a village girl that is the threat but his capacity to aggravate doubt.

In the face of that doubt, Fian's nails are riven, pulled off with pincers, and two needles thrust under every nail "even up to the heads." For the second time, he's put to the torture of the "bootes," and his "legges" are "crushte and beaten together as small as might bee, and the bones and flesh so brused, that the bloud and marrowe spouted forth in great abundance, whereby they were made unserviceable forever." Notwithstanding all these torments, the pamphleteer says, "hee would not confesse anie thing, so deeply had the deuill entered into his heart, that hee vtterly denied all that which he had before auouched, and woulde saie nothing thervnto but this, that what hee had done and sayde before, was oonely done and sayde for feare of paynes which he had endured" (27–28). In denying the authenticity of his previous confession, Fian exposes as mere theatrical pretense both his own penitence and the efforts of the court he has sought to appease. Instead of revealing and making plain, instead of delivering certainty, the gap Fian creates between the invisible world of imagined crimes and the demonstrable world of evidence grows bigger and bigger. It is a gap not only between invisible crime and demonstrable evidence but between first and second testimonies, written and oral confessions, a gap of widening doubt. Even Fian's body refuses to provide certainty in the form of a devil's mark. And in the absence of a theatricalization, a consistent narrative, or a bodily mark that delivers certainty, the court's violence seems to be virtually limitless.

## The Pamphlet's Silences

Almost none of the pamphleteer's additions can be found in Fian's indictment or in the examination records of other defendants that Normand and Roberts provide. Neither the girl from Saltpans, the brother who Fian promises to teach "without stripes," nor the gentleman rival—let alone the amorous cow—exist in any of these materials. Nor is there a reference to a possession reenacted before the king. Equally telling are the pamphleteer's silences, the things he omits from records to which he seems to have had access. He credits Fian with being the "one man suffered" to come to "the Diuels readinges" (18), though examination records and indictments list at least eight other men as present when the devil orders everyone to kiss his ass. The title page of *Newes from Scotland*, which was probably the work of the printer, gives Fian top billing, declaring his "damnable life and death" as a notable sorcerer burned at Edinburgh, and including him among those who tried to "bewitch and drowne his Maiestie in the sea comming from Denmarke."[23] But the pamphlet itself barely connects him with the event, saying only that Tompson confesses to being accompanied "with the parties before specially named" when she christened the cat and threw it into the sea. Moreover, the pamphleteer eliminates the devil's mark on Fian's body, transferring its attention, as we have seen, to what happens when the examiners *don't* find a mark.

Just as additions like the reenactments before the king suggest that creating the sensation of certainty can deflect violence, so the portrait of the examiners hunting for the devil's mark suggests the way violence can intensify when certainty can't be achieved. Although it can hardly be said to offer a science or even a theory of emotion, the pamphlet's attention to the reactions of the examiners exposes this dynamic.

What we see in *Newes from Scotland*, in contrast to the precautions Kramer and Sprenger recommend or Scot's repetitions, is a breakdown of strategies for combating doubt. Defendants in *Newes from Scotland* get tortured in direct proportion to their tendency to aggravate doubt, and in inverse proportion to their ability to create the sensation of certainty. This in turn suggests a way of understanding the relative merits of the different evidentiary procedures; there is a kind of hierarchy of procedures. Theatrical reenactments trump narratives, producing actual "delight." But if a defendant can offer a sustained narrative, particularly a written one, it is possible to strike a pose of appeasement and thus forestall violence. It is when the defendant contradicts himself, compromises the narrative or claims it was merely a theatrical deception designed to avoid pain, that the violence escalates. Both strategies, performances and narratives, suggest justice's attempt to compensate for a waning language of signs. They attest to both the ideal of canon law with its belief in the power of what is seen (two eyewitnesses) and what is heard (confession) but even more to the strain that the law of proof is under. What *Newes from Scotland* suggests is not a static system of evidence in which each piece has a fixed value but a fluid and escalating set of needs on the part of the examiners, an escalating set of attempts to ward off uncertainty. When each fails, the requirements for the next become more rigorous and rigid. When all methods have been exhausted what remains is one last spectacle "for example sake": Fian "put into a carte and . . . first strangled . . . [then] . . . immiedatly put into a great fire, being readie prouided for that purpose" (28). The examiners' violence is echoed in the apparent relish of the pamphleteer's description—the blood and marrow spouting forth in great abundance and the legs crushed and beaten as small as might be.

# Chapter 6

# Spenser's False Shewes

At the end of canto 8 of book 1 of *The Faerie Queene*, Spenser has Una strip the witch Duessa so Red Cross Knight can see who he's been consorting with. Una's goal in stripping the witch is ostensibly to demonstrate what Duessa actually is. "Such is the face of falshood," she tells Red Cross Knight (1.8.49), revealing Duessa's grotesque body so that, "Such as she was, their eies might her behold" (1.8.46). But if Duessa is stripped so that Red Cross (and we) may see exactly what she is, the scene conspires in a number of ways to make this impossible. Duessa's body repeatedly defies categorization. Perhaps more importantly, the speaker reminds us more than once how impossible it is to actually describe Duessa (because what he refers to as his "chaster muse" is too ashamed to do so).

The stripping of Duessa belongs to the long historical tradition we have been examining, a tradition to which both *Newes from Scotland* and the judicial section of *Malleus Maleficarum* belong, a tradition in which justice searches and strips the witch to establish that she is, in fact, a witch. But both Duessa's terminal ambiguity—her "both/and" quality—and the speaker's professed reticence in describing her work against this tradition and thus raise a series of questions: What does looking at Duessa's naked body "do" or accomplish for Red Cross Knight and what is being asked of us when we look with him at something we can't fully see? Does Spenser luxuriate in or incriminate the kinds of practices operative in *Newes from Scotland*? And if he incriminates, what specifically is he incriminating? Like Duessa's body itself, comparison of the scene to the trials and advice to judges of the kind we have been considering suggests a kind of "both/and" answer to these questions. This chapter argues that while Spenser exposes the fantasy of certainty at work in the witch-stripping tradition as just that—fantasy—the scene is nonetheless implicated in the kinds of sexual violence against women endemic to that tradition.

Numerous critics in the past few decades have sought to reconcile apparently misogynistic moments like this one with Spenser's larger designs. With his customary brilliance, Harry Berger argued for misogyny and gynephobia in the poem as displacements of male self-hatred.[1] Joe Campana beautifully describes the absence of compassion that male figures in book 1 exhibit when faced with instances of each other's "abject masculinity."[2] More recently, Stephanie Bahr has argued that Duessa's complaint at the beginning of book 2 that she has been raped has legitimacy.[3] Mindful of Garthine Walker's reminder that the most important legal criterion for rape in the period was vaginal penetration, this chapter stops just short of calling the moment a rape, but asks instead what function sexual violence in the stripping of Duessa serves.[4] I suggest that looking at Duessa's naked body serves as much as an attempt to reconstitute Red Cross's masculinity as it does to expose Duessa's falsehood. Even as Spenser exposes the way that stripping the witch can amount to a pretext for the sadistic pleasures of voyeurism, he implicates the poem and us in the very practices he incriminates.

## Manly Force

Una's stated purpose in stripping Duessa is to reveal to Red Cross what Duessa actually is. ("Such is the face of falshood," she says.) The stripping of the witch in book 1 seems to be the logical culmination of that process which begins with the two magical instruments that make it possible: Arthur's shield and the squire's horn. A number of critics have noted the way that Arthur's shield is tainted by the very "magicke artes" we are told it penetrates, but at least on a literal level, both the shield and horn are presented as having the capacity to penetrate enchantment, to strip illusions of their power to deceive.[5] Both by analogy and by narrative preparation, they create the expectation that Duessa's stripping will provide certain knowledge, the truth behind the face of illusion.

Thus, Arthur's shield is at least initially presented in terms which cast it as the specific antidote to Archimago's magic. Not only does it have conventional shield properties like invulnerability, being made "all of Diamond perfect . . . / That point of speare it neuer percen could" (1.7.33), and not only is it specifically immune to magic ("No magicke arts hereof had any might, / Nor bloody wordes of bold Enchaunters call"), but the shield's key method of combating illusion is to reduce enchantment to its constituent parts: "But all that was not such, as seemd in sight, / Before that shield did fade, and suddeine fall." Where Archimago's magic has the capacity to shape "liquid ayre" into persons, the shield has the capacity to reduce persons to nothing but dust and ultimately air ("Men into stones therewith he could transmew / And stones to dust, and dust to nought at all" [1.7.35]). Similarly, not only is the squire's horn capable of being heard for three miles, echoing itself three times and invoking fear in every wight who hears it, but it is capable of penetrating enchantment:

> No false enchauntment, nor deceiptfull traine
> Might once abide the terror of that blast,
> But presently was void and wholly vaine (1.8.4)

Thus both objects prepare us for the revelation of Duessa's body, offering the fantasy that what is to come will offer certain knowledge. They do so at exactly the moment when we encounter the opposite, the figure Ignaro, whose every answer is, "He could not tell." It is the work done by the shield and horn that creates the expectation that Duessa's body will similarly "open" and reveal what it is, an expectation which takes root as early as canto 2 when Fradubio, admitting that Duessa's "partes" were "hidd in water" that he couldn't see, begins to build the anticipation that eyes more capable than his will see and reveal those hidden "partes" (1.2.41).

What Red Cross and we see, though, in canto 8, undermines this fantasy of certainty in at least two ways. Duessa resists classification. She is figured as both female, her nether parts the shame of "all" her kind, and male, with a great phallic tail at "her rompe." She is both age, her "crafty head . . . altogether bald," and a mockery of age, as if "in hate of honorable eld" (1.8.47). She is both age—a "loathly, wrinkled hag, ill fauored, old" (1.8.46)—and a kind of infantile scatological fantasy of dripping fecal matter. She is both animal and human, and even as an animal is neither one kind nor another, one foot "like an Eagles claw," the other "like a beares vneuen paw" (1.8.48). More significant than whatever Duessa is, though, is the fact that the narrator regularly reminds us he can't actually describe her.[6] "My chaster Muse for shame doth blush to write," he says. "[Her] secret filth good manners biddeth not be told" (1.8.48 and 1.8.46), he adds in an echo of Fradubio's "Her neather partes misshapen, monstruous / Were hidd in water, that I could not see" (1.2.41). Rather than getting a fulfillment of Fradubio's half-veiled description of Duessa's body, what we get is another veil, a reminder that we are seeing not the body but part of the body.[7] We are being reminded that what we see is ultimately fragmentary, partial, extraneous in comparison to what cannot be described.

That what seems to bestow certainty in Spenser often does just the opposite has been widely noted. Susanne Wofford suggests this is the fundamental condition of the poem itself.[8] What is less apparent are the consequences of this particular moment's withholding of knowledge. What are the consequences of being shown something we are told we are not seeing in its entirety? And what does it mean for this partial view to take place at the moment of supposed revelation? A comparison with analogous witch-stripping moments in *Newes from Scotland* and *Malleus Maleficarum* offers one kind of an answer.

Published between the first and second edition of Spenser's *Faerie Queene*, the pamphlet *Newes from Scotland*, as we have seen, like canto 8, depicts the practice of stripping the witch to reveal what she is. But in *Newes from Scotland* what one finds beneath the clothing when the witch—at least the female witch—is stripped is not uncategorizability, not any kind of "both/and," but what the examiners and pamphleteer take to be an indisputable "sign" that demonstrates that the witch is really a witch. The devil's mark signifies a specific history, the occasion on which the devil revealed himself to the accused, getting her to "addict" herself to his service and giving her a mark on some secret place on her body, which remains sore and insensible until their next meeting.[9] The devil's mark is the evidence of the demonic pact and as such carries with it a guarantee that the events leading up to and away from this pact—actions which follow a codified sequence, as James describes them in *Daemonologie*—have actually taken place. Perhaps more importantly, as we've seen, the mark brings about the *sensation* of certainty in the examiner who looks at it, relieving affects of doubt and uncertainty. The discovery of the mark calms David Seaton, Geillis Duncane's master and examiner.

If all we had for comparison were the discovery of the devil's mark on Geillis Duncane and the revelation of Duessa's hybrid body, Spenser would seem to be pointing to the impossibility of certainty, to the fact that it is in fact a sensation, not an actual state of affairs. Where the examiners achieve the sensation of certainty when they discover the devil's mark on Duncane's body, Spenser's narrator repeatedly casts Duessa's body as unknowable, something that "biddeth not be told," something beyond the words used to denote it, words which inevitably fail to describe it. Spenser's narrator repeatedly implies that this body points beyond itself to something which can't be seen and can't be named. (Admittedly, the devil's mark also points to something beyond itself in representing the demonic nature of the event that it commemorates, but by pointing to a specific history, a sequence of codified steps that constitute every demonic pact, it limits and reduces the power of what is "beyond" rather than pointing to something unnameable as Duessa's body does.)

But Geillis Duncane is not the only defendant searched for a devil's mark in *Newes from Scotland*. The defendant who bears the most resemblance to Duessa is not Geillis Duncane (who seems to get by with only being "searched") but Agnes Sampson, who not only has to be "searched" but stripped until the devil's mark is found, not on the forecrag of her throat, but on her genitals. Like Duessa, "loathly, wrinckled . . . ill fauored, old," Agnes Sampson is the "eldest witch of them al," and her treatment at the hands of the examiners, like the stripping of Duessa, suggests the loathing of the older female body at work in these texts. But Sampson's treatment suggests something else as well. That Sampson has not only to be stripped but shaved "on each part of her body" until the devil's mark is found on her "privities," as if the stripping itself were insufficient to produce nakedness and had to be repeated more violently, suggests that whatever else it may register, the sexual nature of Sampson's torture registers the examiners' frustration with her opacity, her unknowability. Thus the stripping of Duessa can be read not only as exposing the impossibility of certainty—and in particular the certainty ostensibly sought in the practice of stripping the witch—but as exposing the way that very search itself serves as a pretext for violence. Una, by comparison, only humiliates Duessa, rather than resorting to physical violence, saying it would be a shame to let Duessa die and allowing her to escape ("To doe her die (quoth *Vna*) were despight, / And shame t'auenge so weake an enimy; / But spoile her of her scarlot robe, and let her fly" [1.8.45]).

At minimum these comparisons give the lie to the claim one critic makes that "surprisingly few of the numerous concerns about witches found in *The Discoverie of Witchcraft*, *Malleus Maleficarum*, and other contemporary treatises about witchcraft . . . emerge as significant topics of interest in *The Faerie Queene*."[10] Taken in isolation, such comparisons might also be said to point to the impossibility of ever satisfactorily revealing the "is" beneath what "seems." But a moment from *Malleus Maleficarum* begins to address the question of what function looking at Duessa's body serves.

It will be recalled that in the *Malleus* one of the more theatrical "practices" the inquisitors urge judges to adopt is the precaution of bringing the witch in backwards in a basket. Witches, the inquisitors tell us, have been known to beg nothing else from their jailors than that they get the first look at the judge and his assessors as they are being brought before them. There have been cases where the witch's gaze has been so powerful that it has disoriented the judge and so completely alienated him from his own judgment that he doesn't dare to convict. For this reason, witches are to be led in backwards. As we have seen, the inquisitors design a variety of procedures, themselves spectacles—which they call "precautions"—which seek not merely to avoid the witch's danger but to neutralize it. Bringing the witch in backwards offers an antidote to the witch's power, turning the witch into the object of the gaze rather than allowing her to be the gazer. What then, is it that stripping Duessa neutralizes? What is looking at her naked body an antidote for?

A look at some of Red Cross's lapses suggests that the stripping of Duessa is not merely an education about the face of falsehood or even a correction to Red Cross's ability to delude himself but rather an antidote to the failure of what the poem calls Red Cross's "manly forces." Stripping and humiliating the witch becomes an attempt to reconstitute Red Cross's masculinity itself.

Early in book I, when Archimago first seeks to seduce Red Cross away from Una, he sends him three temptations, the dream that makes him dream of love and lusty play that nearly melts his "manly hart" away (1.1.47), the sprite who impersonates Una who could have "rauisht" "weaker sence" (1.1.45) and who seeks to seduce Red Cross after the dream he's just resisted, and the sprites who impersonate Una and a lusty squire having sex "in a secrete bed," and "in wanton lust and leud embracement" (1.2.3 and 5). It is in this third temptation, which is essentially a pornographic picture, that Archimago succeeds.

All three of these assaults are presented as scenes of theater, specifically as things to be seen. In the second, most extended of these, Archimago creates a succubus whom he trains, in effect, in theatrical impersonation, not only dressing her "all in white" and casting a black stole over her "most like to seeme for *Vna* fit" (1.1.45) but teaching her "to imitate that Lady trew, / Whose semblance she did carrie vnder feigned hew" (1.1.46). He rehearses in her a histrionic power she is herself quick to exhibit as she tries to seduce Red Cross, "Wringing her hands in wemen's pitteous wise" (1.1.50).

Here Spenser not only casts magic as a generalized kind of theatricality but attributes to it precisely the dangerous powers attributed to theater by those who attacked the stage during the period, the power not only to seduce and titillate but to "ravish" the mind of the spectator in whom such lust is created.[11] Thus the succubus, her "tender partes" framed of " liquid ayre," is "so liuely and so like in all mens sight, / That weaker sence [she] could have rauisht quight" (1.1.45). She is understood, as Stephen Gosson said was the case with plays, not only to "whet desire to inordinate lust" but to "ravish" the senses, even the senses of her creator ("nigh beguiled with so goodly sight" [1.1.45]).[12] And this capacity to ravish grows not only out of the "tenderness" of her erotic "partes" but out of how "like" they are in all men's sight, how accurate an imitation she is, as if the ability to "ravish" lay in the capacity for verisimilitude itself.

Archimago's third assault on Red Cross, and the one that succeeds in separating him from Una, making him "burn" with "gealous fire" and finally leave her, is essentially pornography, theater conceived of as voyeurism. The second sprite, reconstituted as a lusty squire, and the first perform a scene of coitus. The most serious threat, then, the magic most inimical to the self, is explicitly conceived as a moment of intensely sexualized looking. Archimago first describes then presents the scene, inviting Red Cross to "see, where your false Lady doth her honor staine" (1.2.4) and bringing him into "a secret part" where the couple are locked in what the text calls "leud embracement."

In theory, the revelation of Duessa's body should be an antidote to this picture. Grotesque where the previous picture has been erotic, "real" where the previous scene has been false, revolting where the image of the sprites has been titillating, the sight of Duessa's body would seem to be an opposite to Red Cross's early moment of voyeurism, and the experience of looking at Duessa's body would seem to be recuperative. But it is the specific sense in which the experience is recuperative that is disturbing: For the scene suggests that in order to restore masculinity, the woman's body must be stripped and exposed. To see this, we need to look at the events which precede Duessa's stripping.

Earlier in canto 1, when Red Cross defeats Error (who is herself, like Duessa, both androgynous and female) he requires more than "manly force" to do so. But this manliness is immediately dissipated by the dream that Archimago sends, the dream that nearly melts his "manly hart" away. When Fradubio first speaks to him, Red Cross can "no member moue," and it is not till this "passion" passes and his "manhood" is "well awake" (1.2.32) that he can really listen to the story that Fradubio tells.[13] At the beginning of canto 7, dallying with Duessa, he drinks out of a sluggish stream whose waters have the character of the dull nymph they derive from, and his "manly forces" immediately begin to "faile" and flow out of him. And it is at the moment that Red Cross's masculinity is imagined to flow out of him that the giant, Orgoglio, arrives, phallic both in his size ("exceed[ing] / The hight of three the tallest sonnes of mortall seed" [1.7.8]) and in the weapon with which he nearly "pouldres" Red Cross ("a snaggy Oke, which he had torne / Out of his mothers bowelles" [1.8.10]). At the moment of the dismembering of this phallic giant, we hear an inarticulate roar that is like the "kindly rage" of Cymbrian bulls roaring for their "milkie mothers," and the next we see of Red Cross, his "feeble thighes, vnhable to vphold / His pined corse" (1.8.40), his "vitall powres / Decayd" and his "flesh shronk" (1.8.41), he has to be carried by Arthur. It is then at the height of the fantasy that something external can cause the loss of masculinity (contact with a woman, drinking out of a contaminated stream) that the woman's body must be stripped and viewed. It is at the moment of the most intense vision of effeminization, then, that Red Cross must view the naked body of Duessa.

The sense in which the viewing of Duessa is recuperative, then, is not primarily that it reveals "what is" under "what seems," for, in fact, in contrast to the devil's mark in *Newes from Scotland*, Duessa's body resists being known and always points to that thing beyond it which cannot be seen and cannot be said. Rather, the stripping of Duessa offers an antidote to effeminization. Only by stripping the female body can the male protagonist begin to recover from those threats to his "manly forces," the threats that paralyzed him so that he could "no member move." There are two points here. First, that sexual violence, the act of stripping the woman, is offered as an antidote to effeminization, and second, that Red Cross is being trained to understand the female body as a grotesque, being trained further to understand androgyny, mixedness, uncategorizability itself as grotesque.[14]

That this particular antidote to effeminization turns out to be as inadequate at restoring masculinity as it is at restoring certainty is not apparent until canto 9. There, sinews "shrunken" (1.9.20), Red Cross suffers a "secrete breach" in his conscience at Despair's speech, and the "vgly vew of his deformed crimes" disperses all his "manly powers" again, and Una has to grab the knife Despair hands him and explicitly invoke the "manly hart" Red Cross has lost sight of (1.9.52–53) to get him to leave.

## "Disarmd, Disgaste and Inwardly Dismayde"

John Lambe, a quack doctor charged with witchcraft in the early 1600s and ultimately convicted in 1624 of raping a child insisted in his appeal that there had been no rape because no "inward enforcement" had taken place.[15] The most important legal criterion for rape during the period, Garthine Walker reminds us, was vaginal penetration.[16] No depiction of such a penetration occurs in the stripping of Duessa in canto 8. And yet one of Arthur's defining characteristics is in fact his capacity to penetrate, to penetrate not only enchantment but things like castles and solid doors. It is the squire who blows open the castle so that it "quake[s] from the grownd" (1.8.5) and every door flies open, his horn having such power that there is "No gate so strong, no locke so firme and fast / But with that percing noise [it flies] open" (1.8.4). But once inside it is Arthur with all his keys for whom the doors open effortlessly "without any breach" (1.8.34), all doors except the one door that separates him from Red Cross. This "yron doore" Arthur "ren[ds]."

It is a peculiarity of Arthur that though his armor and shield can never be penetrated, the first constructed so that "deadly dint of steele" can never endanger it, and the second hewn out of a massy diamond so that "point of speare" can never pierce it, his heart can be "pierced" or penetrated "with percing point / Of pitty deare." The "ruth" he feels for Red Cross "so fowle forlore" after hearing his "dreary, murmuring voyce" (1.8.38) on the other side of the door asking for death creates a "trembling horrour" that at once has to be thrown off and at the same time seems to motivate him to "rent that yrone dore, / With furious force" and enter.[17] In the moments before the stripping of Duessa, then, the poem, as Stephanie Bahr has noted, seems to rehearse the act of penetration. Although it would be a reach to call these moments rape, they do suggest the way that penetration, the element which legally constituted rape in the period, gets displaced onto physical buildings, the way entrances and piercings get enacted metaphorically. "Locks and keys constituted common metaphors for sex," Walker says. "The image of the locked door in rape narratives implied that the rapist had violated a woman's intimate, sexual, boundaries" (15).[18]

But if the poem rehearses the act of penetration, it also rehearses another pattern in which rage becomes the instrument for reconstituting masculinity. Early in book 1, when Red Cross begins to undergo the long series of threats to his masculinity which punctuate the book, after entering the threatening and almost embarrassingly explicit "darksom hole" of Error's den and finding himself encircled and engulfed in Error's phallic tail which "all suddenly about his body wound" (1.1.18), we are told that it is "shame" rather than an awareness of the "certain peril" he stands in that allows him to mobilize the fury necessary to summon "more than manly force" to successfully battle Error. Similarly, at the end of the canto, when Archimago sends the dream of love and lusty play which nearly melts his "manly hart" away, Red Cross wakes from the bliss he's been "bathed" in in a state of fury, and "halfe enraged," he thinks to kill the sprite he thinks is Una. In both these moments, threatened masculinity (which has been at risk ever since Red Cross handed his "needlesse spere" to the dwarf at the beginning of the book) reconstitutes itself through the mobilization of rage. Two phenomena in the poem, the summoning of rage as a means of fighting threats to masculinity and the repetition of penetration, precede the stripping of Duessa.

But at the moment that Red Cross most needs to mobilize this kind of rage, the moment where his masculinity seems to leak out of him, he is unable to summon this response. Oblivious to the property of the fountain by which "all that [drank] thereof, [did] fainte and feeble grow," Red Cross drinks and immediately his "manly forces [begin] to fayle" (1.7.5–6). Not feeling his "chaunged powres" until his courage and "chearefull blood" melt to "fayntnes chill" and he reaches too late for his "vnready weapons"(1.7.7), he is unable to contend with the bloated and explicitly phallic Orgoglio. If the canto followed the pattern established in cantos 1 and 2, Red Cross would summon the rage necessary to overcome both his enemy and his own weakened state and recoup his collapsed masculinity. But "disarmd, disgraste, and inwardly dismayde . . . faint in euery ioynt and vayne" through the fountain which "him feeble made," he cannot (1.7.11). He is thrown into another dark hole, the dungeon, requiring Arthur to rescue him. The ensuing battle between Orgoglio and Arthur can almost be seen as a contest between two conceptions of masculinity, the bloated and oversized phallus that is Orgoglio (beginning erect and ending flaccid like a bladder lacking wind) and the shield which, like its wielder, is known for its capacity to penetrate.[19]

Although the stripping of Duessa isn't technically or legally a rape, the moments which precede it suggest that key elements of rape are present in the poem like pieces of a puzzle waiting to be assembled. The episode, then, is both implicated in the tradition of violating and stripping the witch to reveal her nature and involved in a critique of that tradition. Even as it calls into question the very idea of certainty by suggesting that there is always something beyond the witch's body that cannot be seen and cannot be said, even as it casts as "unspeakable" and unknowable what the examiners in texts like *Newes from Scotland* imagine as a marker of certainty, the episode participates in the pleasures of sexual violence. Even as it suggests the way that stripping the witch can be a pretext for that violence, it seems to revel in that practice.

A last point of comparison with *Newes from Scotland* may be instructive here. The difficulty the examiners in *Newes from Scotland* have finding a devil's mark on Fian's body is matched only by their failure in getting him to stick to his initial confession. As we have seen, when Fian retracts that confession, saying that he only said what he said to avoid torture, the examiners, assuming he's been newly marked, search for a devil's mark. Put to the torment of the boots when his body fails to yield one, his legs destroyed so that they are no longer recognizable, he is ultimately strangled, burnt, and displayed as an example. Duessa's body occupies a kind of midpoint between the bodies of the women tortured until they yield devil's marks and the destroyed body of the man whose body fails to do so. The experience of looking at her gives the appearance of certainty, while calling attention to all that cannot be known. To return to the question of what it means for us to look at something we can only see part of: just as *Daemonologie* titillates its readers' curiosity by directing our attention to what it won't tell us, Spenser's narrator creates a similar desire to know what it is that is hid in water, what it is we cannot see.

# Chapter 7

# Danger in Words
## Faustus, Slade, and the Demonologists

In act 1, scene 3, of Marlowe's *Tragicall History of Doctor Faustus*, Mephistopheles seeks to disabuse Faustus of the notion that the words he uses in conjuring have magical power. Asked if Faustus's words called him ("Did not my conjuring speeches raise thee? Speak" [1.3.46]), Mephistopheles, in a much-discussed passage, says:

> That was the cause, but yet *per accidens*
> For when we hear one rack the name of God,
> Abjure the Scriptures and his Saviour Christ,
> We fly in hope to get his glorious soul,
> Nor will we come unless he use such means
> Whereby he is in danger to be damned. (1.3.47–52)[1]

Mephistopheles argues (as Epistemon does in *Daemonologie*) that the words of conjuring have no inherent power, no efficacy. They are merely signs of a soul's availability. They mean; they do not "do." But Faustus's central act in the play, his promise of his soul to the devil, would seem to offer the consummate example of words which do something simply by being uttered. In promising his soul, Faustus does not (in Austin's terms) describe what he is doing; he does it. He does not "'describe' a state of affairs," but brings one into being.[2] As such, the play poses a series of interrelated questions: Under what circumstances (if any) does Marlowe imagine speech as an act? Under what circumstances (if any) does he imagine speech not as an "ordinary" act in which (to cite Austin) "to say something is to do something," but as an "extraordinary" act, one which is in a larger sense efficacious? And what relation does the play imagine between necromantic words and other kinds of words like prayers or promises?

Recent attempts to answer such questions have, in important ways, advanced our understanding of *Faustus*'s odd capacity to resonate with speech-act theory, either by arguing that the play exploits Reformation arguments that "magical language has no intrinsic spiritual efficacy" or by noting the way the play exploits that magical language itself on behalf of the early modern stage.[3] But the question of whether words are efficacious is complicated by a peculiar feature of Faustus's promise, the feature of repetition. Faustus does not promise his soul once in the play but over and over again. What is the performative power of a promise if it has to be repeated again and again? Does repetition suggest a prior iteration has been ineffective? One answer to these questions lies in the legal tensions surrounding the notion of promises themselves during the period, tensions that had been building up since the middle of the sixteenth century but ultimately came to a head in what has come to be known as *Slade's Case*.

In an important article on the A and B texts of the play, Leah Marcus argued that what she called "textual indeterminacy" in the drama of the period—in *Faustus* the impossibility of assigning either the A or B text the status of original or "real" text—always involves an element of ideology.[4] The A and B texts, she argued, were each ideologically coherent, if often at odds with each other. I would like to extend the notion of indeterminate moments containing within themselves conflicting but equally coherent ideological positions, not for the purpose of comparing the A and B texts, but to argue that two opposite attitudes toward contract implying two corresponding attitudes toward promise and indicative of two opposite ideological positions operate within the play. Although these tensions have been explored in detail by a number of important critics and legal historians, the precise epistemological anxieties they generate in *Faustus* have been less attended to.[5] *Faustus*'s repetition of the promise both registers these tensions and seeks to navigate them.

## From Aphoristic Knowledge to Heavenly Characters

The fantasy that words have the power not only to "do things" simply by being uttered, but to do magical things, are efficacious, animates Faustus from the very beginning of the play and can be seen in his rejection of the disciplines he has excelled in. He encapsulates each discipline in a motto or aphorism. "Is to dispute well logic's chiefest end?" he says, rejecting the study of logic. "Then read no more; thou hast attained the end" (1.1.8, 10). "The end of physic is our body's health," he says, rejecting medicine. "Why Faustus, hast thou not attained that end?" (17–18). These mottos are metonymic for the disciplines they describe: "Being and not being" for philosophy, "the reward of sin is death" for divinity.[6] Such phrases seek to freeze whole bodies of knowledge and reduce them to the least number of words possible. They mean; they do not do.

In turning away from the disciplines these aphorisms stand for (medicine, law, philosophy, divinity), Faustus turns away not only from the disciplines themselves but also from the whole idea of a kind of knowledge that can be put into aphoristic form, and with it an attachment to language that describes, or "epitomizes." That he does so is echoed by the fact that he turns away from that part of his own work that has been reconstituted as aphoristic knowledge:

Why Faustus [he says], has thou not attained that end?
Is not thy common talk sound aphorisms?
Are not thy bills hung up as monuments,
Whereby whole cities have escaped the plague,
And thousand desp'rate maladies been eased? (18–22)

By the end of the first scene of the play Faustus has turned away from the language of aphorism to the language of necromantic words, "lines, circles, signs, letters, and characters" (53) which he claims will bring "a world of profit and delight" (55). If act 1, scene 3, begins with Faustus thinking that "Jehovah's name / Forward and backward anagrammatised" *enforces* spirits to rise (1.3.8–9), act 2, scene 1, ends with him prepared to believe the pronunciation of words is efficacious and brings "men in armour" (2.1.167).[7]

Mephistopheles, of course, has already repudiated the notion that the words of conjuring are efficacious, saying that Faustus's "conjuring speeches" were only the accidental cause of his being raised, that "rack[ing] the name of God" and "abjur[ing] the Scriptures" and Christ are only signs of a soul in danger of being damned, signs without which Mephistopheles and his ilk would not bother to come ("nor will we come unless he use such means" [1.3.48–51]). Although Mephistopheles's description of the way conjurations work is more complicated than it initially seems—the words used in conjuring do bring devils to the conjurors doing the uttering, but only because such words give the devils the information they need to make travel decisions—this qualification is safely inscribed within a vision of necromantic language as a system of signifiers, indicators of the spiritual states of the conjurors. Necromantic words are, strictly speaking, only things that signify, rather than things that behave. The power is not in the utterances themselves but in the devils who use them as barometers to the spiritual states of those who do the uttering.

In his insistence on this point, Mephistopheles says almost the same thing as Epistemon, James's spokesman in *Daemonologie*, who tells his interrogator, Philomathes, that neither the words nor rites of conjuration have any inherent power: "it is no power inherent in the circles or in the holines of the names of God blasphemouslie used nor in whatsoever rites or ceremonies."[8] None of these have actual power to "raise any infernall spirit" or keep him "perforce" within or outside the circles (17). Nor is there inherent power in the "vaine wordes and freites," the tools the devil gives his apprentices, the magicians, to work with (12). Nor do necromancers really rule, though they may seem to, where witches only serve. It is not by any inherent power they can have but only "ex pacto allanerlie" (9), through a pact. In *Daemonologie* the linchpin necessary to maintain the claim that the words of witchcraft and conjuring have no actual power is the notion of the demonic pact, the contract between the devil and the magician: the devil only encourages the delusion that the words have magical power in order to secure the magician's consent in making that contract.

In *Daemonologie*, we are told that the contract consists of two things: "forms" and "effects." By forms, Epistemon says he means "in what shape or fashion [the devil] shall come unto [magicians] when they call upon him." By effects he says he means the particular services the devil will bind himself to (19). To the "baser sorte" (those with less skill) the devil obliges himself to come in the form of "a dog, a catte, an Ape or such-like other beast, or else to answere by a voyce onlie." To these magicians he binds himself to "effects" like curing diseases in "their own particular menagery" or "such other base things as they require of him" (19). In contrast, to the "most curious [or skilled] sorte" he will oblige himself to appear as a "continuall attender, in forme of a Page" or permit himself to be "conjured, for the space of so many yeres, ether in a tablet or a ring, or such like thing, which they may easely carrie about with them." And he will oblige himself to effects like entering a dead body in order to give more sophisticated information relevant to commonwealths and nations, "such answers, of the event of battels, of maters concerning the estate of commonwelths, and such like other great questions" (20).

There are some meaningful discrepancies in Epistemon's explanation—if it is the magician's skill that determines what the devil will do, at least *some* efficacy is being accorded to the magician. But in other ways, at first glance, the bargain

Faustus makes with Mephistopheles would seem to be a textbook case for the kind of contract Epistemon describes. Faustus, clearly the more "curious" or skilled sort of magician, gets Mephistopheles to "wait upon" him (1.3.37)—what Epistemon calls being an "attender"—and fantasizes about matters concerning the "estates of commonwealths" like chasing the prince of Parma from the land. He demonstrates the kind of "curiositie in great ingines" (8) that Epistemon says the devil uses to draw potential magicians to him. And in his migration from logic through medicine, philosophy, and divinity to necromancy, Faustus moves up what Epistemon calls "the slipperie scale" of curiosity from legal to illegal, innocent to criminal knowledge, in the same way Epistemon says the magician getting ready to make such a contract does. But in contrast to *Daemonologie* (where the word "contract" appears seven times in relation to the magician), the word "contract" never appears in the play. There are moments early on that seem to *imply* the language of contract, but these very soon give way to the language of bequest, deed of gift, and eventually promise.

Nowhere in act 2, scene 1, the scene in which the pact is signed, does the word "contract" appear, although there are numerous moments, early on, which seem to imply contractual arrangements. "Now tell, what says Lucifer thy lord?" Faustus asks (2.1.30), and Mephistopheles answers "that I shall wait on Faustus whilst he lives / So he will *buy* my service with his soul" (31–32, emphasis mine). In its first iteration, Mephistopheles presents the bargain as an exchange of services for goods: Mephistopheles's service for Faustus's soul. In its initial iteration, then, Mephistopheles presents the purchase as limited and not subject to conditions.

As soon as the terms have been named, though, several things begin to happen. On the one hand, the conditions attached to the purchase begin to multiply, and even as they do, the form of the pact begins to harden, materialize. On the other hand, the language used to describe the exchange changes to that of a bequest or deed of gift and eventually a promise. Finally, the promise has to be reiterated over and over again. These processes bleed into one another, but they can also be traced separately.

Thus, if in its first iteration the exchange involves a one-to-one swap of soul for service, in subsequent iterations, the list of demands attached to the bargain (famously) escalates, first on Faustus's part, then later on Mephistopheles's. On Faustus's side, the "scroll" that appears in the second (and written) iteration of the contract reads "that Faustus may be a spirit in form and substance" (97), also that "he [Mephistopheles] shall be in his chamber or house invisible. Lastly, that he shall appear to the said John Faustus at all times in what form or shape soever he please" (102–5). Faustus has on the one hand multiplied his specified conditions to include being a spirit and Mephistopheles being invisible. He has, on the other hand, as others have noted, limited Mephistopheles's service to twenty-four years. At subsequent moments and in subsequent iterations, it is Mephistopheles who adds conditions. Thus when Faustus asks who made the world and Mephistopheles refuses to tell him, and Faustus reproaches him ("Villain, have I not bound thee to tell me anything?"), Mephistopheles says, "Ay, that is not against our kingdom, but this is" (2.3.70–72). In so doing, he adds the unstated condition of not speaking of God or paradise in Faustus's lifetime. In its final iteration in act 5, when Faustus has reneged and offers to ratify his vow again, Mephistopheles tells him to do it quickly and with "unfeigned heart" (5.1.74), adding the conditions of authenticity and sincerity.

Even as the conditions multiply, the language which describes the transaction changes from that characteristic of contracts—even if nobody uses the word—to that of a bequest. Early on, in the same way that Mephistopheles speaks of Faustus buying his service with his soul (2.1.32–50), he talks about Lucifer requiring "security" (36). Faustus himself presents Mephistopheles with a scroll of "articles prescribed between us both" (92). In contemporary law today, all these terms suggest a contract which in turn suggests that consummation cannot occur until a future moment in which both parties have met their obligations. But as the scene progresses, the language suggestive of contract gives way to the language of "bequest" and "deed[s] of gift." Faustus must "bequeath" his soul "solemnly" and write it as a "deed of gift" in blood (2.1.34–35). In contemporary law, in contrast to the language of contract, this language of gift suggests immediate consummation as soon as the deed is written. Even "bequest" suggests a diminution of rights for the bequeather, Faustus.

What is striking is that even as Faustus loses rights—loses them both by virtue of the multiplication of conditions and by virtue of the change from contract to bequest—the devils keep requiring new, increasingly material iterations of his promise. It must be written. It must be written in blood. It must be written in heated ("cleared") blood because the flowing blood has congealed. One might imagine that as the devils get the better of him, as Mephistopheles rewrites the agreement both to include new conditions and to free the devils of obligations, the need for reiteration would diminish. But the promise keeps having to be made over and over again, as if each previous iteration were insufficient or as if the repetition itself were what the devils were after. Why does the promise have to be repeated again and again? And why do the devils require it to take an increasingly material form?

## From Demonic Pacts to Earthly Promises

One answer to these questions lies in the tensions developing in what we now call contract law during the period in which *Faustus* was written, many of which reached a head in what has come to be known as *Slade's Case*. Sometime in 1595 John Slade sold for 16 pounds to Humphrey Morley certain crops, due to ripen on a plot that he leased. When the crops came in months later, Morley failed to pay. Instead of employing customary remedies, which would have consisted in seeking to recover the payment in an "ordinary" action of debt, Slade, through his lawyers, sued Morley in *"assumpsit,"* an action for failure to perform an undertaking, a move akin to our modern sense of breach of promise. The various courts that heard the case split in a series of verdicts, but ultimately Slade was victorious, recovering not only his original sixteen pounds but additional damages. (The case was argued four times between 1596 and its final judgment in November 1602, in a decision involving the whole English judiciary.)[9] The case's importance lay at least in part in the choice it gave subsequent plaintiffs about whether to bring an "ordinary" or an "extraordinary" action (an action for debt, or an action for *assumpsit*) against their defendants. But equally important are the implications the decision has for our notion of contract itself, admittedly a different notion than Sir Edward Coke had when he said on behalf of Slade that "every contract executory importeth in it self an *Assumpsit*" or promise.[10] In its own way, *Slade's Case* can be understood as marking as historically specific, contingent, a phenomenon we tend to think of as inevitable and natural: the embeddedness of promises in contracts.

One thing that is important about *Slade's Case* is the way that claims about "promise," or more properly "undertakings," superseded claims about "contract" (contract in its older sense of an agreement only partially performed) as the superior means of collecting a debt and prosecuting a right. That the devils in the play increasingly require oral, written, and then again oral promises from Faustus, rather than relying on something like "bare contract," reflects the emergence of this principle. But the play registers not only the practices and principles that judges and juries ultimately upheld but also the competing practices they were in the process of downgrading and disabling. Prior to Slade, at least in the view of some courts, unless a plaintiff could somehow prove that the debtor had made a promise *subsequent to and independent from* the original bargain, *assumpsit* as a legal strategy remained off-limits.[11] The devils in the play are hedging their bets. Their demands for Faustus to reiterate his promise over and over again can be seen as attempts to get subsequent and independent promises out of him as well as his original contract. Thus the play does not so much "take a side" on legal positions as it becomes a vector for legal tensions in the period.

Although such tensions reached a head in *Slade's Case*, years after Marlowe's death, they had been building up for decades, between the two primary common-law courts, the Court of Common Pleas and the Court of the King's Bench, in a debate John Baker describes as "primarily about the propriety of using *assumpsit* to recover debts" (1150). For the Court of Common Pleas, the objection to *assumpsit* was in large part an objection to "extraordinary" or special actions. Such actions could only be invoked in cases where no ordinary remedies existed.[12] Since the original statute which provided the authority for special actions had been passed to prevent a failure of justice when no ordinary remedies existed, it could have no application where a remedy existed in common law as it did for debt.[13] Beneath the issue of whether contracts "imported" promises lay another, deeper ideological divide between the two courts over what we would call a duplication of remedies in the legal system. The objection on the part of Common Pleas, says Baker, "was not to two different causes of action arising on the same facts, but to the same cause of action giving rise to two different forms of action" (1154).[14] Exceptions which the Court of Common Pleas acknowledged as warranting "special actions" were situations with additional circumstances, what we might call collateral damages (if the plaintiff's family starved or his business suffered, or the debt were in grain and after the failure to deliver the market value rose). The King's Bench, in contrast, had no objection to *assumpsit*, but argued that it was "imported" by the contract itself. Nor was the King's Bench particularly worried about overlapping remedies.[15] Thus, although *Slade's Case* itself wasn't resolved until after Marlowe's death, the issues at its core had been in play for years, since the middle of the sixteenth century.

In contrast to those scholars who see the growing division between the two courts as largely competition over revenue, Baker argues persuasively that the debate was "symptomatic of a more intellectual conflict, a final confrontation between the old learning and the new . . . the last stand of Tudor legal conservatives against the legal renaissance of the 16th century" (1150) or, to invoke Marcus's terms in another context, what we might call a view of the issue as driven less by economics than by ideology.[16] The King's Bench sought to expand the emerging action of *assumpsit*, and Common Pleas objected fundamentally to the idea of overlapping remedies.

The play's obsession with the material quality of the contract, its written nature, bears witness to growing legal tensions as well. David Harris Sacks offers one reading of the evolving notion of "consideration" (the word we use for what makes contracts enforceable) in a way that suggests the extra protection gained by the devils from the material form that the promise ultimately assumes. In medieval legal contexts, Sacks says, "The agreement would be binding if the party had a reason acceptable in conscience for making it" (29).[17] That "reason"—a spiritual or ethical entity in light of which the contract was presumed to be binding—was the "consideration." But how might a jury know the contents of a man's conscience? As skepticism about this possibility, about the accessibility of one conscience to another, grew during the period, the need for something "materially observable" became more pressing. Increasingly, money or its equivalent—"material consideration"—began to serve that need. That the devils in *Faustus* require not only the reiteration of Faustus's promise but also for it to take an increasingly material form, both in writing and in blood, reflects the need for visible observable evidence of what goes on in the human mind. That they require Faustus to promise again and again suggests both an anxiety about the "force" of a promise as a speech act as well as a set of evolving legal strategies designed to quell that anxiety. The need for repetition of the promise and the demand for visible "proof" of its existence alike suggest an insecurity about whether a promise like Faustus's can really have force—a concern not only for devils but for the play itself. At the same time, such demands are strategies designed to make that promise stick. In contrast to Sacks, commenting on the complexity of "consideration" in the early modern period, Charles Donahue says, "That consideration was required to support an *assumpsit* is clear enough. What that consideration was is not completely clear even in the time of Slade's case. What is clear is that a sealed writing does not require consideration. The writing in blood [in *Faustus*] is like a seal."[18]

From a modern point of view, the legal strategies developed for and around Slade's case ultimately suggest a conception of promises as inhabiting contracts. Rather than simply offering subsequent proofs that contracts have been made, promises assume the role of animating if tacit principles of the contracts themselves. This view is by no means inevitable. That it had to be defended, and Coke had to actually explain it, suggests how contingent it was: "When the plaintiff said 'You shall have my corn' and the other said 'You shall have so much money for your corn' these are express promises. . . . If he says 'I promise' or 'I agree' it is as much as and all one. And if you will deny that there was any promise here, there was no contract either" (36).[19] The approach to language here is not narrowly literal, for the "force" of the contract does not depend on one and only one utterance or set of words. The promise is embedded neither in a single grammatical structure nor in a single rhetorical formula.[20] Coke's terms anticipate (though ultimately challenge) the superiority of what

Austin calls "explicit performatives" over ordinary performative utterances. For Coke, contracts were not dependent on the utterance of the words "I promise" in order to have binding force.

It can be argued that the notion that promises animate contracts was not new even in Slade's time. One scholar argues persuasively that even conservatives on the Court of Common Pleas had been willing to "infer" a promise, or "read [one] in" to a contract all along.[21] But even this formulation still leaves unresolved where or in what sense the promise "exists," whether only in the mind of the person doing the inferring or "reading in," or in and as the animating principle of the contract itself. Thus to some degree the notion that promises animate contracts was a contingent one until *Slade's Case* determined it should not be. Even then, resistance to the verdict suggests that acceptance was a matter of degree. Far from being unanimous, the final decision in *Slade's Case* seems to have squeaked by with a majority of six to five. We now know that Coke's *Report* often presents as resolutions what were in fact his own arguments. And even after *Slade's Case*, courts were still resisting the precedent set by it and reversing decisions which followed that precedent.[22]

It may be recalled from chapter 2 that Bodin is so concerned not to pass on the power of the words used by magicians to his audience that he not only won't utter those words but won't name the magicians who utter them. He lambastes the Master Sorcerer "who does not need to be named [qui ne merite d'estre nome]" and "the great doctor in the diabolical art who I shall not name [grand Docteur en l'art Diaboliqe, qui ie ne nommeray point]."[23] We could say then that where Slade's lawyers were able to use the notion that utterances had performative power in order to "fix" these utterances and give them a predictable set of consequences in the world of the courts, and thus to secure rights for their client, Bodin saw such utterances as so unstable, so autonomous, as not to be "securable," and therefore had to resort to more radical and rigid means for securing their speakers, the witches. Both traditions sought a response to the perceived performative power of utterances, but Bodin's, unable to imagine a way to "fix" or secure utterances—in Bodin's case even when he sought to restrict himself to those already in a written record—needed to eliminate their speakers instead.

How does Marlowe's play ultimately navigate such crosscurrents, aside from making the devils the better lawyers in the play, the ones who avail themselves of the best legal strategies? If the words of necromancy lack efficacy, are there other kinds of words which are efficacious? Has the play transferred the fantasy of the efficacious word from charms and conjurations to the promise Faustus makes? The Evil Angel makes precisely this point when, halfway through the play, he says that it is "too late" to repent (2.3.78), as if the promise were irreversible. But the old man implies that the promise is more or less beside the point when he tells Faustus to pray, to "call for mercy." Is the play, then, transferring the fantasy of the efficacious word, now not to the promise but to the notion of prayer?

But Faustus never does pray. Most of act 5 revolves around what he does instead. If the Old Man says, "call for mercy and avoid despair" (57), the moments that follow display a series of substitutes and failures to do so, utterances that are ultimately misfires. "I do repent" in line 64 has the potential to be a speech act, and in being one, an act of repentance, but its place in an antithesis of "I do repent, and yet I do despair" marks it as one of a pair of constatives, descriptions of feelings. As for prayer, Faustus engages in a series of invocations, but they are not to God but to pieces of the universe and to the devil. (In this sense, he's a textbook case of the claims some reformers made that man always substitutes a false god for God.[24]) To the universe, Faustus says: "Stand still, you ever-moving spheres of heaven / That time may cease" (5.2.68–69); to Lucifer: "Ah, rend not my heart for naming of my Christ!" (5.2.80). When Faustus does turn to God, it isn't to call for mercy but to put a limit to his damnation. The scene dramatizes the failure to utter the one speech act that the play suggests might in theory have been efficacious, showing us instead a series of misfires. In so doing, it suggests it is not the utterance but the failure of the utterance that is dangerous. Does the play ultimately preserve the fantasy of a word which simply by being uttered is efficacious? In this way as in so many others the play remains indeterminate and withholds an answer. In the prayer for mercy Faustus never utters, the act of repentance he never makes, the play preserves what could be called a nostalgia for an efficacious word, but insofar as this word never takes place in the mouth of man, this idea remains, if not hypothetical, an idea never realized in action.[25]

CHAPTER 8

# Paulina and the Theater of Shame

In the middle of II.iii of *The Winter's Tale*, Leontes throws Paulina out of his chambers, calling her a "mankind witch" (67) and threatens to have her burnt (113). "I care not," Paulina tells him, "It is an heretic that makes the fire, / Not she which burns in't" (114–15).[1] Paulina argues, in effect, that the crime is in the mind of the beholder, the one who makes the accusation and sets the fire, not the body or the actions of the burnt. Leontes implies, by contrast, that the crime of witchcraft is real and in the actions of the woman he orders burnt as a witch. The play has at its center, then, the fantasy of witch-burning, articulated from two different viewpoints, that of the witch-hunter and that of the hunted, who in this case is also the critic of the system. Which of these constructions lies closer to the heart of the play? And what is the significance of their juxtaposition?

The question is complicated by the fact that the two positions themselves correspond roughly to two central and opposite positions offered during the period about the reality of witchcraft: one articulated by Reginald Scot, whose 1584 *Discoverie of Witchcraft*, as chapter 3 argued, took the position that most witch hunts were, in fact, misogynistic scapegoating practices aimed at poor, old, and often menopausal women, and that the "witchcraft," if any, was in the mind of the victimizers; and the other position articulated by King James VI of Scotland and I of England—Shakespeare's own spectator at the time of *The Winter's Tale*. As we have seen, unlike Scot, James insisted that witchcraft was real and that witches could be identified and should be punished. What does it mean for the play to invoke these two opposite points of view about witchcraft in the exchange between Paulina and Leontes? One thing it means, as the first section of this chapter will suggest, is that *The Winter's Tale* exposes the latter position, King James's, for its inconsistencies. Through Leontes, *The Winter's Tale* suggests the way that conceptions of witchcraft like those at work in *Daemonologie* actually spring from anxieties about the male body. For this to emerge, it is necessary to return to the arguments Scot and James make to see how deeply they inform *The Winter's Tale*.

## Dogmatism and Its Discontents

Although Reginald Scot never flatly denies the existence of witches or witchcraft, he does advance the position that most charges of witchcraft are erroneous, coming on the accusers' part from motives as various as guilt at turning a hungry neighbor away, a sense of powerlessness at a cow or a child dying, or a fundamental misogyny aimed at old menopausal women themselves. Witchcraft for Scot, as we have seen, is not the ability to create material change, turn one substance into another, or raise the dead, but something much more like sleight of hand. The snake charmer Scot believes in, he says, is the one who takes out the snake's teeth with a rag before the performance.

The central focal point for what presents itself as witchcraft really being sleight of hand is, it will be recalled, the witch of Endor story in 1 Samuel 28, in which Saul, distraught, goes to the witch of Endor, who summons up for him the dead Samuel. What, Scot asks, happened at Endor? The so-called witch of Endor must have thrown her voice, and Saul, delusional, hungry, sleep-deprived, and gullible, imagined it was Samuel speaking. Paulina does not rehearse the specific details or recapitulate the logic of Scot's argument, but she does express his main point, which is that the crime, the heresy or evil, is in the mind and subsequent actions of the accuser, not the actions of the one who is called witch.

Many people took objection to Scot's position during the period, but the person who took the loudest objection was James, then king of Scotland. As we have seen, James incorporates Reginald Scot's position on the witch of Endor into his dialogue *Daemonologie* in the person of his questioner and straight man, the foil, Philomathes, and he energetically refutes Scot's position in the voice of his point-of-view character Epistemon, the knower of things, who gives the answers. Philomathes reproduces Reginald Scot's arguments in short form at the very beginning of *Daemonologie*, clearly so that they can be, once and for all, eliminated: Saul must have been starving, guilty, distracted out of his wits, for God surely wouldn't let Samuel be summoned out of the bosom of Abraham, because he wouldn't let the blessed be woken by every passing witch. As important, Philomathes argues, God wouldn't let the devil take the form of Samuel because it would be "inconvenient" for the prophets, who would then never know when it was an angel speaking to them or when they were being deceived. To this last and crucial epistemological concern, Epistemon argues that the devil could indeed have taken the form of Samuel. From an epistemological point of view, his shapeshifting provides no "inconvenience" to the prophets since God never allows his own to be deceived but only those who first deceive themselves. ("Neither could that bring any inconvenient with the visiones of the Prophets, since it is most certain, that God will [only] . . . permit him [the devil] so to deceive . . . such, as first wilfully deceives them-selves" [4].)

*Daemonologie* begins, then, by eliminating Reginald Scot's position (a position echoed ultimately in *The Winter's Tale* by Paulina) and argues that witchcraft is real. At *Daemonologie*'s center is a kind of dogmatism that knowledge is possible. To whom is it possible? "His [God's] own." A claim which presumably includes the author of the book, himself an examiner. What are the payoffs of it being possible? It is possible to determine who is a witch and who is not and therefore to accurately prosecute. How is it possible? As we have seen, the book offers various "signs" to distinguish demonically induced behavior from natural maladies. It is possible to tell a witch from a melancholic, for instance, because melancholics are lean, pale, constantly "bewraying" themselves, and confess to witchcraft voluntarily, where witches are "fatte or corpulent in their bodies" and given over to "the pleasures of the flesh" (30), and confessions have to be extorted from them under torture "which witnesseth their guiltines" (30). It is possible to tell a possessed person from a person suffering from mania or frenzy because possessed people have chests like iron ("an ironie hardnes of . . . sinnowes"), speak in "sundrie languages" previously unknown to them, and demonstrate the strength of more than six "of the wightest and wodest" men, whereas manic and frenzied people do not. One of the hallmarks of the book's insistence that knowledge is possible, then, is an implicit faith in the evidence of the senses in the form of a checklist: weight, coloring, chest-hardness, strength, speaking in previously unknown languages.

But even as the text asserts that it is possible to know a witch from another person, it is beleaguered by an unacknowledged doubt that it is not. As we have seen, witches confess, says Epistemon, to a category of information which while not a lie is also not true. Some witches confess to flying through the air in the "likenesse of a little beast or foule" (39) and penetrating solid walls ("pearc[ing] through whatsoever house or Church, though all ordinarie passages be closed" [39]), and this is certainly not possible—first, because the property of a solid body is to be solid, and both witches and walls retain that property; second, because it would be too much like transubstantiation ("so like to the little transubstantiat god in the Papistes Masse" [40]); and finally, because when Peter got out of prison he did it not by passing through a solid wall, but rather by opening a door, and witches cannot do anything that Peter could not do. How is it, then, that witches go to their death confessing to having traveled in the shapes of small beasts and fowl and penetrating solid walls? The devil ravishes their "thoughtes" and dulls their "sences," deluding them, often leaving tokens of false evidence behind so that many witches share (and swear to) the same collective delusion ("For he being a spirite, may hee: not so rauishe their thoughts, and dull their sences . . . that he maie deceiue them with the greater efficacie, may hee not at that same instant . . . illude such other persones so in that same fashion . . . he makes them to beleeue that they mette; that all their reportes and tokens, though seuerallie examined, may euerie one agree with an other" [41–42]). There is then, as we have seen, a category of information which, while not a lie, is also not true, which implicitly means that not every confession can be trusted to be reliable. The problem is not an inconsistency in what Epistemon has said about deception—those witches who are deceived are those who first deceive themselves—but rather a problem with how we know whether to trust a confession. Some confessions are (implicitly) unreliable. This disparity is never noted or acknowledged by either of the speakers in the book, but the anxiety it generates grows more acute as the book proceeds. Set against a dogmatism that knowledge is possible is an anxiety of rising doubt.

One characteristic of *Daemonologie*, then, is that it vacillates between dogmatic assertions that knowledge is possible and a rising (if unacknowledged) fear that it is not. But this dogmatism comes in response to another kind of anxiety as well. Just as *Daemonologie* asserts that false thoughts entering the mind are only possible if one first deceives oneself, so it argues that the devil only gains power if one first gives him what Epistemon calls "entresse." But this polemical claim is undermined by what turns out to be the narrative of the book. For what follows is an extremely graphic narrative of "entresse" in which things penetrate the body, particularly the male body, without permission, a narrative which begins with the fear of witches penetrating solid walls, escalates to a fear of spirits penetrating solid walls, and culminates in a fear of spirits in the form of succubi and incubi draining the sperm out of the male body. The human body, the male body in particular, is imagined as penetrable, porous, susceptible to invasion.

How does any of this inform the debate between Paulina and Leontes in II.iii of *The Winter's Tale*? As we shall see, the portrait that emerges of Leontes in the first three acts of *The Winter's Tale* looks very much like the picture of *Daemonologie* with its vacillation between dogmatism and doubt, between dogmatism and the fear of penetrability. In this way the play offers an important meditation on the way anxieties about masculinity like those at work in *Daemonologie* became externalized in the witch hunts of the period.

## Gates Rammed Open

*The Winter's Tale* opens, as *Daemonologie* does, with its protagonist insisting on the possibility of knowledge. When he concludes that his wife has cheated on him, Leontes appeals to a checklist of visible "signs." His belief in the possibility of knowledge, in other words, is grounded in a faith in the evidence of the senses. "But to be paddling palms and pinching fingers, / As now they are, and making practised smiles / As in a looking-glass" (I.ii.114–16), he says, rattling off what he takes to be the visible signs of adultery, and later to Camillo adds, "Is whispering nothing? / Is leaning cheek to cheek? Is meeting noses? / Kissing with inside lip? Stopping the career / Of laughter with a sigh?—a note infallible / Of breaking honesty!" (I.ii.281–85). Thus his first decision that Hermione has betrayed him ("Too hot, too hot!") specifically rests in a belief in ocular evidence.

What is startling is the way Leontes is able to consider in a speculative way exactly the dogmatism, the faith in ocular evidence, he is about to slip back into. He considers the possibility that the senses are fallible when he acknowledges the way that nature, affection, can trick a person, making him mistake a son for a self of twenty-three years ago (154), but immediately acts as if the senses were reliable again when he says of Hermione, "How she holds up the neb, the bill to him! / And arms her with the boldness of a wife / To her allowing husband" (I.ii.181–83).

The pattern more or less repeats itself in II.i. Leontes begins by considering the possibility that the mind doesn't merely distort but makes its own reality when he describes the poison in the spider's cup:

There may be in the cup
A spider steeped, and one may drink, depart,
And yet partake no venom, for his knowledge
Is not infected; but if one present
Th' abhorred ingredient to his eye, make known

How he hath drunk, he cracks his gorge, his sides
With violent hefts. (II.i.39–45)

The passage locates the poison less in the external world, in the spider, than in the mind. It argues, in effect, that the mind in part makes reality. But no sooner has Leontes recognized this possibility than he retreats back into a position which ignores it, a position of dogmatism: "I have drunk, and seen the spider" (45). When, at the end of the scene, the lords attempt to defend Hermione, Leontes reiterates the supremacy of his own senses ("You smell this business with a sense as cold / As is a dead man's nose; but I do see't and feel't, / As you feel doing thus," he says, even as the text replicates his situation by keeping us in the dark about what "doing thus" is [151–53]). The play, then, reveals the same structure in Leontes that appears in *Daemonologie*, a vacillation between dogmatic certainty, the belief that knowledge is possible, and a slippage into radical doubt. One could say that as is the case in *Daemonologie*, Leontes's assertions of dogmatism grow more vehement in response to the panic that there is no certainty, in response to a growing doubt. But they grow more vehement in response to something else as well.[2]

It is not just the structure of vacillation between dogmatism and radical doubt that Leontes shares with *Daemonologie*. Beneath Leontes's dogmatism and beside the vacillation lie the same fears about the penetrability of the male body that characterize *Daemonologie*. The first thing to note about Leontes's "charges," his own attacks, is the way they expand—both in nature and in reference to whom they're aimed at—throughout the first three acts of the play. He begins by fearing that Hermione has slept with Polixenes ("Too hot, too hot!"), continues by fearing that she has been unfaithful for years (To Mamillius: "Art thou my boy?"), and erupts in III.ii in a charge of attempted regicide. The indictment reads that Hermione is "accused and arraigned of high treason in committing adultery with Polixenes, King of Bohemia, and conspiring with Camillo to take away the life of our sovereign lord the King, thy royal husband" (III.ii.13–16). The anxiety expands from the charge of a single adultery to a charge of years of adultery to a charge of attempted regicide. As the charge grows, Leontes also accuses more and more of the people around him of being traitors: "a nest of traitors!" (II.iii.82), "Traitors!" (72), "thou, traitor" (130). He accuses himself of weakness as well ("It is but weakness / To bear the matter thus; mere weakness" [1–2]), and he accuses himself of being a feather ("I am a feather for each wind that blows. / Shall I live on to see this bastard kneel / And call me father?" [153–55]).

We are told at the very beginning of the play by Archidamus that if Leontes comes to Bohemia he shall see "great difference betwixt our Bohemia and

108   CHAPTER 8

your Sicilia" (I.i.3–4). But difference, or rather the feared collapse of it, seems to be precisely what is at stake throughout the first few acts of the play. Act 1 tells, in effect, a story about difference, a story that begins with a nostalgia for a world without difference and culminates in a terror of what it would mean to lack difference. When Hermione, questioning Polixenes about his shared childhood with Leontes, attempts to establish "difference," asking Polixenes who was the "verier wag o' th' two" (I.ii.65), Polixenes insists that the world they shared was a world whose fundamental principle was the absence of difference.[3] This is what it meant to be a "boy eternal" (64); they were interchangeable: "We were as twinn'd lambs that did frisk i' th' sun / And bleat the one at th' other" [I.ii.66–67]). To be "boy eternal" was not simply to live in the absence of sexual difference, though that certainly, but to live in the absence of difference between two human beings: to be "twinn'd lambs." The tone of the speech is rosy, nostalgic, elegiac.

In seventy lines, Leontes himself makes a similar speech. Asked by Hermione if he is "moved" ("You look / As if you held a brow of much distraction. / Are you moved, my lord?" [147–49]), Leontes lies and pretends his mood is due to a "trick of nature," to slipping into a memory in which he mistook Mamillius for his former childhood self:

>   No, in good earnest.
> How sometimes Nature will betray its folly,
> Its tenderness, and make itself a pastime
> To harder bosoms! Looking on the lines
> Of my boy's face, methoughts I did recoil
> Twenty-three years, and saw myself unbreeched,
> In my green velvet coat; my dagger muzzled
> Lest it should bite its master, and so prove,
> As ornaments oft do, too dangerous.
> How like, methought, I then was to this kernel. (I.ii.149–58)

Although the speech is a lie, it reveals a truth about Leontes, a regression, a momentary slip to a time before difference, "myself unbreeched"—literally not in pants yet—"my dagger muzzled / Lest it should bite its master, and so prove / As ornaments oft do, too dangerous." Although the memory of being undifferentiated, "unbreeched," phallus "muzzled," is cloaked in nostalgia, in memories of the green velvet jacket, it is brought on by the violence of the rage ("too hot") and the sense of cuckolding ("to the infection of my brains / And hard'ning of my brows") that precedes it.

By the next time Leontes articulates these ideas, they have changed from a kind of benign regression to a complete horror of porousness, from a nostalgia for the absence of difference to a fear of the loss of it. At the moment of his greatest dogmatism, Leontes's greatest faith in ocular evidence ("How she holds up the neb, the bill to him! / And arms her with the boldness of a wife / To her allowing husband"), Leontes articulates a horror at penetrability, views himself as someone porous, someone capable of being fished out of. The passage begins with the sense that the wife can be fished, sluiced, penetrated:

> There have been,
> Or I am much deceived, cuckolds ere now,
> And many a man there is, even at this present,
> Now, while I speak this, holds his wife by th'arm
> That little thinks she has been sluiced in's absence. (I.ii.188–92)

But by degrees, the wife who is sluiced becomes the means by which the husband is fished: "And his pond fished by his next neighbor, by / Sir Smile, his neighbour" (193–94). The speech culminates in a vision in which the male body becomes rammed open against its own will ("Nay, there's comfort in't / Whiles other men have gates, and those gates opened, / As mine, against their will" [194–96]). It is as if by contamination the wife's porousness or penetrability leads to the husband's. "Be it concluded, / No barricado for a belly. Know't; / It will let in and out the enemy / With bag and baggage—Many thousand on 's / Have the disease and feel't not. How now, boy?" (201–5). If Epistemon seems incapable of putting to rest the notion of things getting into the body, Leontes's words, too, culminate in a vision of penetrability, porousness, a set of holes.

It's fitting then, that in the next scene, Leontes seems obsessed with the country's holes ("How came the posterns so easily open?" [II.i.52–53]) and that he worries a moment later that there is literally too much of Hermione "in" Mamillius: "Give me the boy. I am glad you did not nurse him. / Though he does bear some signs of me, yet you / Have too much blood in him" (56–59). No wonder then that in II.iii Leontes explodes at seeing another child, seeing, in effect, what has been "in" Hermione.

We could say then that the play's early depictions of Leontes present him as sharing more than one analogy with the James of *Daemonologie*. Not only is he characterized by a vacillation between rigid dogmatism and rising doubt, but the rigid dogmatism seems designed to quell, as it does in *Daemonologie*, the sense of the body as well as the mind as susceptible to invasion. These fears soon coalesce around Paulina. At the moment she puts the infant child in front of him, she becomes to him not only a "mankind witch" but the quintessential midwife-witch of demonological tracts: "lady Margery, your midwife there" (159), a "gross hag" (107), "lewd-tongued" (171), "a most intellgencing bawd,"

"Dame Partlet" (75), "a callet of boundless tongue" (90–91) who makes her husband "woman-tired," "unroosted" (74).

We have a partial answer to the question of what it means for the play to invoke two opposite positions about witchcraft. For in exposing anxieties about penetrability as being the ones behind Leontes's attacks on both his wife and on Paulina, the mankind witch, the play would seem to critique that structure of scapegoating which vents outside onto women the anxieties about the body the man experiences within. In so doing it does not simply reveal, as other critics have suggested, the anxieties about masculinity at work in any number of Shakespeare plays, but rather suggests the precise role of these anxieties in precipitating the spectacle of witch-hunting itself and thus takes a very definite stand against the kind of witch hunts that characterized James's early reign.

Does this mean that, almost by default, the play takes the stand that Reginald Scot did, that criminality lies in the mind of the oppressor rather than in the body and actions of the oppressed? Is Paulina the mouthpiece for Reginald Scot in the play? In one sense the easy answer to this question is yes. A skeptical line of thought about witchcraft does indeed run through the play—not only in the argument Paulina voices when in II.iii she says it is the heretic that makes the fire, "not she which burns in it," but in the very mechanics of the ending of the play. Paulina not only voices the arguments that Scot does, her actions in relation to Hermione are legible as making that argument. In one way, Paulina is the witch of Endor as that witch was understood by Scot, creating in her chosen spectator the belief that she has raised the dead.

## Paulina and the Construction of Belief

For Scot, as for many biblical commentators of the period and of periods before him, the basic question produced by the book of Samuel was: What happened at Endor? The witch couldn't have summoned up Samuel, because if she had it would mean that those asleep in the bosom of Abraham could never get any rest but could rather be summoned up by every passing witch. She couldn't have summoned up Samuel because the souls of the dead await judgment and can't be moved around. Nor is it likely, says Scot, that God would answer Saul by a dead Samuel when he wouldn't answer him by a living one (113).

But if the witch didn't summon up Samuel, what (or whom) did she summon? Not a devil, says Scot, because if God wouldn't answer Saul by a prophet, he certainly wouldn't answer him by a devil. Not a devil, because devils don't talk the way that whatever the witch raised talked to Saul. It's "the devil's condition to allure the people unto wickednes . . . not . . . to admonish, warne and rebuke them for evill" (119–20), says Scot. ("This [I say] is no phrase of a divell, but of a cousener, which knew before what Samuel had prophesied concerning Saules destruction" [119].) Not only does whatever the witch summoned not talk like a devil, it doesn't behave like one either. The divell can't stand the name Jehovah, which is repeated five times in the episode ("of which name the divell can't abide the hearing" [115]). Even if it lay in a witch's power to summon a devil, Scot says, it wouldn't be in the witch's power to work a miracle.

But if the witch didn't raise Samuel and she didn't raise the devil, who or what was it that spoke to Saul? As we have seen, Scot's answer is that it is the witch herself who spoke to Saul: she is the consummate theatricalist, a charlatan, a strumpet ("Now commeth in Samuel to plaie his part: but I am persuaded it was performed in the person of the witch hir selfe, or of hir confederate" [119]). Scot's approach to the problem can be summed up in his claim: "But we shall not need . . . to descend so lowe as hell, to fetch a divell up to expound this place" (114). It is ridiculous, Scot says, "to leave manifest things, and such as by naturall reason . . . can be conceived, nor tried by anie rule of reason" (114). His faith in the natural explanation behind apparently supernatural phenomena is embodied in the rhetorical question "For what need so farre fetches, as to fetch a divell supernaturallie out of hell, when the illusion may be here by naturall meanes deciphered?" (119). No need to posit a devil when a natural explanation is available. What is the natural explanation? The witch was a ventriloquist: "speaking as it were from the bottome of hir bellie," "cast[ing] hir self into a transe, and so . . . answering to Saule in Samuels name in hir counterfeit hollow voice" (121).

Scot makes much of the fact that Saul never actually set foot in the witch's chamber but only heard her cousening words. For him the story is a parable about ocular evidence, not because such evidence is fundamentally unreliable, but because Saul was so morally depraved and such a gullible fool, so "bewitched and blinded in the matter" (116), that he failed to examine it, though "doubtlesse a wise man wold have perchance espied her knaverie" (116). Much of Scot's treatment of the story of the witch of Endor, then, is spent revealing and iterating the idea that what lies behind the appearance of witchcraft, especially witchcraft that takes the form of conjuring a dead person, has a perfectly rational natural explanation behind it.

It is easy to see the analogies between Scot's argument and the way the play dangles the fantasy that the dead Hermione may have been living and tucked away in Paulina's chapel all along. Like Leontes, we are set up to understand Hermione's reanimation as if it can only be a return from the dead, a resurrection. As Stephen Orgel has argued, it is not simply Leontes but we who are made to understand that Hermione is actually dead when Paulina says, "I say she's dead—I'll swear't" (III.ii.201) and when Leontes himself asks Paulina to "bring me / To the dead bodies of my Queen and son. / One grave shall be for both" (232–34).[4] (Even as late as V.iii, Leontes is still saying "I saw her, / As I thought, dead, and have in vain said many / A prayer upon her grave" [V. iii.139–41].) From a dramaturgical standpoint, the inconsistency between the death at the end of the trial scene and the living Hermione at the end of the play seems designed to create in us the same sequence of responses that Leontes undergoes (a sense of certainty, an undermining of certainty, and an opening up of doubt).

When Hermione says at the end of V.iii that, hearing from Paulina that the oracle gave word Perdita might have survived, she stayed alive in order to see the "issue," the moment creates the same sensation of a natural explanation behind the appearance of the supernatural that Scot's scene does when he announces the witch of Endor is a ventriloquist, although Orgel has argued Hermione doesn't need to hear this from Paulina, having heard the oracle's pronouncement herself in III.ii. When the second gentleman in V.ii mentions that Paulina has had "some great matter there [at her chapel] in hand" and that "ever since the death of Hermione [she] visited that removed house" (V. ii.102–5), the moment seems to offer a punch line, the revelation of the same kind of "trick" under the special effects that Scot reveals. *The Winter's Tale* "answers" *Daemonologie* not only by exposing the anxiety about masculinity at the core of *Daemonologie* but by deepening and rehearsing Scot's argument, though as we shall see there are differences between Paulina and Scot. The "natural trick" argument is only one way—and perhaps the least significant one—in which the play "rehearses" Scot.

Scot's deepest interest in the witch of Endor story lies not in the witch's ventriloquism, nor in her technical ability to cast illusion, nor even in the story's power to confirm Scot's pet axiom that the natural explanation is the best way to explain ostensibly supernatural phenomena. Scot's fiercest and least integrated response to the story lies in his outrage at the witch's ability to detect and exploit Saul's capacity for fear. Central to Scot's reading and to his skepticism is his sense of the way one person can exploit another's capacity for fear and channel it into belief. Thus Scot is emphatic in his portrayal of Saul as a person terrified, "in despaire of the mercies and goodnes of God" (115), "straught of mind, desperate, and a verie foole" (115). This, he says, the witch knows and uses. By Saul's own admission, by his own betrayal of his emotional state, the witch might easily conjecture that his heart failed, and "direct the oracle or prophesie accordinglie" (119).

To accomplish this direction she utilizes a specific rhetorical strategy, speaking in general terms, telling part of the truth, and leaving the rest to Saul's suggestibility: "Lo now the matter is brought to passe, for I see woonderfull things" (118), she says, and Saul falls for the bait, longing "to know all, [he] asked her what she saw" (118). When pressed, she remains just general enough for Saul to supply the rest, to project his own interpretation. Saying she sees angels and gods ascending, but not specifying any particular angel, the witch of Endor knows the right way to word such an answer to make Saul draw the conclusion that it was Samuel—to make him create the image that she needs him to see: "Then proceedeth she with her inchanting phrases and words of course: so as thereby Saule gathereth and supposeth that she hath raised a man" (118). Otherwise his next words ("what fashion is he of?") don't "depend" on anything: "For otherwise his question dependeth not upon anything before spoken" (118). Saul's question "hangeth not upon hir last expressed words" (118). Like a good manipulator, she doesn't have to use names, saying only that she sees "an old man lapped in a mantell" (118) and letting Saul's mind do the rest by creating the image of Samuel. In this way her skill—and Scot's interest in her—lies less in any technical ventriloquism than in her ability to "conjecture that his [Saul's] heart failed" (119) and her knowledge of how to "direct the oracle or prophesie accordinglie" (119).

It is in this way that Paulina offers the closest analogy to Scot's version of the witch of Endor, in her ability to exploit Leontes's capacity for guilt and fear. But where the witch of Endor invokes the use of partial truths and vague generalities to make her auditor create the image she desires him to have, Paulina employs a rhetoric of opposites and negation to escalate Leontes's fear. She begins her harangue in III.ii by depicting not the set of torments Leontes will actually have to undergo but the ones that she claims he has created for her, the wheels, racks, fires, the flaying, boiling "in leads or oils" (174–75) she predicts he'll subject her to in retaliation. She works by substituting discrete tortures for indefinite and inchoate ones, physical torments for emotional losses, her own hypothetical punishment for the catastrophe Leontes himself is about to undergo, scrambling physical and emotional, discrete and indefinite torture, unbalancing Leontes by conflating author and victim of torture, victim and victimizer.

But this "unbalancing" rhetoric is only a first, preparatory step for the rhetoric of opposites that is to come: "That thou betrayedst Polixenes, 'twas nothing" Paulina says, "nor was't much / Thou wouldst have poisoned good Camillo's honour" (183–86). The "nor was't much" speech works by saying the opposite of what it means. It *was* something to have betrayed Polixenes; it *was* much to have poisoned Camillo's honor; it was monstrous (not none or little) to have cast forth his daughter to crows, and directly his fault that his son has died. Even this sort of unbalancing rhetoric is itself only in the service of Paulina's final strategy. She intensifies Leontes's affect by barring it an outlet in action, telling him "not [to] repent these things," that they are "heavier / Than all thy woes can stir" (206–7), that no amount of repentance can earn forgiveness:

> A thousand knees,
> Ten thousand years together, naked, fasting,
> Upon a barren mountain, and still winter
> In storm perpetual, could not move the gods
> To look that way thou wert. (208–12)

Still in a sense invoking the rhetoric of opposites, she tells Leontes not to repent, to run "mad indeed, stark mad" (181) and to "betake thee / To nothing but despair" (207–8). Like Ulysses, who shows Troilus Cressida's betrayal and then intensifies his reaction by barring it an expression in action, urging him to contain himself lest he "break out" (V.ii.51), lest his displeasure "enlarge itself" (37), lest he "flow to great distraction" (41), Paulina intensifies Leontes's affect by barring it an expression in penitential action. In this way, she works to create despair, and out-Endors the witch of Endor. Shakespeare is at pains not only to suggest, as Scot would, the possibility of a natural trick under what looks like the supernatural but the very mechanisms and rhetorical practices of intimidation that create belief itself. He deepens Scot's argument, saying not only, "There may be a natural explanation for what looks like witchcraft" or "Male tyrants who scapegoat women do so in response to their own crumbling sense of self," but "behind the creation of belief is a discourse of intimidation, a set of practical strategies which work through the exploitation of fear."

In the service of what does Shakespeare show us these practices? What work does the play envision such rhetoric doing? In another moment, in the hands of another rhetorician like Ulysses, we might expect the effect of such a speech to be the creation of radical doubt ("This is, and is not, Cressid," Troilus says [V.ii.146]) or the dissolution of self ("I will not be myself," he says, grasping at the dissolving "guard of patience" he claims stands between his will and all offenses [V.ii.63]). But after Paulina's speech, Leontes does not descend into either radical doubt or rage, having already exhibited both sets of responses to the world at the beginning of the play without the help of anybody's rhetoric.[5] What then is the effect of Paulina's rhetoric, and the ensuing picture of her the play proposes?

From her first appearance onstage, Paulina talks about curing Leontes. "These dangerous, unsafe lunes i' th' King, beshrew them! / He must be told on't," she says, "and he shall" (II.ii.29–30). She appoints herself to the job, saying that the "office" becomes a woman best (30). She professes herself his "physician / Your most obedient counselor; yet that dares / Less appear so in comforting your evils, / Than such as most seem yours" (II.iii.54–57). She comes, she says, with "words as medicinal, as true" (37), words to "purge" him of the humor "that presses him from sleep" (38–39). Her method for effecting a cure will consist of harsh speech: "If I prove honey-mouthed, let my tongue blister, / And never to my red-looked anger be / the trumpet any more" (II.ii.32–34).[6] Are Paulina's harsh(er) words to Leontes after the trial scene (harsh even to the point of claiming that Hermione is dead) simply a part of that cure? And if so, at what precise point in the play does such a "cure" take effect?

We expect Leontes to have changed in the sixteen years that take place before act 4, but as late as act 5 there are signs that no real transformation has occurred. While he remembers Hermione and her virtues, he cannot forget his blemishes in them: he says, "and so still think[s] of / The wrong I did *myself*" (V.i.8–9, emphasis mine). Although he is perfectly willing to submit to Paulina's governance and to swear to what she asks, the line clearly suggests that Leontes is still, sixteen years later, thinking of his own losses, not what he did to others. Nor does the scene present him as regenerate in other ways. Paulina's castigation that he killed his wife falls on resistant if not deaf ears: if one by one you wedded the world, she says, and took something good from each to make a perfect woman, "she you killed, / would be unparalleled" (15). Leontes acknowledges the truth of what she says ("I did so") but tells her to "say so but seldom" (19). Where he welcomed her harsh words sixteen years earlier as "truth, which I receive much better / Than to be pitied of thee" (III.ii.231–32), he is appreciably less eager to have his crimes recounted to him now. As the scene progresses, he becomes even less eager. At Paulina's relentless reminders that Mamillius would have been the same age as Florizel, Leontes tells her to "cease" (V.i.118), that Mamillius "dies to me again when talked of" (119) and that her words will bring him to consider that which will "unfurnish [him] of reason" (123). Looked at from the standpoint of the willingness to remember, the capacity to think of what he's done as a wrong to others and the willingness to hear the past retold, Leontes is not presented as particularly "cured" in V.i. His innuendo about begging Polixenes for Perdita ("the precious thing" Polixenes holds but a "trifle") adds to the picture of an untransformed and incomplete penitent.

## Piercing of the Soul

But if Leontes has not redeemed himself in sixteen years, when does such a transformation take place? In a kind of twin fantasy at the beginning of act 5, Leontes and Paulina imagine the reanimation of the dead Hermione. A worse wife but "better used," Leontes says, would make Hermione's "sainted spirit / Again possess her corpse" (57–58). Although he still seems bent on bloody thoughts ("She . . . would incense me / To murder her I married" [61–62]), the exchange nonetheless begins to identify the work that is necessary for reformation or "cure." Paulina says,

> Were I the ghost that walked . . .
> I'd shriek, that even your ears
> Should rift to hear me, and the words that followed
> Should be, "Remember mine." (63–67)

For spiritual change to take place, the passage argues, it is necessary first to remember. And in order to begin the work of remembering, one needs the shriek that will rive the general ear, the organs of perception. Just as Cleomenes has described the "burst / And the ear-deaf'ning voice o' th' oracle," which, "kin to Jove's thunder, so surprised my sense / That I was nothing" (III.i.8–11), the senses need to be split, to be broken, to become as nothing, before change can occur. Leontes will eventually articulate precisely this "piercedness" or "burstness" at the sight of the statue. To Paulina's claim that the statue's wrinkles are a tribute to the carver, making Hermione "as she lived now" (V.iii.32), Leontes says: "As now she might have done, / So much to my good comfort as it is / Now piercing to my soul" (V.iii.32–34).

Taken in isolation what the moment suggests is the degree to which the affective experience of being "pierced" is crucial to spiritual transformation. But the moment has a number of other resonances as well. Where in I.ii Leontes's moment of greatest hysteria, his dogmatism that he knew Hermione had cheated, was punctuated by the fear of being "sluiced" or rammed open, here the articulation of what it is to be "pierced" by sorrow precedes his acceptance of what is contradictory and chaotic, what cannot be proven. When Paulina offers to draw the curtain forty lines later, Leontes repudiates the "settled senses of the world" for "the pleasure of that madness" (72–73). Thus, the scene argues that reason itself is a lesser mode of perception than what one apprehends when one is being "pierced." Memory is pictured as both facilitating this piercing and flowing from it: Leontes describes the "evils" the statue has "conjured to remembrance" (40) in a line that makes the real magic in the play the ability to call up the memory of his own wrongdoing.

What is the relation between Paulina's earlier rhetoric of despair and this piercing of the soul? The relation is that of a prologue or rehearsal. Her words soften the incomplete penitent, prepare him, by reducing him to despair for the soul-piercing that is to come. In the service of what does Shakespeare show us such rhetorical practices? In the service of showing us the machinery behind the awakening of faith. Paulina is and is not Reginald Scot, then: she is, in the sense of revealing the practices of intimidation by which humans compel faith out of each other, but in embodying these practices she is not, because Reginald Scot would never admit the legitimacy of faith even partially compelled in this manner.

But there is another aspect to Paulina's rhetoric that bears comment. Why does she choose the particular rhetorical strategies she does, conflating victim and victimizer, speaking in a language of opposites and negation, and especially, why does she utilize the technique of barring affect an outlet in action? Why are these the chosen strategies for softening a potential penitent? To put the question differently, to what are these verbal strategies the antidote, corrective, or cure?

We can best answer these questions if we look at the rhetorical and theatrical strategies Leontes himself offers in the trial scene, the strategies to which Paulina responds. From the very beginning of the trial scene, Leontes seems to approach the trial as a means of "clearing" himself. That is, although he ostensibly seeks to establish Hermione's guilt, he seeks as forcefully to remove his own. Nominally conceding that the "party tried" is Hermione, Leontes looks at the trial as a means of "clearing" himself.

> This sessions, to our great grief we pronounce,
> Even pushes 'gainst our heart. The party tried,
> The daughter of a king, our wife, and one
> Of us too much beloved. Let us be cleared
> Of being tyrannous, since we so openly
> Proceed in justice, which shall have due course
> Even to the guilt or the purgation. (III.ii.1–7)

Much of what follows in the scene can be seen as Leontes's attempts to stage, make visible, his "clearness" or innocence. That the scene aligns his expansion of the charges against Hermione from adultery to regicide with the fact that he regards himself as on trial suggests that Leontes's attacks on others intensify in proportion to the degree he feels himself culpable.

In fact, the energy with which he seeks to script the scene he does is marked by the resistance he meets, first on the part of Hermione and then on the part of Paulina, each of whom has an alternative script in mind. Hermione holds fast to the position that she is in a morality play. Seven times in III.ii she articulates the "theatrical" nature of the dilemma she finds herself in, claiming that "if powers divine / Behold our human actions, as they do" (27–28) she will eventually be vindicated. Her claim is premised both on the idea that though her human audience won't believe her, the same evidentiary binds don't bind divine audiences, and on the generic assumptions that govern morality plays that "innocence shall make / False accusation blush and tyranny / Tremble at patience" (29–31).[7]

But the more vividly Hermione describes the way the scene ought to go, the play she would like to be in, the more it becomes apparent that this divine theater is circumscribed by a very different kind of play, with different generic assumptions on earth. Describing her dilemma as if it were a "play" history "pattern[ed] to take spectators," she increasingly specifies her unhappiness as owing to the fact that she is being made into public spectacle:

> For behold me . . .
> The mother to a hopeful prince, here standing
> To prate and talk for life and honour fore
> Who please to come and hear. (36–41)

The speech implores, in effect, to be outside the theater, to be indoors and alone, though Hermione will eventually scale this back to a plea for a better, more compassionate audience:

> The Emperor of Russia was my father.
> O that he were alive, and here beholding
> His daughter's trial! that he did but see
> The flatness of my misery, yet with eyes
> Of pity, not revenge! (117–21)

Like Cleopatra, refusing to be displayed in the public market like a strumpet, Hermione, who earlier said she would not weep or theatricalize her grief, laments being staged as a whore:

> Myself on every post
> Proclaimed a strumpet; with immodest hatred
> . . . hurried
> Here, to this place, i' th' open air . . . (99–103)

The first half of III.ii, in which Leontes seeks to "clear himself," is a trial in which Hermione is staged as a strumpet. This itself suggests the mechanism at work for Leontes: the scene staged "the strumpet," the event staged "the conviction of the strumpet," is in the service of "clearing" or purging the guilt that Leontes cannot clear himself of. In this version of theater, as in *Newes from Scotland*, what is staged externalizes through another person what is feared at the heart of the self. Here justice seeks to dump "outside" what it cannot tolerate within.

Paulina's rhetorical strategies, her very theatricality itself, constitute an antidote to Leontes in the mechanism by which they work.[8] In Leontes we get a trial whose mechanism, whose principle of theatricality, is to push outwards, to stage as "other" what is sensed to be criminal at the heart of the self. In Paulina we get a rhetorical strategy whose mechanism is to push inside the spectator a sense of criminality. To what end does the play juxtapose these two mechanisms of theater? In having Paulina "answer" Leontes the way she does, the play suggests that this first kind of theater, which externalizes what is criminal at the heart of the self by staging an "other" as the criminal, is in need of correction.

But a theater which stages as "other" what is feared at the heart of the self is practically a working definition for the kinds of trial scenes described in demonological treatises of the period. Thus if at the heart of *Daemonologie* is a fear of penetrability, a fear that the body can, like a wall or a door, be entered wheresoever the air can enter in at, *Newes from Scotland* manages this fear by showing female bodies, if not penetrated, then stripped, shaved. If *Daemonologie* fears that the mind can be "ravished" and made unable to tell illusion from what is real, *Newes from Scotland* stages knowability by marking and delimiting and exhibiting these bodies. When the pamphlet depicts Agnes Sampson shaved, with a devil's mark on her genitals, it converts her from a penetrator and knower of secrets—someone who knows what James said to his bride on their wedding night—to a thing whose secrets and secret places are known. That *The Winter's Tale* should hold this kind of theater up for correction is itself remarkable, but that it should do so in the way it does is more so.

That it is the "mankind witch" who offers a countertheater and corrective to Leontes is telling in light of the long history of justice offering a countertheater to the alleged spectacles attributed to witches. As we have seen in the judicial section of *Malleus Maleficarum*, the inquisitors Kramer and Sprenger advise future judges to adopt a set of theatrical "precautions" to neutralize the power of the witch. In III.ii of *The Winter's Tale*, in contrast, it is male justice that needs to be neutralized and cured. When Paulina says it is the heretic that makes the fire, not she who burns in it, she announces what she will subsequently dramatize, that criminality is in the mind of the oppressor, not the body or actions of the one on trial.

# Epilogue
## This Is and Is Not Magic

Midway through *The Tempest*, Ariel, in the shape of a harpy, tells Alonso, accompanied by Sebastian and Antonio, that the "powers" have "bereft" him of Ferdinand because of his crimes against Prospero. Ariel tells all three, "I have made you mad" (III.iii.58).[1] In so doing, he seems to employ the same rhetoric for spiritual rehabilitation Paulina does when, in III.ii of *The Winter's Tale*, she tells Leontes to "run mad indeed" and to betake himself to nothing but despair (III.ii.181, 207–8). On the one hand, both plays present madness and specifically the madness induced by loss as a stage on the way to spiritual change. On the other, Prospero himself doesn't go through the kind of visibly induced madness Alonso does or in fact any kind of obvious madness at all. Yet he makes claims to have changed, claims that though he is "struck to th' quick" with "their high wrongs" (V.i.25), he will forgive his enemies.

What is being said through the comparison? In its juxtaposition of the two reversals—Alonso's, which is systematically engineered and induced, and Prospero's, which is so hasty that it often seems to critics inauthentic—the play seems to raise a series of questions: Under what conditions does spiritual change take place? Can it be engineered or must it come spontaneously from within? What is "real" spiritual change? And are we supposed to believe that Prospero has undergone it?[2] These questions are complicated by the fact that *The Tempest* gives us at least two kinds of lenses under which to examine the possibility of change, one induced by explicitly theatrical means and the other implicitly anti-theatrical, involving the shedding or at least apparent shedding of theatricality. Both vehicles for change invoke the languages of witchcraft and magic in the terms James articulated these in *Daemonologie*, but they do so in ways which interrogate that book. If *The Winter's Tale* juxtaposes two kinds of rival theaters, a trial staged by Leontes designed to clear himself of blame and a rhetoric of blame articulated by Paulina designed to break him down and soften him up, *The Tempest* seems to collapse that opposition. There are no rival theaters in the play, only alternate expressions of theatricality on the part of Prospero.

## Making Men Mad

On the one hand, *The Tempest*, like *The Winter's Tale*, offers a vision of madness as a stage on the way to spiritual transformation. From the very beginning of the play, Prospero has demonstrated an interest in producing madness in his victims. "Who was so firm, so constant, that this coil / Would not infect his reason?" he asks Ariel about the shipwreck (I.ii.207), and Ariel replies, "Not a soul / But felt the fever of the mad" (I.ii.207–10). From the very beginning, too, Prospero has Ariel perpetrate the fiction of loss first on Ferdinand and then later on Alonso. Thus, though Ferdinand says Ariel's music allays both the waves' fury and his own passion, that music seeks specifically to convince him in the "full fathom five" song that his father is dead. And although Alonso already fears Ferdinand has drowned ("My son is lost" [II.i.107] he says, asking, "what strange fish / Hath made his meal on thee?" [II.i.110–11]), Prospero agitates and sharpens this fear when he has Ariel appear in III.iii as a harpy and say: "Thee of thy son, Alonso / They [the powers] have bereft" (75–76). Thus, like Paulina telling Leontes to betake himself to nothing but despair, Prospero seeks to create despair and madness.

Both Alonso's and Gonzalo's responses testify to the success of this endeavor. Alonso, blaming his own trespass against Prospero for the fact that his son "i' th' ooze is bedded," vows to follow Ferdinand "deeper than e'er plummet sounded" (100–101) in order to drown himself, and Gonzalo, describing the "great guilt" of the three men, "like poison given to work a great time after," sends others after the king to prevent him from drowning himself and to prevent the other two from whatever "this ecstasy / May now provoke them to" (108–9). Whatever sanity may remain to the three after III.iii is further compromised by Prospero's charms. When, in act 5, Prospero asks him how they are, Ariel says that all three men are "confined together" (V.i.7) and "abide all three distracted" (V.i.12). A few dozen lines later we see them enter frantically, twitching, presumably in madness. Thus, from the very beginning, the creation of the belief that a son has died is in the service of inducing madness and eventual despair.

But if Prospero has Ariel sustain the illusion necessary to drive Alonso and his confederates mad, Ariel also suggests that this madness may be a step on the way to "a clear life ensuing" (III.iii.82), that the "desolate isle" itself will protect the three from the wrath of the powers which "else falls / Upon [their] heads" (79–81). On the island, two different states of affairs exist which are paradoxically intertwined—"heart's sorrow" and a "clear life ensuing." Thus Ariel's speech holds a distant promise of some sort of purification or "clearness" to be obtained by the heart's sorrow, and implicitly by the loss of the son and the madness that have brought that sorrow about. Like the tempest itself, then, which makes its victims' garments fresher than before, Ariel invokes madness as a stage in a kind of purgative or penitential process. In a manner reminiscent of the instruction Prospero has offered him about Sycorax at the beginning of the play, Ariel presents the beginning of this penitential process as an exercise in memory ("But remember—/ For that's my business to you—that you three / From Milan did supplant good Prospero" [68–70]).[3]

Such a state of affairs seems very similar to that operative in *The Winter's Tale*. There, where Leontes is told to "run mad indeed" and to betake himself to nothing but despair, Paulina agitates both his guilt and his sorrow, rhetorically urging him to madness. There, like Ariel, she insists that he remember, telling him that if she were the ghost of Hermione watching him remarry, she'd shriek to rive his ears, "Remember mine" (V.i.67). But where we are shown a whole mechanics, a technology of magical effects by which Ariel instigates Alonso's change, and where we are shown a whole panoply of rhetorical effects by which Leontes is made to change, very little precedes Prospero's apparent reversal. It seems to happen in a moment.[4] When he asks Ariel in V.i "How fares the King and's followers?" (7), Ariel describes their distraction: "the King, / His brother, and yours, abide all three distracted, / And the remainder mourning over them / Brimful of sorrow and dismay" (11–14). Prospero's charms work so strongly on them, Ariel tells him, that if Prospero beheld them, his affections "would become tender" (18–19). Apparently upbraided and ashamed at the idea that a nonhuman spirit is more capable of human feeling than he himself is ("Hast thou, which art but air, a touch, a feeling / of their afflictions, and shall not myself / One of their kind . . . Be kindlier moved than thou art?"), Prospero says that though he is "struck to th' quick" with "their high wrongs" (25), he'll take part with his nobler reason against his fury and forgive his enemies ("They being penitent, / The sole drift of my purpose doth extend / Not a frown further" [28–30]).

As others have pointed out, two of Prospero's three enemies are clearly not penitent.⁵ We hear almost nothing from Antonio or Sebastian after Prospero confronts them with their crimes. Sebastian says, "The devil speaks in him!" (129) when Prospero says he could tell Alonso things about them that would "pluck" a frown. And later when he sees Ferdinand playing chess with Miranda, he says "A most high miracle" (177). But neither he nor Antonio say much else before the play ends, except to speculate on Caliban's market value at home (Sebastian: "What things are these, my lord Antonio? / Will money buy 'em?" [263–65]. Antonio: "Very like. One of them / Is a plain fish and no doubt marketable" [265–66]). Neither gives the slightest evidence of being sorry. After being shown in such detail the means by which Alonso's regret and subsequent change is effected, what does it mean for Prospero's about-face to be displayed as so unprompted, and perhaps more importantly, so dependent on false premises? What argument is being made through the juxtaposition?

## How to Make Men Mad

One aspect of the difference between the two reversals is the means by which they come about, the first engineered by expressly theatrical means, the second seeming not only to come out of nowhere but announcing itself as a kind of anti-theatricality, a repudiation not only of "rough magic" but of the props and costumes used to implement the illusions of that rough magic. Alonso's change is instigated by means which are explicitly and flamboyantly theatrical, and Prospero's at least seems to take place in the context of a process of a divestment of theatrical accoutrements.

Thus, Ariel and his rabble act out the moment from the *Aeneid* on the turning islands of the Strophades in which the harpies descend on Aeneas and his men, polluting their banquet and leading them to despair of ever reaching Rome. In so doing, they rework their subject matter to suit Prospero's purposes. There, on the Strophades, the harpy Celaeno predicts that Aeneas and his men will suffer such a terrible hunger that they will gnaw their platters with their teeth (309–10). There, the prophecy, like the prophecies in *Macbeth*, is technically correct but misleading in its ability to scare and demoralize: the platters, not revealed till much later in the *Aeneid*, will be made of wheaten cakes (VII, 120) and as such serve as a guidepost, a geographical marker, for where the men are in relation to Rome. In contrast, Ariel's words are not technically true but a lie: "Thee of thy son, Alonso, / They [the powers] have bereft," he says (III.iii.75–76), though Ferdinand is alive and well hauling wood nearby. The pronouncement serves not as a guidepost for a journey to come but as a trick to scare and humble Alonso, madness and despair apparently being the necessary preconditions for change. Ariel also reworks the part of Celaeno to incorporate one of the central tropes of James VI's *Daemonologie*, the trope of the magician's familiar who fetches dainties from all over the world. Epistemon describes this phenomenon in book 1 of *Daemonologie*, where among the "effects" he says Satan affords magicians are "faire banquets and daintie dishes, carryed in short space fra the farthest part of the worlde" as well as "faire armies of horse-men and foote-men . . . castles and fortes" (22). All these things are "but impressiones in the aire" easily gathered by the spirit, because the spirit itself "draw[s] so neare to that substance" of air. Faustus has Mephistopheles execute the same task when he fetches grapes for the duchess, but Prospero and Ariel revise the trick, sending the banquet from the magician instead of retrieving it for him and taking it back before anyone can eat.

Thus, in Ariel's performance the play aligns an overt and flamboyant theatricality, a theatricality built out of illusion, with one of the tropes of magic, presenting the dark arts in the terms James conceived of and articulated. In contrast, Prospero's reversal is presented not as the product of a theatrical trick but as spontaneous, free of the taint of pose or dissimulation and part of a declaration of anti-theatricality. Although the first half of the play proliferates with his capacity to make illusions, Prospero spends the second half of the play stripping those illusions he creates of their illusionary power, until he ultimately "discases" himself and presents himself as Prospero, duke of Milan. Thus the play begins with Prospero's use of Ariel to create illusions, "flam[ing] amazement" (I.ii.198), dividing and burning in many places, impersonating flame itself. It continues with Prospero's instruction to Ariel to make himself a "nymph o' th' sea" (I.ii.301) yet invisible to all eyes "but thine and mine" (302). Like those spirits attending magicians in *Daemonologie* who can appear as dog, cat, ape, or voice only, Ariel appears as a disembodied voice during the "yellow sands" and "full fathom five" songs and then again, later in the play, when he turns Stephano and Caliban against Trinculo. In these moments, "theatricality" and the tropes of *Daemonologie* are synonymous. At the beginning of the play, when Prospero's thirst for revenge on those from Milan is at its sharpest and his zenith depends on his "auspicious" star, he most obsessively employs Ariel in this capacity of illusion-maker and as illusion itself. Ariel as harpy ("bravely . . . performed" and "with good life / And observation strange" [III.iii.79–85]) is his consummate example. But as the play progresses, Prospero begins to strip even his most elaborate theatrical production, the masque in IV.i, of its illusionary power. When Ferdinand asks if he's used spirits to create his "majestic vision," Prospero willingly discloses the mechanics behind the illusion as "Spirits, which by mine art / I have from their confines called to enact / My present fancies" (IV.i.120–22). He takes the process further when he tells Ferdinand and Miranda, "These our actors, / As I foretold you, were all spirits and / Are melted into air, into thin air" (IV.i.148–50), and yet further when, after commenting on the fact that no one from Milan or Naples who looks at him recognizes him, he sends Ariel for his cape and rapier so he can "discase" himself and "[himself] present / As [he] was sometime Milan" (V.i.85–86). If the play presents Alonso's reversal as the product of a theatrical trick, it presents Prospero's as a stage in a progression of his self-proclaimed divestment of theatricality.[6]

But the distinction between theatricality and anti-theatricality depends on the assumption that there is a "real" and an "artificial," and it is just this distinction that Prospero undermines after interrupting the masque when he says that the cloud-capped towers, the gorgeous palaces, the great globe itself, and all that inherit it will dissolve like the "insubstantial pageant" his spectators (and we) have just watched.[7] If the world we take to be real is itself an insubstantial pageant, the distinction between real and imitation dissolves. Nothing stands outside a theater. Prospero as he was "sometime Milan" is as much a role as it is the "real" Prospero discased. And as much as the epilogue seems to step outside the play and mark itself as real, its request that we release Prospero with our "good hands" puts us into the play as if we had the ability to control its action. From this point of view what appears to be an anti-theatrical divestment of theater may be just one more role, one more of theater's guises.

Does this mean Prospero's claim that he will "passion" as Ariel does or take part with his noble reason against his fury is similarly a pose? And can the same be said for his claim that he will abjure his rough magic, the second claim following on the heels of and seemingly implicated in the first?

For Shakespeare to have Prospero relinquish his magic would seem to criminalize it, as James does magic in *Daemonologie*. Such a gesture would make Prospero what James (as he is portrayed in *Newes from Scotland*) wanted Dr. Fian to be, the magician turned penitent who repudiates the dark arts.[8] (Fian, it should be recalled, ultimately retracts his renunciation, but until he does so he claims to forsake his "wicked wayes" and acknowledge "his most ungodly lyfe," showing that he's "too much folowed the allurements and entisements of sathan ... by coniuring, witchcraft, inchantment, sorcerie" [25]) Like the magician in *Daemonologie* who moves up the "slipperie scale of curiosity," Prospero has moved from knowledge of the liberal arts to a knowledge of magic. Like the magicians in *Daemonologie*, once learned men "overbare ... of the spirit of regeneration" who move from licit to illicit knowledge "and so mounting from degree to degree, vpon the slipperie and vncertaine scale of curiositie; ... are at last entised, that where lawfull artes or sciences failes, to satisfie their restles mindes, even to seeke to that black and vnlawfull science of *Magie*" (10), Prospero, by his own account reputed "in dignity" and "for the liberal arts without a parallel," became similarly "transported / And rapt in secret studies" (I.ii.73–77). Neglecting worldly ends but "dedicated / To closeness and the bettering of [his] mind," he awaked an "evil nature" (89–93). But unlike Epistemon's magician or Doctor Faustus who follows a similar trajectory, the "evil nature" Prospero awakes is not in himself but in his brother. Rather than moving toward damnation, Prospero moves toward temporal loss and someone else's corruption. Although his tempest is like those localized tempests that witches in *Daemonologie* and *Newes from Scotland* create and although he works amatory magic, Prospero's tempest makes the mariners' garments fresher than before, and the charms he uses that bind Miranda and Ferdinand promote chastity rather than interfering with it. Thus, the play uses but inverts the force or moral sense of central tropes in *Daemonologie*. Its presentation of the dark arts themselves has already redefined those arts. Whatever it is Prospero renounces or doesn't renounce is already distinct and different from magic as James conceptualizes it.[9]

For all of Ariel's more spectacular magical effects, the thunder and lightning, disappearing banquet, and attendant spirits do less to produce change in Alonso in III.iii than Ariel's words. The real instrument for beginning the process of spiritual change in this scene seems to be language, those words which make even more hopeless a man who has already said "Even here I will put off my hope" (III.iii.7). But even these words only begin the process. Neither Ariel's spectacle nor his rhetoric does more than foster Alonso's distraction. If Ariel's words like Paulina's are preparatory, it takes Prospero's magic circle and "solemn music" to undo the charm and restore Alonso to his wits. In light of this, what are we to make of the magic circle? What exactly happens in it? Does Prospero relinquish his rough magic, and is it heavenly music that cures the "three men of sin," or is what happens an extension of the rough magic Prospero has just promised to abjure?

Practically everything that takes place surrounding the magic circle makes it impossible to answer this question. When Ariel leads the three men of sin and their various attendants and caregivers into the magic circle, we see them racked in frantic gesture. The stage direction reads:

> *Solemn music: Here enters Ariel before; then Alonso, with a frantic gesture, attended by Gonzalo, Sebastian and Antonio in like manner, attended by Adrian and Francisco. They all enter the circle which Prospero had made, and there stand charmed; which Prospero observing, speaks.*

In one way, "the frantic gesture" suggests not only the madness the play has already ascribed to the men but actual possession. Both Ariel's initial characterization of the three men as "distracted" (12) and unable to budge "till your release" (111) and the boatswain's description of the mariners echo descriptions of possession in the period. Compare the boatswain's description of the mariners as "dead of sleep" (230)—"Where but even now with strange and several noises / Of roaring, shrieking, howling, jingling chains . . . / We were awaked" (232–35)—to Reginald Scot's description of the feigned possession of the witch of Westwell's "roring, crieng, striving and gnashing of teeth" (102), or even to *Newes from Scotland*'s description of the possessed rival gentleman's "great scritch" before he falls into "a madness, sometime bending himselfe, and sometime capring so directly vp, that his head did touch the seeling of the Chamber" (21).[10] Similarly, both Prospero's narration of the release of the men from their madness and Alonso's own recounting of his experience cast the scene as a dispossession ("The charm dissolves apace," says Prospero [64]; "Th' affliction of my mind amends, with which / I fear a madness held me," says Alonso [115–16]). But the scene is unlike an exorcism not only in that no devils are named but because Prospero specifically says music ("a solemn air") is the best comforter of an "unsettled fancy," of "brains, / Now useless" (60).

And if there is ambiguity in what happens in the magic circle, the ambiguity about when Prospero makes the circle is equally pronounced. Orgel explains, "F at l.57.5 has the shipwreck victims 'all enter the circle which Prospero had made' but gives no indication of when he makes it. Either here or when he begins his 'airy charm' at l.52 would be appropriate" (note at line 32). If Prospero makes the magic circle at line 32, it's possible to imagine him abjuring his rough magic after he makes it. But if he makes the magic circle after he abjures his rough magic, the drawing of the magic circle itself undermines the abjuration. And if it's going to be music that calms the frantic men (if an airy charm is a piece of music that is calming rather than a charm that happens to be musical), why does Prospero need a magic circle at all?

*Daemonologie*, notwithstanding its contradictions on this point, insists the magician's circles are merely deceptions designed to make the magician think he wields power ("it is no power inherent in the circles, or in the holines of the names of God blasphemouslie used: nor in whatsoever rites or ceremonies at that time used," Epistemon says).[11] But *The Tempest* never suggests the circle that Prospero has the men step into is anything but efficacious. What function does it have in the play and what is its relation to Prospero's own reversal?

Alonso, Sebastian, and Antonio are not the first or only people in the play to step into a circle of one kind or another. From the very beginning of the play, characters are locked in circles or threatened with being locked in them. Having been locked in one tree trunk, Ariel is threatened with being "pegged" in the knotty entrails of another. Some sixty lines later Miranda tells Caliban that Prospero has "deservedly confined" him in "this rock." Over and over, Prospero locks or threatens to lock people and things into enclosures and circles which trap them. Even Caliban's cramps and pinches are imagined as circular enclosures. When Prospero explains to Ariel the mechanism by which they work, it turns out they are "side-stitches" that "pen . . . up" Caliban's breath (I.ii.326). In a way, the most extreme version of an enclosure the play offers is not confinement in an oak or a rock but the confinement of being locked or "confined" in a disordered mind, a fate suffered not only by Alonso, Sebastian, and Antonio but by Caliban, who describes the visual and auditory illusions that Prospero sends him in terms of a tightening circle ("sometime am I / All wound with adders, who with cloven tongues / Do hiss me into madness" [II.ii.12–14]). Over and over, Prospero locks or threatens to lock up people and things in circles.[12] The magic circle that Alonso, Sebastian, and Antonio are led into is, paradoxically, simply the latest and most vivid image of such a container and, at the same time, ostensibly the means of escaping such containment.

But if Prospero locks others into circles, he complains that he himself has been similarly encircled. At the beginning of the play, he describes his own entrapment not in a tree of the kind he threatens to peg Ariel in but *as* the tree itself. He is the one being choked, not by the trunk but by the ivy in the form of his brother Antonio, who threatens to suck out his vitality or power. (Antonio, seducing the officers with the office he is usurping, is "the ivy which had hid my princely trunk, / and sucked my verdure out on't" [I.ii.86–87], Prospero says.) The island itself is the most visible version of the circles which confine him.

The play poses a relationship between the circle Prospero draws and the circle he complains of having been encircled by, between the need to imprison others and having been imprisoned. The real object of dispossession, or at any rate the person in need of dispossession from his own fury, is Prospero himself. And if this is so, the sentiments of the epilogue suggest the value of the exorcism is as much for the exorcist as for the exorcised. If we extend the logic of the epilogue, with its claims that if we would be pardoned, we should likewise pardon, the value of Prospero's release of his enemies from distraction and madness lies less in their release than in his own possible release from fury. To dispossess them is to begin to exorcise himself, to escape the choking of the verdure.

To answer an earlier question, Prospero's apparent reversal may lack the elaborate machinery Alonso's reversal necessitates because the importance of Prospero's reversal is internal—less an atonement paid for crimes committed or grieved for, susceptible to being righted by the restoration of a dukedom, than a release from a need for vengeance itself. That such an exorcism is at best unfinished, deeply incomplete, is clear not only from Prospero's turn to us for help at the end of the play, with its sense that he is still in danger of being trapped in his "bands," not only from his complete lack of interest in what happens to Caliban, and not only from the fact that two of the three men of sin have clearly not changed, but from the affect through which he articulates his ostensible pardon of Antonio ("to call [you] brother / Would . . . infect my mouth," he says [130–31], as he claims to be forgiving Antonio's "rankest fault" [131–32]). His announcement that he will take part with his reason against his fury, then, seems reducible to neither dissimulation nor a full, sincere act of repentance but something more like a rehearsal of an act of forgiveness, an attempt to bring into being through patterned action a state of affairs which internally has not yet taken place, as if spiritual change were as much an action to be practiced and rehearsed as an inward sentiment.

In many ways, demonological texts record a history of imagining a malevolent "other," for the inquisitors the witch, for Reginald Scot the witch-mongers themselves, for James in *Daemonologie* both the witch and Reginald Scot as well as Johannes Weyer. These texts revolve around strategies for how to manage, neutralize, deflect, and see into the inside of enemies who are imagined to be as perilous as they are malevolent, strategies that vary from gestural maneuvers like carrying a witch in backwards to neutralize the power of her gaze and touch to scripts which seek to control future trials by stabilizing the words of future witnesses and defendants who don't yet exist. Prospero rehearses and ultimately exhausts a number of these strategies. Having been encircled, he seeks to encircle and designs counterperformances to neutralize malevolent others. And like Bodin, he designs paradigms to avoid seeing affinities between himself and the "thing of darkness" he only partially acknowledges as his own as well as to avoid seeing affinities between his own potential as a usurper and Antonio's actual usurpation. At the same time, *The Tempest* interrogates both the meaning and the possibility of exorcism, suggesting its utility may lie as much in what it is imagined to do for the one performing the exorcism as the one the exorcism is performed upon. If Reginald Scot exorcises those analogies he shares with the witch-mongers he ridicules through the compulsive repetition of their tropes and formulas, Prospero's exorcism of his rage seeks to work through the exorcism of the three men of sin of their "unsettled fancy." As a reflection on the debates about the efficacy of words and images which characterize so much Reformation and Counter-Reformation discourse, the play seems to suggest that efficacy consists not in whether the bread is the body or a figure, the circle real or illusion, but the use to which one puts it. And to rid oneself of one's demons, the play seems to suggest, it is necessary to forgo the demonization of others.

# NOTES

## Introduction

1. II.iii.67 and 113–15 in Shakespeare's *The Winter's Tale*, edited by Stephen Orgel (Oxford and New York: Oxford University Press, 1996). All subsequent quotations are taken from this edition and included in the body of the text.

2. James VI, *DÆMONOLOGIE, IN FORME of a Dialogue Diuided into three Bookes. EDINBVRGH, Printed by Robert Walde-graue, Printer to the Kings Majestie. An. 1597*; the text from Elizabethan and Jacobean Quartos, ed. G. B. Harrison, from the series Bodley Head Quartos, published by John Lane, Bodley Head Ltd., London 1922–26. The original of this text is in the Bodleian Library. All subsequent citations incorporated in the body of the text. See also Reginald Scot, *The Discoverie of Witchcraft* (1584 London; Totowa, NJ: Rowman and Littlefield, 1973). All quotations are taken from this edition and will be incorporated into the body of the text. For an exhaustive genealogy of commentators on the witch of Endor story during the period and a reading of these in relation to *Macbeth*, see Stuart Clark's fine "Sights: King Saul and King Macbeth," in *Vanities of the Eye: Vision in Early Modern European Culture* (Oxford: Oxford University Press, 2007). All subsequent quotations taken from this edition and incorporated in the body of the text. For Clark on the supernatural and natural, see my chapter 3, note 10 of this work. For a treatment of the change in visual images of the story, see Charles Zika's compelling discussion of visual treatments of the Endor story in *The Appearance of Witchcraft: Print and Visual Culture in Sixteenth Century Europe* (New York: Routledge, 2007), 156–61.

3. See Jean Bodin, *De la Demonomanie des Sorciers* (Paris: Chez Iacques du-Puys, 1587). The edition cited in this book can be found here: https://archive.org/details/BodinDemonomanieBNF1587/page/n1/mode/2up.

4. Henricus Institoris (Heinrich Kramer) and Jacobus Sprenger, *Malleus Maleficarum Vol. 1: The Latin Text*, ed. Christopher S. Mackay (Cambridge: Cambridge University Press, 2006).

5. *NEWES FROM SCOTLAND declaring the damnable life and death of DOCTOR FIAN, a notable SORCERER (1591)*; the text from Elizabethan and Jacobean Quartos, ed. G. B. Harrison, from the series Bodley Head Quartos, published by John Lane, Bodley Head Ltd., London 1922–26. The original of this text is in the Bodleian Library. All subsequent citations are included in the body of the text.

6. For Foucault's description of an episteme as an epistemic field, "a middle region" which "makes manifest the modes of being of order" ("Thus, in every culture, between the use of what one might call the ordering codes and reflections upon order itself, there is the pure experience of order and of its modes of being"), see *The Order of*

*Things: An Archaeology of the Human Sciences* (New York: Vintage Books, 1973), xxi. For his initial description of the "two great discontinuities in the *episteme* of Western culture: the first [of which] inaugurates the Classical age (roughly half-way through the seventeenth century) and the second, at the beginning of the nineteenth century, [marking] the beginning of the modern age," see xxii. For his elaboration on what he ultimately comes to call "the sixteenth-century episteme," see 17–45.

For a critique of the way this model posits change, see, for instance, Stuart Clark, *Thinking with Demons: The Idea of Witchcraft in Early Modern Europe* (Oxford: Oxford University Press, 1997): "Above all, Foucault seriously underestimated the extent to which the natural and cultural accounts of signification had always been available as alternatives and continued to coexist during much of the seventeenth century. That a language made sense because of conventions that it should was defended not only throughout the Renaissance but in medieval scholarship too, in a debate going back to Plato's *Cratylus*," 286–87. See, too, Mary Floyd-Wilson's challenge to Foucault's episteme in *Occult Knowledge, Science and Gender on the Shakespearean Stage* (Cambridge: Cambridge University Press, 2013), 2 and 4.

7. I read Bodin as more contradictory than Clark does but agree with his claim that "in a sense, the diametrically opposed approaches of Bodin and Scot were the only logical solutions to this problem. By attempting to be reasonable about witchcraft without giving up his belief in its fundamental features James tried to find a compromise between common sense and faith. Like Weyer's it involved too many inconsistencies to be really successful." See Stuart Clark, "King James's *Daemonologie*: Witchcraft and Kingship," in *The Damned Art: Essays in the Literature of Witchcraft*, ed. Sydney Anglo (London: Routledge, 2011), 173.

8. J. L. Austin, *How to Do Things with Words*, ed. J. O. Urmson and Marina Sbisà, 2nd ed. (Oxford: Clarendon Press, 1975), 6. All subsequent quotations are taken from this edition and included in the body of the text.

9. For Clark's argument about the inefficacy of "signs" see *Thinking with Demons*, 290. The quote from *Daemonologie* is from book 1, chapter 5, 16–17.

10. See Stephen Gosson, *School of Abuse* (1579; repr., London: Shakespeare Society, 1841), 19, and Phillip Stubbes, *The Anatomie of Abuses* (1593; repr., Netherlands: Da Capo Press, 1972), sig F5V, respectively, the first for the claim that theater effeminates the mind and the second for the claim that costumes "adulterate" male gender. For Gosson's repetition of the Deuteronomic code, the claim that garments are "set down for signes distinctive between sexe and sexe," see his *Playes Confuted in Five Actions* in Arthur F. Kinney, *Markets of Bawdrie: The Dramatic Criticism of Stephen Gosson, Salzburg Studies in Literature*, vol. 4 (Salzburg: Institut für Englische Sprache and Literatur, 1974), 175. For my earlier discussion of the contradiction between the anti-theatrical use of the Deuteronomic code and the fear of effeminization, see Laura Levine, *Men in Women's Clothing: Anti-theatricality and Effeminization, 1579–1642* (Cambridge: Cambridge University Press, 1994), 3–4 and 19–25.

11. Eamon Duffy, *The Stripping of the Altars: Traditional Religion in England 1400–1580* (New Haven, CT: Yale University Press, 1992). All subsequent citations are incorporated in the body of the text.

12. Keith Thomas, *Religion and the Decline of Magic* (Oxford: Oxford University Press, 1997). All subsequent citations are incorporated in the body of the text.

13. Margaret Aston, *England's Iconoclasts Volume 1: Laws against Images* (Oxford: Oxford University Press, 2003). All subsequent citations are incorporated in the body of the text.

14. For an example of a "switchback" or "zigzag" in England during Henry VIII's reign, consider the persistent vacillations of antipathy to images which expressed themselves in the *Articles* and *Royal Injunctions, Bishop's Book,* and *King's Book* between 1536 and 1543. On July 11, 1536, the sixth of the *Ten Articles*, "On Images," allowed images as "representers of virtue," "good examples," "stirrers of men's minds," and things to make men remember and lament sins and offences (especially the image of Christ) but it forbade censing. A month later, the first set of royal injunctions issued by Cromwell forbade "set[ting] down or extol[ling]" images. A year later, *The Bishop's Book*'s wording of the second commandment forbade making any graven image, and the commentary on the commandment argued both that "we be utterly forbidden to make or have any graven similitude or image to the intent to bow down to it, or to worship it" and ordered bishops and preachers to teach people that "God in his substance cannot by any similitude or image be represented or expressed." In early 1538, the Rood of Boxley was exposed as fraud and destroyed at Saint Paul's, and by fall 1538, the second set of royal injunctions ordered parochial clergy to "take down and delay" images (according to Aston, leaving terminally ambiguous whether "delay" meant "destroy" or only "take down"). In contrast, by 1543 *The King's Book* had narrowed down the second commandment to "Thou shalt not have any graven image, nor any likeness or anything that is in heaven above or in earth, beneath or in the waters under the earth, *to the intent to do any godly honour and worship* unto this" (emphasis mine), implying it was acceptable to have images for other purposes. *The King's Book*'s commentary had replaced the 1537 phrase "by these words *we be utterly forbidden*" with "by these words *we be not forbidden* to make or to have similitudes or images, but only we be forbidden to make or have them to the intent to do godly honour unto them" (emphasis mine). By 1543 the commentary had completely eliminated the sentence that God in his substance couldn't by similitude or image be presented or expressed.

For the *Articles* under Henry VIII and the Henrician, Edwardian, and Elizabethan Injunctions, see Gerald Bray, *Documents of the English Reformation*, 3rd ed. (Cambridge: Lutterworth Press, 1994), 141–52. For the first set of Henrician Injunctions (1536), see 153–56. For the second set of Henrician Injunctions (1538), see 157–60. For the Edwardian Injunctions (1547), see 217–26. For the Elizabethan Injunctions (1559), see 300–312. For Aston's comparison of *The Bishop's Book* and *The King's Book*, see 239–43 (quotations for the two books taken from Aston). Other kinds of contradictions during Henry's reign include but were not limited to the contradiction between creed and opportunities for exploitation, like the Fourth Injunction's claim that "it shall profit more [the] soul's health, if they do bestow that on the poor and needy, which they would have bestowed upon the said images or relics" just as the monasteries were being dissolved and pillaged. For Aston's description of the tension between the 1561 royal order that rood lofts be taken down as far as the beam while Elizabeth's royal chapel "proved resistant to reform," see 312–13. For Aston's claims that "Henry VIII and Elizabeth I had more in common with Mary than is sometimes allowed for," see 341. For one of the many instances of the circularity between the arguments that images were dangerous if they were abused and the claim that they should be destroyed because men would abuse them, see Aston's description of the growing problem of the absence of a criterion for "abuse" of images in Edward's reign, 246–77, especially 256–62. For Bucer, see Martin Bucer, Jacobus Bedrotus and William Marshall, "A Treatise Declarying and Shewing . . . That Pyctures & Other Ymages . . . Ar in No Wise to Be Suffred in the Temples or Churches of Cristen Men," 1535, in *Letters and Papers, Foreign and Domestic, of the Reign of Henry VIII, IX*, nos. 357–58, ed. J. S. Brewer. J Gairdner, and R. H. Brodie, (London: 1892–1910), STC 24238-9. On the one hand, Bucer says that images must be "plucked out of church," because there will always be those who "put of their cappes unto them / . . . and make curtesye to them: yea / to kysse their feete / to praye to them" but on the other hand, Bucer grants that "karvers & paynters craftes / are craftes both gyven by God and also lawfull."

15. Carlos M. N. Eire, *War against the Idols: The Reformation of Worship from Erasmus to Calvin* (Cambridge: Cambridge University Press, 1986), 57 and more generally 54–65. For Eire's treatment of Luther's response to Karlstadt's iconoclasm, see 65–73.

16. See Eire, *War against the Idols*, 84 and footnote 124. For his more extended discussion of Zwingli's iconoclasm, see 76–86. In a different context, Sophie Read argues that for Zwingli the eucharist itself was a way to "imagine" Christ's passion (though not to participate in it). For the "spectrum" of possible beliefs on the eucharist from Catholicism to Zwingli and the four "broad positions on the nature of Christ's presence in the eucharist" it implies, see *Eucharist and the Poetic Imagination in Early Modern England* (Cambridge: Cambridge University Press, 2013), especially 18.

17. Nor do I mean to suggest that all Catholicism imagined images as efficacious. Kimberly Johnson argues that "the variety of opinion on the manner and mode of signification in the sacrament dispels any illusion that Christianity enjoyed, even long before the Reformation, a monolithic and uncomplicated understanding of the rite [of the eucharist]" and details the way that "much of the diversity of opinion from the early medieval church through the era of Reformation can be traced to the competing influences of Ambrose of Milan and Augustine of Hippo." See *Made Flesh: Sacrament and Poetics in Post-Reformation England* (Philadelphia: University of Pennsylvania Press, 2014), 11, and 7–21 more generally. Clark argues that for Catholics, while "words did have a uniform, automatic, but, of course, supernatural power to bring about physical changes," such words were the apparent exception that proved the rule, "performative utterances of a particularly pure kind . . . since sacramental efficacy, above all, could not rest on the power of the words themselves, only . . . on an instrumentality that they acquired from heaven" (*Thinking with Demons*, 291).

In contrast, see Eire's description of the way that pre-Reformation piety ended up endowing images with power: "As the material expansion of the cult [of saints] progressed, the veneration of the saints became so tied up with images that the visual representations threatened to overshadow the spiritual element behind their worship. . . . The growing cult of images had no safeguard built in to prevent the people from confusing the image and what it sought to represent" (14). Similarly, for Eamon Duffy's claim that medieval piety often came close to magic, incantation, and exorcism, see especially his discussion of prayers against the devil which came "very close to litany or invocation, at times closer to spells or charms than anything else" (269). For his claim that "it would be a mistake" to see various "'magical' prayers as standing altogether outside the framework of the official worship and teaching of the Church," see 279 and 266–98 more generally.

For Sarah Beckwith's penetrating analysis of the way the isolation of the eucharist and purgatory from "the practices of penance" in Greenblatt's *Practicing New Historicism* simplifies the complexity of a medieval inheritance, see her "Stephen Greenblatt's *Hamlet* and the Forms of Oblivion," *Journal of Medieval and Early Modern Studies* 33, no. 2 (2003): 261–80. For Greenblatt's argument, see his book cowritten with Catherine Gallagher, *Practicing New Historicism* (Chicago: University of Chicago Press, 2000).

18. The difference can easily be overstated. Carlo Ginzburg's *The Night Battles* (Baltimore, MD: Johns Hopkins University Press, 1983) for instance could be described as tracking a contradiction between early and late testimonies on the part of the Benandante, or testimonies before the inquisitors had disseminated witchcraft beliefs and after they had done so. Marion Gibson identifies contradictions about the dismissal of servants in a pamphlet about the Earl of Rutland. As noted below, in *Demon Lovers: Witchcraft, Sex and the Crisis of Belief* (Chicago: University of Chicago Press, 2002), Walter Stephens argues that confessions about the demonic pact were necessary not because they were obvious but *"because the concept of sex with demons needed constant reinforcement"* (7). At the same time, Clark's call to avoid reducing demonology to "epiphenomena" or anachronism and his care to emphasize the integrity of witchcraft belief especially as an early form of scientific investigation has led to an avoidance of a depiction of demonology as contradictory. See Marion Gibson, "Understanding Witchcraft? Accusers' Stories in Print in Early Modern England," in *Languages of Witchcraft: Narratives, Ideology and Meaning in Early Modern Culture*, ed. Stuart Clark (New York: St. Martin's Press, 2001). All subsequent references to Ginzburg, Stephens, and Gibson are taken from the editions cited above and are included in the body of the text. For Quentin Skinner's description of the "mythology of coherence" and the discomfort with the possibility of actual contradiction, see "Meaning and Understanding in the History of Ideas," *History and Theory* 8, no. 1 (1969): 3–53, especially 19–20.

19. "All orthodox theorists, inside and outside Germany, allowed for an important measure of delusion in witchcraft matters," Clark says. "All contributors to the field of demonology, whether we call them 'believers' or 'doubters,' had to differentiate demonic from non-demonic, true from illusory phenomena; allocating individual aspects of witchcraft was always more a question of emphasis than of dogma." *Thinking with Demons*, 209–10 and the chapter "Believers and Sceptics," more generally 195–213.

20. Michel Foucault, *Discipline and Punish: The Birth of the Prison*, trans. Alan Sheridan (New York: Vintage Books, 1977), 34. "Torture is a technique; it is not an extreme expression of lawless rage," says Foucault (33). It is "not the expression of a legal system driven to exasperation and, forgetting its principles, losing all restraint" (34–35); "judicial torture was not a way of obtaining the truth at all costs; it was not the unrestrained torture of modern interrogations" (40).

21. The claim that spectacles which involve torture offer antidotes to doubt, or are in any way compensatory, would seem to run counter to claims made by Foucault for whom the notion of torture as spectacle implies the corollary that knowledge is always the absolute privilege of the prosecution (35). But precisely because Foucault is so intent on demonstrating the way that power "produces" knowledge and truth, his analysis never makes possible a discussion of the way that "power's" propulsion to theatricality might itself be compensatory or recuperative or aimed at quelling anxieties within power itself. The texts this book examines suggest that violent spectacle itself

can be an expression of an exaggerated need for certainty, an expression of a sense of *knowledgelessness*. In different ways the writers examined here turn to, or understand others as turning to, spectacle as a way of addressing that knowledgelessness.

22. Edmund Spenser, *The Faerie Queene*, ed. A. C. Hamilton, Hiroshi Yamashita, and Toshiyuki Suzuki, rev. 2nd ed. (London: Routledge, 2013). All subsequent quotations are taken from this edition and included in the body of the text.

23. See Stephen Greenblatt, "Shakespeare Bewitched," in *New Historical Literary Study: Essays on Reproducing Texts, Representing History*, ed. Jeffrey N. Cox and Larry J. Reynolds (Princeton, NJ: Princeton University Press, 1993), 108–35.

24. Stuart Clark explains the logic of examining motifs in demonological treatises for their typicality or membership in the same "language game" in "Inversion, Misrule and the Meaning of Witchcraft," *Past and Present* 87 (1980): 98–127, and *Thinking with Demons*, 440. For Clark's discussion of the "different notion of language [that] will have to be considered" and the "linguistic circumstances that enabled the utterances and actions associated with witchcraft belief to convey meaning," as well as his claim that "the animating principle of this alternative account of language and meaning is the relationship not of reference but of difference," see *Thinking with Demons*, especially 6–9. Clark closes "Inversion, Misrule and the Meaning of Witchcraft" with the sentence, "The primary characteristic of demonological texts as historical evidence is not their supposed unverifiability but their relationship to what J. L. Austin called a 'total speech situation,'" 127. But as Jonathan Culler has pointed out in response to Austin's very notion of the "total speech situation," "total context is unmasterable, both in principle and in practice. Meaning is context-bound, but context is boundless." See "Convention and Meaning: Derrida and Austin," *New Literary History* 13, no. 1 (1981): 15–30, especially 24.

25. Stephens, *Demon Lovers*, 10–11. Although Stephens doesn't explicitly centralize the principle of contradiction as a starting point of investigation, it is implicit in his claim that confessions about the demonic pact were necessary not because they were obvious but *"because the concept of sex with demons needed constant reinforcement,"* 7.

## 1. Judicial Procedure as Countermagic in *Malleus Maleficarum*

I would like to thank Larry Rosenwald for many stimulating discussions about medieval Latin, as well as Jesse Njuss and Melissa Vise. Any faults in translation are my own.

1. In isolation, the relevant passage leaves ambiguous who is to be wearing the words Christ uttered and the blessed wax, the judge himself or the witch. The question seems to come down to a fundamental ambiguity in the phrase *collo eius*, which can mean either "his neck" or "her neck." Christopher Mackay's fastidious translation of *Malleus Maleficarum* translates it as "her neck," which Mackay explains in terms of "the naked body and the inability to tolerate 'such things,' especially the remains of saints, [leaving] no doubt that it is the witch being talked about" (personal correspondence). My thanks to him as well as Hans Peter Broedel, Jennifer K. Nelson and Larry Rosenwald for their various thoughts on this passage. I gratefully consulted Mackay's English translation of *Malleus Maleficarum*, but ultimately made my own translations. All quotes from *Malleus Maleficarum* are taken from Henricus Institoris (Heinrich Kramer) and Jacobus Sprenger, *Malleus Maleficarum, Vol. 1: The Latin Text*, ed. Christopher

Mackay (Cambridge: Cambridge University Press, 2006), and included in the body of the text.

Throughout this chapter I refer to the "inquisitors" for the reader's convenience. Although there is doubt about how much of parts 1 and 2 Sprenger contributed, Kramer is generally conceded to be the author of part 3. He referred to himself as Institoris. See Mackay's Kramer and Sprenger, *Malleus Maleficarum*, 64, for the claim that Institoris's "authorship of the legal sections of the *Malleus* is undeniable through comparison with the content of the *Memorandum* and *Nuremburg Handbook*," and Hans Peter Broedel for the claim that "indeed, so estimable were Sprenger's intellectual and spiritual attainments, that some have questioned the actual extent of Sprenger's contribution to the *Malleus*"; Hans Peter Broedel, *The* Malleus Maleficarum *and the Construction of Witchcraft* (Manchester: Manchester University Press, 2003): "Although Sprenger certainly wrote the 'Apologia auctoris' which prefaces the *Malleus*, and did so in terms that strongly suggest his active participation in its writing, nonetheless because the work is of one piece stylistically (and Institoris definitely wrote the third part of the text single handedly), and because the *Malleus* throughout reflects Institoris' known preoccupations, it is likely that beyond lending the work the prestige of his name, Sprenger's contribution was minimal" (Broedel, *The* Malleus Maleficarum, 18–19).

2. See Stuart Clark's *Thinking with Demons* for a discussion of some of these precautions as "almost sacramental," and Walter Stephens for the claim that Kramer's "counterdemonic practices" actually function to keep "his fear and witch hatred in a constant state of alarm," *Demon Lovers*, 196. For his distinctions between *maleficia, superstitiosi*, and the legitimate rites of the Church many people used "to achieve the same effects as magicians" as well as all the "ambiguous ground between" in the *Malleus*, see Broedel, *The* Malleus Maleficarum, 148. For his claim that the moral valence of a supernatural or preternatural power could be understood in terms of its effects, see 150–52. Similarly, see 151 for the claim that "the *Malleus* appears almost as much a justification of popular Christian ritual as a condemnation of witchcraft." For his description of the five criteria practice had to conform to in order to qualify as valid religious observance, see 154.

3. Sydney Anglo notes the contradictoriness of the Inquisitors' claim that magistrates and examiners are among the privileged whom witches cannot harm in the face of the lengths they go to protect themselves from witches, in "Evident Authority and Authoritative Evidence: The *Malleus Maleficarum*," in *The Damned Art*, 1–31. Stuart Clark, noting the way the precautions judges are to take are at odds with the Inquisitors' claims that magistrates are protected against witchcraft, says:

> At odds with their earlier arguments were the precautions which Kramer and Sprenger advised judges to take against *maleficium*, including even the avoidance of a witch's touch, 'especially in any contact of their bare arms or hands.' Judicial officials . . . were to guard against the bewitching power of the words spoken by the accused during torture, and against the mollifying power of their glances in the courtroom. The authors of the *Malleus* warned solemnly that for this reason, 'the witch should be led backward into the presence of the Judge and his assessors.' Even at the point of arrest, witches were to be carried off without them being able to touch the ground and thereby replenish their powers of

resistance and of staying silent under cross-examination—powers which their apprehension had initially nullified. (*Thinking with Demons*, 576–77)

For Eamon Duffy's description of the symbiotic relationship between the official practice of the Church and superstitious practices and prayers in *Malleus Maleficarum*, see *The Stripping of the Altars*, 285–86.

4. Describing a whole "penal arithmetic" (37), "a whole casuistry of legal bad faith" (35), "an arithmetic modulated by casuistry" (37), Foucault in *Discipline and Punish* describes the way that judges could catch the accused out in false questioning, keep the nature of the action from him, and keep the nature of the evidence from him. For critics of Foucault's model from the standpoint of the unpredictability of behavior on the part of the condemned, see Thomas W. Laqueur, "Crowds, Carnival and the State in English Executions, 1604–1868," in *The First Modern Society: Essays in English History in Honour of Lawrence Stone*, ed. A. L. Beier, David Cannadine, and James M. Rosenheim (Cambridge: Cambridge University Press, 1989), 305–55. For a critique of the limits of Foucault's reliance on spectacle as a model for discussing England's trial and for an analysis of the problem of "inwardness" in English crime, see Katharine Eisaman Maus's "Proof and Consequences: *Othello* and the Crime of Intention," in *Inwardness and Theater in the English Renaissance* (Chicago: University of Chicago Press, 1995), 104–27.

For an astute critique of the unfortunate conjunction between the limits of Foucault and the new historicist coupling of Foucault with synecdoche, see Elizabeth Hanson's introduction to *Discovering the Subject in Renaissance England* (Cambridge: Cambridge University Press, 1998). For a sustained critique of the model offered in *Discipline and Punish* in relation to the issue of gender, see Frances Dolan's "'Gentlemen, I have one more thing to say': Women on Scaffolds in England 1563–1680," *Modern Philology* 92, no. 2 (November 1994): 157–78, and, more generally, Catherine Belsey's treatment of women's opportunity to speak on the scaffold in *The Subject of Tragedy: Identity and Difference in Renaissance Drama* (London: Methuen, 1985), 190–91. Finally, see Lorna Hutson's important critique of the application of Foucault's argument in *Discipline and Punish* to the "English understanding of evidence or of what constitutes or who decides the 'truth' of what happened in a criminal case" (70), as well as her broader remarks that "England did not, in the sixteenth century, adapt the methods of canon law inquisition to a secular criminal procedure involving professional prosecutors" (66) in *The Invention of Suspicion* (Oxford: Oxford University Press, 2007). I differ from these powerful critiques in my attempt to account for why some judicial procedures require a theatrical performance and others do not, a problem which *Discipline and Punish* fails to engage.

In "Shakespeare and the English Witch-Hunts," in *Enclosure Acts: Sexuality, Property and Culture in Early Modern England*, ed. Richard Burt and John Michael Archer (Ithaca, NY: Cornell University Press, 1994), 96–120, Deborah Willis describes the way a neighbor falls ill after denying charity to a poorer woman and enumerates the possibilities the neighbor has at his or her disposal (turning to the church, to prayer, trying to appease the witch, or, with the benefit of the passage of the 1563 Witchcraft statutes, appealing to the local justices of the peace). Willis notes that "the trial itself functions as a kind of countermagic, with judges and jury taking over some aspects of the role of the cunning folk, as the witch's exposure and forced confession also dissolve her magical powers" (107). My argument here and throughout this chapter takes as a sustained proposition about judicial spectacle that the procedure is carefully and deliberately structured as a kind of counterperformance or countertrial.

5. Similarly, anti-theatrical tracts in England during the early modern period were organized into "actions" and "scenes." See Levine, *Men in Women's Clothing*, 2.

6. Differently, Mackay explains how the "Heresy of Sorceresses" was a "mixed crime (*crimen mixtum*) in that it contained both ecclesiastical and secular elements. This dual nature derives from the notion that this heresy consisted of two elements: heresy / apostasy on the one hand and the infliction of temporal losses on the other"; Kramer and Sprenger, *Malleus Maleficarum*, Vol. 1, 64. But see as well Broedel, *The* Malleus Maleficarum, 20 and 33.

7. In at least one case, there is reason to think this attempt at control failed. James Sharpe notes that, in 1538, the Spanish Inquisition urged inquisitors not to believe everything Kramer and Sprenger said (*Instruments of Darkness: Witchcraft in England 1550–1750*. London: Hamish Hamilton, 1996, 22). In *Servants of Satan: The Age of the Witch Hunts* (Bloomington: Indiana University Press, 1985), Joseph Klaits addresses this need for control in terms of centralizing rulers' "attempts to exert control over judicial officials" through the "promulgation of elaborately detailed written law codes meant to standardize and regularize court procedure" (131). Klaits, following Christina Larner, classifies witchcraft as a kind of heresy (135), but fails to note the inquisitors' own vacillating needs to segregate and conflate the two crimes. For a compelling description of the torture so transparently conducted to elicit even a manufactured confession that the German executioner begged the accused to confess anything in order to avoid what was ahead, see Klaits's description of the torture of the German burgomaster Johannes Junius, arrested in 1628 (128–30). For Stephens's analysis of the same case as an illustration of the claim that "interrogators needed to hear *a certain kind* of answer" in particular, see *Demon Lovers*, 5–7 and 15–16.

For the "rank hypocrisy" with which the church "relaxed" to the secular courts those it would have been "unseemly" to execute, see Mackay. He explains:

> Church courts had the right to impose ecclesiastical punishments (the most severe being excommunication, or exclusion from participation in the sacraments of the church). These courts could not, however, inflict corporeal penalties . . . the decision of whether someone was guilty of heresy was decided in an ecclesiastical court, and if such a court wished the accused to be burned, it "relaxed" (i.e., handed over) the convict to the secular authority, which did not try the case over in its own right but simply inflicted the secular penalty on the basis of the ecclesiastical conviction. . . . As noted in the *Malleus*, the decision of the ecclesiastical court turning over the convict to the secular court would ask that court to refrain from bloodshed, but this request was the rankest of hypocrisy. As the *Malleus* makes clear on numerous occasions, it was taken for granted that the penalty was a most unpleasant death by fire, but it was simply felt to be unseemly for the church to participate openly in the imposition of the death penalty. The thoroughly insincere plea for mercy (whose rejection was assumed) was the solution.

For Mackay's discussion, see 63–64 of his introduction to *Malleus Maleficarum*, Vol. 1.

8. The sense of this seems to be, in part by way of Nicholas Eymeric, author of the *Directorium Inquisitorum*, that such people be present to avoid errors in sentencing.

9. For Mackay's discussion of the three ways of initiating a process and the risks associated with the first two, and the first in particular, see Kramer and Sprenger, *Malleus Maleficarum*, Vol. 1, 74–75. For a rich discussion of the background of inquisitorial process as Kramer inherited it, see Kramer and Sprenger, *Malleus Maleficarum*, 67–73.

10. This is consistent with John H. Langbein's analysis of the way judicial discretion increasingly crept into the continental legal systems. See particularly "The Revolution in the Law of Proof" in his *Torture and the Law of Proof: Europe and England in the Ancien Régime* (Chicago: University of Chicago Press, 1976), 45–60. But see as well Broedel's discussion of the importance the inquisitors ascribed to personal experience in conflicts between authority and personal experience (especially in the context of Thomistic "epistemological optimism") and the attendant importance of narratives as the form this experience took, *The Malleus Maleficarum*, 94–95.

11. For previous discussions of these precautions, see notes 2 and 3.

12. For recent discussions of the degree to which *Malleus Maleficarum* is or is not a misogynist text, see in particular Stephens, *Demon Lovers*, 34–36, for an evaluation of Pico Mirandola's claim that the book is a "hammer for smashing *skeptics*" not women and a discussion of the way the book's depictions of women serve to substantiate the reality of demonic copulation and more than that, it "*contradicts* the accusation that Kramer has an overactive imagination," 35–36. On a different note, see Tamar Herzig's "Fear and Devotion in the Writing of Heinrich Institoris," in *Emotions in the History of Witchcraft*, ed. Laura Kounine and Michael Ostling (Houndmills, UK: Palgrave Macmillan, 2016), 19–35, for the claims that "Institoris' attitude toward charismatic religious women was in fact characterized by fascination, rather than by anxiety" and "as far as Institoris was concerned women's frightening proclivity to witchcraft and the admirable experiences of ascetic women mystics were two sides of one, singularly somaticized and emotional understanding of the female nature" (20), as well as for a review of some of the older debates. See as well Herzig's related argument in "Witches, Saints and Heretics: Heinrich Kramer's Ties with Italian Women Mystics," *Magic, Ritual and Witchcraft* 1, no. 1 (2006): 24–55. For a more typical reaction, see Anglo's claim that the "monkish misogyny of the *Malleus* is blatant," "Evident Authority," 16.

13. See my introduction for the distinction between subscribing to a formal creed and behaving as if words and images had performative power. In contrast, Mackay sees this passage as an example of the way Kramer seeks to upgrade the witch's threats from circumstantial evidence (*indicia*) to evidence of the deed (*indicia facti*): ". . . ecclesiastical law held that 'evidence of the deed,' that is a manifest instance of guilt, was grounds for conviction, and an example of this is that preaching heresy is 'evidence' of the crime of being a heretic. The threat of the supposed sorceress is then equated with this situation. . . . Since the harm is inflicted invisibly through the independent operation of Satan, it is necessary to use the threatening words as a guide to the identity of the culprit, whose guilt is then corroborated through her reputation or other such acts." Mackay concludes that "this methodology was certainly a violation of the normal mode of conviction according to the inquisitional procedure of the secular courts. . . . Faced with the situation delineated by Institoris [Kramer] for a conviction by presumption, a secular court would have no choice but to examine the accused under torture and to acquit her if she refused to confess." See Kramer and Sprenger, *Malleus Maleficarum*, 77–78. The primary difference between my reading of

the witch's threat and Mackay's is that I see the inquisitors endowing the witch with performative power where he understands the threat as gerrymandered "evidence."

14. In *Dangerous Familiars: Representations of Domestic Crime in England, 1550–1700* (Ithaca, NY: Cornell University Press, 1994), Frances Dolan discusses the way seventeenth-century writers viewed witches' anger as a source of their power and speech as a primary means of communicating that anger (196–98). Her discussion takes place in the context of an evaluation of the ways the witch was imagined or not imagined to have agency (skeptics like Scot deny her agency to minimize her accountability and guilt; conservative writers maximize her agency). Where for Dolan, conservative writers conceive of the witch's agency as existing in her contract with the devil, for Willis, the devil's contract becomes a method of compensating for the witch's power. For a discussion of Willis's treatment of the demonic contract, see her chapter on James in *Malevolent Nurture: Witch-Hunting and Maternal Power in Early Modern England* (Ithaca, NY: Cornell University Press, 1995). For a reading of the way that not speech but writing implicated women in the crime of witchcraft, see Dolan's "Ridiculous Fictions," *Differences* 7, no. 2 (1995): 82–109.

## 2. Broken Epistemologies

This chapter was presented in an earlier form at the former Mary Ingraham Bunting Foundation. Of the various colleagues who commented on it, I would particularly like to thank Katharine Park, Larry Rosenwald, and Ann Blair.

1. Although I frequently differed from it, I benefited from consulting Randy A. Scott's elegant translation of Bodin's *Demonomanie* (Toronto: Centre for Reformation and Renaissance Studies, 1995).

2. *Newes from Scotland*, 21.

3. In dealing with the related topic of judicial punishment as spectacle during the period Foucault fails to address the question of under what circumstances authority might relinquish or not relinquish theatricality. See chapter 1, note 4 for notable critiques of Foucault and the introduction, note 6 for critiques of the episteme in particular.

4. My argument in this chapter differs both from that of Stuart Clark's and also from the earlier tradition Clark responds to. Like Clark, I understand Bodin as viewing witchcraft as the opposite to ideal justice, but unlike Clark, I read the *Demonomanie* as straining against the possible resemblances between its own prescribed judicial practice and the practices of witchcraft itself. In his chapter on Bodin at the end of *Thinking with Demons*, Stuart Clark lays out in its most emphatic form the position that *Demonomanie* springs from the same principles that can be found at the core of the *République*. Read correctly, he argues, the *République* offers divine authorization for absolute monarchy with as much force as divine right theory (672). For Clark, Bodin thought in terms of such an enmity between witchcraft and the magistrate that "we could almost predict" that Bodin would want to locate protection against witchcraft in the "inviolability" of the magistrate (676). In both texts, Clark says, Bodin draws out the implications of a certain philosophy of order, and *Demonomanie* becomes a "regulatory" effort, to restore that order in a dangerously negligent and sick commonwealth and reinstate the ideal order so terribly lacking in France at the moment of its composition. For such a reading, crime in general and witchcraft in particular must

necessarily be the opposite of ideal justice, rather than something justice can see itself mirrored in. Responding to an earlier tradition which sought to segregate the *Demonomanie*, asking, in effect, how the enlightened Bodin of the *République* could write it, Clark offers an important argument for the value of understanding *Demonomanie* and *République* in relation to each other (672).

In contrast, for earlier responses to a critical tradition which sought to segregate the *Demonomanie* from Bodin's other work, see E. William Monter's "Inflation and Witchcraft: The Case of Jean Bodin," in *Action and Conviction in Early Modern Europe*, ed. Theodore K. Rabb and Jerrold E. Seigel (Princeton, NJ: Princeton University Press, 1969) and (more generally preoccupied with "false paradoxes" critics have found within the *République* and between it and various other works of Bodin), see P. L. Rose's "Bodin's Universe and Its Paradoxes: Some Problems in the Intellectual Biography of Jean Bodin," in *Politics and Society in Reformation Europe*, ed. E. I. Kouri and Tom Scott (New York: St. Martin's Press, 1987).

5. For an analogous discussion of the same problem from a different perspective, see Katharine Maus's discussion in *Inwardness and Theater*: "Elizabeth and Jacobean statutes leave it unclear whether witchcraft is essentially a mental, inward crime—consisting in the secret allegiance to evil powers—or whether it is prosecuted because, like murder or theft, it ruins the lives and properties of others. . . . English juries were notoriously reluctant to convict in the absence of material damages, but strictly speaking the blasted livestock, the wasted children, the possessed neighbors, the milk that refused to become butter were merely the effects or symptoms of witchcraft and not its essence" (110–11).

6. At the beginning of *How to Do Things with Words*, J. L. Austin distinguishes between the notion of the constative which describes or refers and the performative utterance which "does" something simply by being uttered. The work of the book is to undo this distinction, although, I would argue, Austin does so in two different and potentially contradictory ways. The first of these ways consists of demolishing both terms, showing both to be ideals of language or dimensions of assessment. The second way of demolishing the opposition lies in the very conception of a "speech act" which preserves not just as an ideal or dimension of assessment the characteristics associated with performativity, but the notion of a performative as a thing in itself: "Once we realize that what we have to study is *not* the sentence but the issuing of an utterance in a speech situation, there can hardly be any longer a possibility of not seeing that stating is performing an act" (139). This method of resolving the original opposition works not by demolishing both "constative" and "performative" and revealing them as only dimensions of assessment, but only by demolishing "constative." I detail the tension between these two strategies in an essay in progress, "Austin's Two Endings."

In distinguishing between "illocutionary" acts ("'He urged [or advised, ordered, &c.] me to shoot her'") and perlocutionary acts ("'He persuaded me to shoot her'" or "'He got me to [or made me, &c.] shoot her,'" 102), Austin makes a distinction about what he calls "consequence language," which is useful in thinking about Bodin. After acknowledging that "illocutionary acts invite by convention a response or sequel" (117), he says that it is "a commonplace of the consequence-language" that "this [response or sequel] cannot be included under the initial stretch of action" (117). In the fear of barbarous signs and characters, curses, and charms that Bodin manifests, he seems to conceive of an utterance including in an "initial stretch of action" not only a response or sequel but a chain effect of magical actions and material changes, as if by being uttered an utterance could not only "do" but do something catastrophic, could not only precipitate a response or sequel but a series of responses and sequels taking the form of material change.

In contrast to Clark's claim that demonologists are "to a man" modern (*Thinking with Demons*, 290), that is, that for them words are not efficacious, see D. P. Walker's still monumental study, *Spiritual and Demonic Magic from Ficino to Campanella* (Warburg Institute, University of London, 1958; repr., Liechtenstein: Kraus Reprint, 1969), 175 for the claim that Bodin also "himself believed in the magical power of words."

7. In Austin's terms, for its emphasis on a statemental ideal of language.

8. One of the things that is interesting about this passage is Bodin's unabashed admiration for this female hostess's knowledge of the dark arts and his complete lack of recognition that the woman he admires (who imparts her knowledge orally) shares many attributes with the women he attacks and advocates putting to death. In discussions of witchcraft persecution, one long-standing feature of debate has been the issue of a male medical profession's response to female healers. In *Witchcraft and Religion* (Oxford, UK: Basil Blackwell, 1984), Christina Larner, while disputing the suggestion that the "major purpose of the witch-hunt was to purge the land of female healers in order to make way for the emergent male [medical] profession" (151), nonetheless says, "I think the scenario of a male takeover of medicine from the sixteenth to the eighteenth centuries is almost certainly accurate" (150) and argues that while "[the] distinction between official and unofficial medicine can be partially made along lines of theory and practice—official medicine was more interventionist, more heroic both for doctor and patient and also more prepared to explain and justify its methods in terms of scientific expertise" in many ways "one is bound to say that one of the principal distinguishing marks was gender. All official healers were male; most unofficial healers were female" (149). For a contrast with Bodin's attitude toward the hostess and her knowledge, see the bailiff David Seaton's anxiety at Geillis Duncane's healing powers in *Newes from Scotland*, 8–9. For earlier discussions of this, see my *Men in Women's Clothing*, 121, and Deborah Willis's discussion in *Malevolent Nurture*, 126. For a discussion of the way writing (rather than oral knowledge) got Anne Bodenham into trouble, see Frances Dolan's "Reading, Writing and other Crimes," in *Feminist Readings of Early Modern Culture: Emerging Subjects*, ed. Valerie Traub, M. Lindsay Kaplan, and Dympna Callaghan (Cambridge: Cambridge University Press, 1996), and for a fascinating account of the way that a capacity for telling the right story, a narrative both strange and yet enough within the parameters of the familiar to be recognizable and thus creditable, see her "'Ridiculous Fictions': Making Distinctions in the Discourses of Witchcraft," *Differences* 7, no. 2 (1995): 82–110. For discussion of the way witches raised anxiety for mothers, see both Willis's *Malevolent Nurture* and Lyndal Roper's description of the ways that recent mothers, separated from infants and coping with pain, attributed demonism to the older single women who nursed and cared for their infants, especially during the first six weeks of life, in *Oedipus and the Devil: Witchcraft, Sexuality and Religion in Early Modern Europe* (London: Routledge, 1994). Approaching completely different materials, Willis and Roper's arguments complement each other.

9. For Austin's argument on the law's largely performative nature despite a penchant for insisting that "utterances used in, say, 'acts in the law,' *must* somehow be statements," see Austin, *How to Do Things with Words*, 19.

10. Note the exact opposition here between Bodin and Scot, for whom nothing not naturally possible is legally possible.

11. Clark articulates a common position on Bodin when he says that Bodin "considered and rejected three of the most important theories of knowledge available to him—'that of Plato and Democritus that only the intellect is the judge of truth, next a crude empiricism attributed to Aristotle, and lastly the total scepticism of Pyrrho'— before choosing a fourth, derived from Theophrastus, in which the 'common sense' mediated between sense data and their interpretation by the mind" (*Thinking with Demons*, 176; the internal quotation is from Richard H. Popkin's *History of Scepticism*, rev. ed. [Assen: Von Gorcum, 1964], 84–85). But this seems to me to assimilate *Demonomanie* to a position which doesn't include its vacillation and contradictions. In her compelling study on Bodin's *Theater of Nature*, *The Theater of Nature: Jean Bodin and Renaissance Science* (Princeton, NJ: Princeton University Press, 1997), Ann Blair describes the importance of the collection or commonplace method for compiling and organizing thoughts in an age when information was expanding at a rate that made traditional rubrics of organization unable to contain what they had to contend with. The method allowed, among other things, for contradictory propositions to be contained within the same book. While not in any sense arguing for *Demonomanie* as composed this way, it does not seem outlandish to imagine it as having to contend with the same kinds of contradictions, often in unsynthesized and unreconcilable ways that the commonplace book had to deal with.

12. The preface of this edition has only penciled pagination.

13. Compare this phenomenon, for instance, with the claim made in *Newes from Scotland* that the devil's mark is an epistemological marker, a "sign," and that until it is discovered the witch will not confess (*Newes from Scotland*, 12–13).

14. See Ann Blair's discussion on the "theater of nature" and the "theater of the book" in *The Theater of Nature*. But unlike nature, there is a component of witchcraft, like the mysteries and intelligences themselves, that cannot be staged, acted out, or reenacted.

## 3. Our Mutual Fiend

1. See Reginald Scot, *The Discoverie of Witchcraft*, ed. Brinsley Nicholson (1584; repr., Totowa, NJ: Rowman and Littlefield, 1973). All quotations are taken from this edition and will be incorporated into the body of the text.

2. See, for instance, Philip Almond, who says, "As a consequence of its comprehensiveness *The Discoverie of Witchcraft* was also an invaluable source of information on magic, demonology, witchcraft, spirits, divination of many kinds and legerdemain" (4). See Philip C. Almond, *England's First Demonologist: Reginald Scot and* The Discoverie of Witchcraft (London: I. B. Tauris, 2014). He argues that "paradoxically, the comprehensive account of magic, witchcraft and legerdemain contained in *The Discoverie of Witchcraft* fostered European demonologies in England, helped the spread of indigenous witchcraft traditions, and inaugurated the English tradition of secular magic and conjuring" (2). Lawrence Normand and Gareth Roberts, too, say, "Scot was an important agent of transmission of demonological information to British readers from continental works such as Bodin's *Demonomanie* and the *Malleus Maleficarum*, two works which he cites in translation at some length." See Normand and Roberts, eds., *Witch-*

*craft in Early Modern Scotland: James VI's Demonology and the North Berwick Witches* (Liverpool: Liverpool University Press, 2000), 330.

3. For Austin's initial claim, see *How to Do Things with Words*, 1: "It was for too long the assumption of philosophers that the business of a 'statement' can only be to 'describe' some state of affairs, or to 'state some fact,' which it must either do truly or falsely." For his final description of it as an ideal, see Austin, 145–46: "With the constative utterance, we abstract from the illocutionary (let alone the perlocutionary) aspects of the speech act, and we concentrate on the locutionary: moreover, we use an oversimplified notion of correspondence with the facts—over-simplified because essentially it brings in the illocutionary aspect. This is the ideal of what it would be right to say in all circumstances, for any purpose, to any audience, &c. Perhaps it is sometimes realized." I discuss this passage in chapter 2, footnote 6 of this book.

4. For opposite positions on the issue of what enabled Scot to arrive at the skepticism about witchcraft he did, see Sydney Anglo, who after distinguishing Scot from Pomponazzi concedes that in the end it is "impossible to distinguish Scot's argument from the Sadduceean argument which he rejects" (134) and sees as "central to Scot's thesis [that] demons are merely evil impulses" (131); "Reginald Scot's *Discoverie of Witchcraft*: Scepticism and Sadduceeism," in *The Damned Art*, ed. Sydney Anglo (London: Routledge, 1977). Leland L. Estes argues, in opposition to Anglo, that Scot was a "deeply religious man," unscientific in the sense of being uncommitted to systematically testing phenomena experientially, but nonetheless uninclined to reduce the role of spirits to metaphors or impulses. For Estes, Scot merely denies them [spirits] a corporeal reality. See "Reginald Scot and His *Discoverie of Witchcraft*: Religion and Science in the Opposition to the European Witch Craze," *Church History* 52 (1983): 444–56, especially 446. Stuart Clark vacillates between the positions articulated by Anglo and Estes, explicitly saying what Estes says, but implying what Anglo says. Like Estes, he says, "In fact, Scot's most telling argument was his reduction (in a 'Discourse on Divels' added to his *Discoverie of Witchcraft*) of all demonic agents to a noncorporeal condition, thus removing them from physical nature altogether" (211–12). But like Anglo, he says, "The only logical alternative left was to remove devils from the physical world altogether and turn spiritual demonism into a metaphor. . . . Scot . . . attempted both" (211). Katharine Eisaman Maus argues that for Scot devils are "pure hallucinations, projections of a guilty imagination" in *Inwardness* (Chicago: University of Chicago Press, 1995), 91. For David Wooton's claim that Scot offers metaphorical readings of the Bible "because this was orthodox Familism" and his larger argument about Scot's relation to Abraham Fleming and The Family of Love, see "Reginald Scot / Abraham Fleming, / The Family of Love," in *The Languages of Witchcraft: Narrative, Ideology and Meaning in Early Modern Culture*, ed. Stuart Clark (New York: St. Martin's Press, 2002), 119–38, especially 132. For Stephen Greenblatt, Scot's whole project is to *disenchant* (115). For Greenblatt's Scot, "figurative speech . . . supported by visual illusion . . . lies at the heart not only of the discourse of witchcraft, but of the practices and persecutions that are linked with this discourse" (116). See "Shakespeare Bewitched," in *New Historical Literary Study: Essays on Reproducing Texts, Representing History*, ed. Jeffery N. Cox and Larry J. Reynolds (Princeton, NJ: Princeton University Press, 1993), 108–35. For Diane Purkiss's description of the way various male historians (including Anglo, Thomas, and Sharpe) valorize Scot's skepticism because what "Scot knows" and what they "know" amount to the same thing, and for the attendant

suggestion that in so doing historians (like Scot) reify the female witch as "completely powerless," see *The Witch in History* (London: Routledge, 2002), 59–88 but especially 63–65.

5. For Almond, it was a hammer against Catholics that Scot was to use continually in *The Discoverie of Witchcraft* (*England's First Demonologist*, 15–16). See too Pierre Kaptitaniak's detailed description of Scot's "anti-Catholic campaign" and his argument that "Scot's interest in witch trials was not enough to provoke him into writing a whole treatise on the subject" (48) and that "behind the displayed humanistic concern for the innocent and the poor that so appeals to modern readers, Scot has a religious agenda: to discredit as much as possible the Catholic dogma and liturgy, and to promote a strongly Calvinist position that made some historians suspect him of being a non-conformist" (49) See "Reginald Scot and the Circles of Power: Witchcraft, Anti-Catholicism and Faction Politics" in *Supernatural and Secular Power in Early Modern England*, eds. Marcus Harmes and Victoria Bladen (Farnham, UK: Ashgate, 2015), 41–66.

6. See, especially, Greenblatt's "Loudon and London," which, though it does not deal extensively with Scot, identifies his influence on Harsnett in associating exorcism with theatricality. First published in *Critical Inquiry* 12 (1986): 326–46, and expanded in *Shakespearean Negotiations: The Circulation of Social Energy in Renaissance England* (Berkeley: University of California Press, 1988). See, too, Greenblatt's more extensive treatment of Scot's "obsession with the exact operation of sleights of hand . . . his careful exposition of the hidden mechanisms by means of which certain theatrical illusions . . . are achieved," as well as Greenblatt's sustained attention to Scot's diatribes about illusions and figuration and his discussion of Scot's larger project of disenchantment in "Shakespeare Bewitched," 114–15.

7. For a description of Scot's antipathy to both Bodin and Brian Darcy, the latter presiding over the pretrial examinations of those accused of witchcraft during the St. Osyth trials and a great admirer of Bodin, see Philip Almond's fascinating account, *England's First Demonologist*, 18–20 and 40–42. Almond notes Bodin's attendance during the Duc d'Alençon's visit to Elizabeth in 1581–82 as well as Darcy's devotion to Bodin's *Demonomanie*. Almond argues that it was "the tactics and techniques" of Darcy that Scot saw as "representative of the impropriety of judicial processes in the trials of witches" (40–41), including Darcy's adoption of Bodin's method of offering immunity to those who confessed (to the detriment of Elizabeth Bennet who acceded to the inducement and was burnt) (44–45). For a description of Scot's rhetorical strategy as a response to Bodin (Scot's strategy "was to increase Bodin's two categories of the criminal and the heretical into three, the criminal, the heretical and the false or impossible"), see Almond, *England's First Demonologist*, 48. See too Kapitaniak, "Reginald Scot and the Circles of Power" for the argument that Scot's indignation was directed against Bodin rather than Darcy (45–49).

For Brian Levack's argument that all possessions in the early modern period, "not just those that were feigned or otherwise volitional, were theatrical productions in which the demoniacs and also their families, neighbors, physicians, pastors and exorcists played their assigned roles" (30), see *The Devil Within: Possession & Exorcism in the Christian West* (New Haven, CT: Yale University Press, 2013), particularly 139–68. For his treatment of the different "scripts" that Catholic and Protestant possessions enacted, see 156–68. Building on work by both Michel de Certeau and Stephen Greenblatt, Levack argues that neither fraud nor illness is sufficient to explain possession.

8. For a comprehensive account of the ways various commentators during the period approached this question (as well as the way the arguments fell out among Catholics and Protestants), see Clark's "Sights: King Saul and King Macbeth," in *Vanities of the Eye* (Oxford: Oxford University Press, 2012), 236–65. Clark credits Pierre Kapitaniak with identifying forty-eight contributions to the debate (about the witch of Endor) between 1486 and 1636, "showing that the Catholic writers on witchcraft tended to side with their Protestant counterparts in tracing the episode to a demonic illusion" (261, footnote 34). See P. Kapitaniak, "Spectres, fantômes et revenants dans le théâtre de la Renaissance anglaise" (PhD diss., Paris-Sorbonne University, 2001). See Zika's fascinating treatment of the way Jacob Cornelisz van Oostsanen's *The Witch of Endor* (1526) breaks from "traditional medieval iconography" introducing elements "from the new iconography of witchcraft" into the traditional story (156). See too his fascinating treatment of Johann Teufel's *King Saul, the Witch of Endor, and Samuel* (1569) for his description of the way the placement of the Samuel figure within the magic circle and the Saul figure outside of it interprets the Saul figure as a ghost (161).

9. For Almond's claim that this interpretation became dominant in part because of the Geneva Bible's endorsement of it in the marginal gloss, see *England's First Demonologist*, 129, as well as 218, note 50.

10. Clark suggests that an explanation of witchcraft in terms of "natural" causes is, in effect, no real challenge to a belief in witchcraft, for though demonic magic might seem "to exceed nature" it, in fact, "worked entirely through the natural powers of demons, and only seemed miraculous by comparison to the natural powers of men and women" (*Thinking with Demons*, 153). Scot's argument here is phrased in terms of the opposition between "manifest things" and "unknown things," (it is "ridiculous . . . to leave manifest things, and such as by naturall reason may be prooved, to seek unknowne things"), the "ridiculous" here being to seek the unknown when the manifest is available (114). But throughout his narrative of the witch of Endor story, he seems to think the existence of natural (in the sense of material, visible, "manifest") facts is a challenge to witchcraft.

11. See my discussion of this contrast in chapter 2.

12. Stephen Orgel suggests that "surely the point isn't that Christ couldn't *have* one, but that he couldn't *leave* one for the offending spirit" (private correspondence).

13. This etiology anticipates closely Alan Macfarlane's explanation of witchcraft persecution in Essex, in which a person was refused some small object and was believed in her anger to retaliate by bewitching her refuser; that is, "It was the victim who had reason to feel guilty and anxious as having turned away a neighbour, while the suspect might become hated as the agent who caused such a feeling" (174). Macfarlane, influenced by Evans-Pritchard, seeks to make historiography accountable to the techniques of anthropology, and his analysis of Essex indictments is impressively grounded in concrete evidence. But to the degree his claims about causation are related to his beliefs about why the witch hunts died out, there remains an inference that cannot be grounded in evidence. This seems to me not a shortcoming peculiar to Macfarlane but one inevitable in the methodology. The step from record to belief will at some point involve an inference. See Macfarlane, *Witchcraft in Tudor and Stuart England* (London: Routledge, 1970). Gibson comments on this kind of etiology in "Understanding Witchcraft?" She says, "The most authoritative analysis of accusers' stories about

witches is still that pioneered by Reginald Scot and George Gifford in the sixteenth century and taken up by Keith Thomas in the twentieth" (45). For her comparison of "denial narratives" and "revenge narratives," see 45–49.

14. For Scot, part of this antifeminism lies in the belief that various falsehoods (like the belief in "Faerie") are ones that we have taken in through *female* speech in particular: "But in our childhood our mothers maids have so terrified us with an ouglie divell . . . whereby we start and are afraid when we heare one crie Bough" (*Discoverie of Witchcraft*, 122). Where Frances Dolan identifies the contradictoriness of Scot's defense of women as consisting in his denial of their agency, for me the uncomfortable contradiction lies in the way Scot's "natural" explanations frequently veer toward the kind of repugnance at women's bodies those he attacks manifest. For Dolan's discussion of the kinds of contradictions built into Scot's conception of female agency, see *Dangerous Familiars: Representations of Domestic Crime in England, 1550–1700* (Ithaca, NY: Cornell University Press, 1994), 207–10. See too Purkiss, *The Witch in History*, especially 64–67. She says, "Scot's scepticism and Jean Bodin's elaboration of the theory of pact witchcraft can be seen as similarly misogynistic responses to the idea that women might act as agents of supernatural causation" (64). "Scot's contempt for women accused of witchcraft actually exceeded that of his contemporaries" (65).

## 4. Strategies for Doubt

This chapter and chapter 5 build on and extend ideas developed in *Men in Women's Clothing*.

1. For Clark's characterization of demonology as "an epistemological debate—a debate about the grounds for ordered knowledge of nature and natural causation," see "The Scientific Status of Demonology," in *Occult and Scientific Mentalities in the Renaissance*, ed. Brian Vickers (Cambridge: Cambridge University Press, 1984), 368. Clark says, "The key questions faced by demonologists were thus of a causal and criterial kind: What was the exact causal status of demonic effects? What laws did they obey or disobey? What were the criteria for distinguishing between their true and illusory aspects? Along what point on the axis from miracles through natural wonders to ordinary natural contingencies were they to be placed? Tracking such questions involved making distinctions that were critical for any explanation of phenomena, whether demonic or not—distinctions between what was possible and impossible, or really and falsely perceived, and between both supernature and nature, and nature and artifice" (353–54). He calls demonology "one of the 'prerogative instances' of early modern science" (356).

2. For an earlier analysis of this narrative, see Levine, *Men in Women's Clothing*, 108–19, especially 114–17.

3. See Popkin, *The History of Scepticism*, xiii–xxii, for a comparison of dogmatic claims about knowledge to the attempts to suspend such claims in classical thought and for the ways these problems were reworked in the early modern period.

4. In the preface to *Daemonologie*, James claims to have written the book "to resolve the doubting harts of many, both that such assaultes of Sathan are most certainly practized. & that the instruments therof, merits most severly to be punished: against the damnable opinions of two principally in our age, wherof the one called SCOT An Englishman, is not ashamed in publike print to deny, that ther can be such a thing as

Witch-craft, and so mainteines the old error of the Sadduces, in denying of spirits. The other called WIERVS, A German Phisition, sets out a publick apologie for all these craftesfolkes, whereby, procuring for their impunitie, he plainely bewrayes himself to have bene one of that Profession" (xi–xv).

5. See Clark, "Believers and Sceptics," in *Thinking with Demons*, 195, 209 and 210, especially 195 for the claim that "demonology presupposed doubt." See 198–208 for a discussion of the similarity of the claims of a skeptic like Weyer and a "believer" like Boguet. See 208 for the intriguing claim that Weyer's form of doubt "was not, after all, a very *effective* form of doubt" (emphasis mine). See too Clark's "King James's *Daemonologie*: Witchcraft and Kingship" in *The Damned Art*, ed. Sydney Anglo," 156–82, especially 162. Clark adds, "It seems quite compatible then for James to have always accepted the principles of witchcraft and yet, in each individual attribution that came to his notice, to have felt the need to be convinced" (163). On the subject of James's possible skepticism, Diana Purkiss says, James "was soon just as ready to deploy scepticism as belief in examining cases of witchcraft and possession, asserting belief in the case of the Essex divorce and scepticism in numerous cases of possession, carefully unmasked as fraudulent by the detective powers of the king." See *The Witch in History* (London: Routledge, 1996), 201.

The closest James comes to acknowledging the rift between the book's assumptions that knowledge is possible and any doubt is Epistemon's attempt to avoid what he calls the Charybdis of skepticism and the Scylla of absurdity ("And by these meanes shall we saill surelie, betuixt *Charybdis* and *Scylla*, in eschewing the not beleeuing of them altogether on the one part, least that drawe vs to the errour that there is no Witches: and on the other parte in beleeuing of it, make vs to eschew the falling into innumerable absurdities." [42]). For Julian Goodare's refutation of Jenny Wormald's "sceptical" construction of *Daemonologie*, see "The Scottish Witchcraft Panic of 1597," in *The Scottish Witch-Hunt in Context*, ed. Julian Goodare (Manchester: Manchester University Press, 2002), particularly 64–66, which concludes with the assessment, "The conclusion that can be drawn here is that if James' supposed doubts in 1597 influenced his public behavior at all it was to spur him into action to defend demonological orthodoxy—both in print, and by means of faggot and stake."

6. For the position that James's arguments in *Daemonologie* are the "stock-in-trade of orthodox European demonology," see Stuart Clark's claim in "King James's *Daemonologie*." In contrast, for the claim that James repeats verbatim new Protestant arguments in *Daemonologie* as did John Cotta in 1616, see Genevieve Guenther's "Why Devils Came When Faustus Called Them," *Modern Philology* 109, no. 1 (2011): 46–70. Although it has become a commonplace to argue that James simply repeats the claims of earlier demonologists (whether Protestant or Continental ones), such a claim assumes a kind of "inventory" approach to treatises in which items like night-flying or the anal kiss either do or do not appear, and ignores the order in which these things occur.

7. See Levine, *Men in Women's Clothing*, especially 114–16.

8. For a more sustained argument about the implications this narrative has for masculinity and a discussion of the Galenic (two-seed) theory of conception, see Levine, *Men in Women's Clothing*, 116–17.

9. On the inviolability of the magistrate, see the chapter with that name in Clark, *Thinking with Demons*, 572–81. Clark says of this inviolability that though Protestant

opinion on it was divided, one of its "staunchest supporters" was James who, conscious of his own "rather fragile authority" and the strength of "aristocratic factionalism in Scotland," used the privilege of inviolability "to set public magistrates like himself decisively apart from ordinary men and their concerns" (576). In part because of Clark's influence and in part because of the degree of interest registered in James himself since the 1980s, most recent readers of *Daemonologie* have seen the book as an extension of James's political philosophy and in particular his attitude toward monarchy. But the narrative of entresse I have just described evinces a kind of "violability" or porousness as well. And just as Clark argues that the principle of "inviolability" was erected in Scotland at a moment of politically "fragile authority," so *Daemonologie* erects the power of the magistrate at a moment of fragile masculinity. See, too, Goodare's description of a kind of political fragility arising out of the tensions between the radical Presbyterian movement and the king in the 1590s. "The Scottish Witchcraft Panic of 1597," 52. For Clark's early description of *Daemonologie* as an expression of James's political philosophy, see his "King James' *Daemonologie*." For the evolution of these ideas in *Thinking with Demons*, see especially 578 and 648 and more generally 549–71 and the discussions that follow in "Witchcraft and Politics." See as well Daniel Fischlin's "'Counterfeiting God': James VI (I) and the Politics of *Dæmonologie* (1597)," *Journal of Narrative Technique* 26, no. 1 (Winter 1996): 1–29.

10. Thus Epistemon transfers the blame for delusion from the perceiver to the perceived over the course of *Daemonologie*. *Daemonologie* begins by insisting that delusion is literally "in" the mind of the perceiver and ends by suggesting that delusion is "in" the similitude of the person perceived as well, a position which makes knowledge almost irrelevant.

## 5. *Newes from Scotland* and the Theaters of Evidence

1. Although James Carmichael, minister of the town of Haddington, is the most likely candidate for authorship of *Newes from Scotland*, in light of the problems in assigning authorship both to the pamphlet itself and to different parts of the pamphlet, I have referred to the writer as "the pamphleteer." For a discussion of composition dating and the particular problems of authorship, see Normand and Roberts, *Witchcraft in Early Modern Scotland*, 291–97.

2. For three recent essays which have sought to categorize the kinds of narratives defendants at witch trials offered, see Peter Rushton, "Texts of Authority: Witchcraft Accusations and the Demonstration of Truth in Early Modern England," 21–39; Gibson, "Understanding Witchcraft?," 43–55; and Malcolm Gaskill, "Witches and Witnesses in Old and New England," 55–80, all in *Languages of Witchcraft: Narratives, Ideology and Meaning in Early Modern Culture*. In contrast, I seek to compare narratives to performances.

3. In "The Spectacle of the Scaffold," Foucault gives a vivid instance of this in the "penal arithmetic" which did not remain inert until assembled, to establish a verdict of guilty or not guilty, but had an "operational function." Describing the way that justice, "in the classical period, operated the production of truth," Foucault says:

> The different pieces of evidence did not constitute so many neutral elements, until such time as they could be gathered together into a single body of evidence that would bring the final certainty of guilt. Each piece of evidence aroused a par-

ticular degree of abomination. Guilt did not begin when all the evidence was gathered together; piece by piece, it was constituted by each of the elements that made it possible to recognize a guilty person. Thus a semi-proof did not leave the suspect innocent until such time as it was completed; it made him semi-guilty; slight evidence of serious crime marked someone as slightly criminal. In short, penal demonstration did not obey a dualistic system: true or false; but a principle of continuous gradation; a degree reached in the demonstration already formed a degree of guilt and consequently involved a degree of punishment. (*Discipline and Punish*, 42)

See Foucault's discussion leading up to this passage, particularly 36–38. For his hierarchy of evidence, see Jean Bodin, *De la Démonomanie des Sorciers*.

4. Langbein, *Torture and the Law of Proof*, 7. For a discussion of the medieval ordeal as "a testament to men's faith in God's immanence but not to their efforts to use the law as an effective instrument of social control" (65–66) and a discussion of the "change from the old [accusatorial] system to the new" (inquisitorial system) as being stimulated partly by the revival of the formal study of Roman law, but mostly from the growing realization that "crime—both ecclesiastical and secular—was increasing and had to be reduced," see Levack, *The Witch-hunt in Early Modern Europe* (London: Longman, 1987), 66–67. For his analysis of the Scottish criminal process as "something of a hybrid between the English and Continental models," see 68. For his sustained treatment of changes in criminal procedure, especially those involving torture and his elaboration of Langbein as well as his comparison of English legal procedures and continental procedures, see 63–93.

5. As noted earlier, in *Discipline and Punish*, Foucault says it is "not an extreme expression of lawless rage" (33), not an expression of "a legal system driven to exasperation and, forgetting its principles, losing all restraint" (34–35), "not the unrestrained torture of modern interrogations" (40).

6. See Frances E. Dolan's discussion of a parallel issue regarding the status of court records in *Whores of Babylon: Catholicism, Gender, and Seventeenth-Century Print Culture* (Ithaca, NY: Cornell University Press, 1999), especially 1–15. She says, "Whereas I once resorted to court records, albeit slyly, for more reliable or more direct access to 'what really happened,' I now view court records as themselves representations, shaped by occasion and convention, rather than as standards against which to check the accuracy of, say, plays" (2).

7. Normand and Roberts make a similar connection about pricking: "Pricking, which was a kind of trial by ordeal, involved sticking a pin into several places on the body until a place was found which was insensible to pain.... Pricking sought to determine a person's criminality by 'an appeal to God, a miracle attesting to the innocence or guilt of the accused'" (*Witchcraft in Early Modern Scotland*, 99). For an analysis of pricking in relation to English law, see Orna Alyagon Darr, *Marks of an Absolute Witch: Evidentiary Dilemmas in Early Modern England* (Burlington, VT: Ashgate, 2006). To the extent that the examiners insist that they *find* the devil's mark, their epistemology differs from the one implicit in Foucault's claim that judicial torture "must mark the victim" (*Discipline and Punish*, 34). In practice the torture that the two texts describe may be indistinguishable, but they serve alternative needs and rationales. Because for Foucault the establishment of truth is always "the absolute right and exclusive power of the sovereign and his judges" (35), the discussion precludes an analysis of the ways attempts to produce "knowledge" might be

recuperative, responsive to anxieties about knowledge within power itself. In *Newes from Scotland*, I would argue, the mark is compensatory, frequently the process by which the examiners themselves seek to achieve or recuperate a sensation of certainty. For earlier discussion, see Introduction, note 21.

8. See document 1 in Normand and Roberts's *Witchcraft in Early Modern Scotland*, which the authors place sometime before December 1590, which actually assigns Sampson a role in the plot. She confesses to "that article [point of accusation] of David Seton, and that which was like the glass was glass indeed mixed with pieces of cords and things to gar it work [make it efficacious] which the devil gave to her"; also "she confesses that they made their consultation there to know how they might wrack David Seton" (138–39). See, as well, document 20, Sampson's dittay from January 27, 1591, item 49, which elaborates on the same set of events. All other references to the examinations and dittays are from Normand and Roberts.

9. Normand and Roberts gloss "Commer" in the song Duncane is supposed to have accompanied as "a female gossip or intimate friend" (315).

10. Normand and Roberts say "the extant dittays and depositions contain no record of an Agnes Tompson among the names of witches, although they mention a Bessie Thomson and Margaret Thomson. Bessie Thomson's name occurs in both the dittays and the depositions frequently, often after that of Geillis Duncan. The name Agnes Tompson here is likely to be an error, because later in *News* information ascribed to her is actually provided in the dittays by Agnes Sampson" (312).

For Craigie's characterization of the two as different witches (but his attribution to Sampson of the attempt to get the king's linen), see James Craigie, *Minor Prose Works of King James VI and I* (Edinburgh: Scottish Texts Society, 1982). For Pitcairn (who is one of Craigie's sources), see Robert Pitcairn, *Ancient Criminal Trials in Scotland*, Vol. 1 (Edinburgh: Maitland Club, 1833), 230–41. For his rationalization of "Tompson" as Sampson, see 217–18. For an earlier discussion of this question, see Levine, *Men in Women's Clothing*, 172, note 5.

11. For an earlier discussion of the questions of why one witch receives more torture than another and the pamphlet's anti-theatrical bias and attitude toward sympathetic magic, see Levine, "Magic as Theatre, Theatre as Magic: The Case of *Newes from Scotland*," in *Men in Women's Clothing*, 120–33.

12. See Normand and Roberts, *Witchcraft in Early Modern Scotland*, document 2, 144–46, and for a brief retelling of part of the same event, see document 19, item 39, 239.

13. In an early article Clark suggests there may have been actual venom, but I can find no evidence of this in either pamphlet or the trials and dittays, and the sources Clark mentions seem more removed. See Clark, "King James's *Daemonologie*," 158 and footnotes 5 and 6, 178.

14. For the distinction between sympathetic and contagious magic see Sir James George Frazier, *The Golden Bough* (New York: Macmillan, 1960), 12–52.

15. Normand and Roberts, *Witchcraft in Early Modern Scotland*, document 4, Sampson's January 1591 examination before the master of work, 155.

16. Normand and Roberts, *Witchcraft in Early Modern Scotland*, document 20, item 41, 240.

17. Normand and Roberts, *Witchcraft in Early Modern Scotland*, document 20, Sampson's dittay, item 51, 245. For an account of a similar attempt on the life of Queen Elizabeth, see Almond, *England's First Demonologist*, 35.

18. See Levine, *Men in Women's Clothing*, 120–33.

19. Normand and Roberts make this point as well (*Witchcraft in Early Modern Scotland*, 298).

20. Normand and Roberts, *Witchcraft in Early Modern Scotland*, document 19, item 5, 228, and item 12, 229.

21. Normand and Roberts, *Witchcraft in Early Modern Scotland*, 299.

22. Normand and Roberts, *Witchcraft in Early Modern Scotland*, document 19, item 2, 226.

23. See Normand and Roberts, 296, for a discussion of the title page, 299–300 for an evaluation of competing possibilities for the origin of the story of Fian and the heifer, 294 for the claim that "the raw material" of much of the pamphlet would have been the pretrial examinations, not the dittays, and 205–6 for their fascinating reading of Fian's dittay itself. See 295 for their argument that the pamphlet's production was subject to both "ideological and market forces, with the Scottish writer having to satisfy James's wish for self-justification, and the English publisher having to satisfy rapidly the market for sensational pamphlets."

## 6. Spenser's False Shewes

1. Harry Berger, "Archimago: Between Text and Countertext," *Studies in English Literature* 43, no. 1 (2003): 19–64.

2. Joseph Campana, *The Pain of Reformation: Spenser, Vulnerability and the Ethics of Masculinity* (New York: Fordham University Press, 2012). For Campana, book 1 dramatizes the consequences of Reformation religious ideology, in particular "the diminishing importance of the suffering Christ," as opposed to morality "expressed through heroic masculinity," and the consequent "inability to apprehend the suffering of others and to respond compassionately" (49). His most sustained reading of this in book 1 is of Red Cross's encounter with Fradubio, though Campana echoes this moment in powerful ways in his discussion of Arthur's rescue of Red Cross Knight from the dungeon, the stripping of Duessa, and his description of the house of holiness.

3. Stephanie Bahr, "'Ne spared they to strip her naked all': Reading, Rape, and Reformation in Spenser's *Faerie Queene*," *Studies in Philology* 117, no. 2 (2020): 285–312. For earlier readings of Spenserian moments that stop "blaming the victim," see Katherine Eggert's "Spenser's Ravishment: Rape and Rapture in *The Faerie Queene*," *Representations* 70 (2000): 1–26. For her discussion of Sheila Cavanagh as similarly "caution[ing] us not to read past rape" and Maureen Quilligan and Susan Frye as identifying an agenda of "men terrorizing women" in relation to Busirane and Amoret, see 1–2 especially.

4. See Garthine Walker, "Rereading Rape and Sexual Violence in Early Modern England," *Gender and History* 10, no.1 (1998): 1–23, especially 3 and 13 for the legal requirement for rape.

5. Both Kenneth Gross and Susanne Wofford point to the paradoxical nature of canto 7's introduction of the shield, what Gross calls the "maddening paradox" of the way the poem suggests that "the shield's magic power is not only unaffected by magic but also, perhaps, not dependent on it all," and the way that the fiction of magic quickly returns, and more strongly, when the shield's power is "explained" as being a creation of Merlin. For the most comprehensive argument on the tendency of iconoclasm to slip into an idolatry as insidious as that it seeks to avoid, see Kenneth Gross, *Spense-*

rian *Poetics: Idolatry, Iconoclasm, and Magic* (Ithaca, NY: Cornell University Press, 1985). See 136 for his discussion of the paradox of the shield. For a rigorous analysis of the kinds of defenses Spenser adopts against the possibility Gross calls attention to, and especially the way Spenser's "consciousness of false speaking and false reading shapes particular sections of the poem," see A. Leigh DeNeef's *Spenser and the Motives of Metaphor* (Durham, NC: Duke University Press, 1982), especially 92–103. See Wofford for her discussion of the same contradiction in the shield Gross discusses and for her discussion of the tension between the shield's perfection and its associations with petrification and death, *The Choice of Achilles: The Ideology of Figure in the Epic* (Stanford, CA: Stanford University Press, 1992), especially 260–62. For Ernest B. Gilman, the shield reveals Spenser's "shield of faith" as "antiartifact"; see *Iconoclasm and Poetry in the English Reformation* (Chicago: University of Chicago Press, 1986), 66.

6. Melinda J. Gough elegantly describes this as a "turning" from what the speaker sees, ultimately derived from Ariosto. See "'Her filthy feature open showne' in Ariosto, Spenser and *Much Ado about Nothing*," *Studies in English Literature, 1500–1900* 39, no. 1 (1999), especially 45–46 and 52–53. In contrast, for Bahr, Duessa's "new 'openness' suggests not just penetration but also interpretive clarity" (296). Her argument and mine, though developing along parallel lines, come to different conclusions about Duessa's interpretability.

7. Pat Parker argues even more comprehensively that the poem itself refuses to allow us to remove its "veils." For a discussion of this in the context of the poem's tendency toward "dilation," its narrative strategy of postponing indefinitely an anticipated if apocalyptic end, see *Inescapable Romance: Studies in the Politics of a Mode* (Princeton, NJ: Princeton University Press, 1979). For Jonathan Goldberg on the poem's endless capacity for deferral (particularly in book 4), see *Endlesse Worke: Spenser and the Structures of Discourse* (Baltimore, MD: Johns Hopkins University Press, 1981).

8. Wofford says, "The premise from which I begin—one of the fundamental 'rules' of *The Faerie Queene*—is that the characters do not know they are in an allegory and cannot and do not 'read' the signs of their world as figurative pointers to another arena of understanding. They *do not know*, in other words, the one fact that they would need to know in order to act ethically in their fictional world" (*The Choice of Achilles*, 220; emphasis mine).

9. James VI, *Daemonologie*, 33

10. For this claim, see Sheila Cavanagh's *Wanton Eyes and Chaste Desires: Female Sexuality in The Faerie Queene* (Bloomington: Indiana University Press, 1994), 56.

11. I differ from Wofford in my understanding of Archimago's theatricality (in the first two cantos of book 1 especially) as mimicking the specific tropes of early modern anti-theatricalism rather than reproducing the Aristotelian categories of pity and fear that Wofford discusses. For Wofford's treatment of the "theatrical analogy" and for book 2's capacity to trouble "the situation of the pitying spectator by defining its moral questions in terms of spectacle and theater," see *The Choice of Achilles*, chapter 4, and particularly the discussion following 404.

12. Stephen Gosson, *The School of Abuse, Containing a Pleasant Invective against Poets, Pipers, Players, Jesters, &c.* (1579; rpt. London: Shakespeare Society, 1841). For Gosson on effeminization, see 19. For my discussion of the fear of effeminization in antitheatrical tracts, see Levine, *Men in Women's Clothing*, 10–25.

13. For Campana this paralysis "embodies the shock of masculinity faced with a materiality that is neither docile nor silent; he faces, instead, the threat of the voice of another person's pain" (*The Pain of Reformation*, 56–57).

14. Where Theresa Krier treats the stripping of Duessa as a moment which evokes disgust, it seems to me to elicit sexual fascination, to escalate to its fullest the sexual looking which begins in book 1. For Krier's treatment of this scene in the larger context of her discussion of the consequences of vision, and in particular of moments in which those viewed experience a loss of selfhood or integrity through the experience of being looked at, see *Gazing on Secret Sights: Spenser, Classical Imitation, and the Decorums of Vision* (Ithaca, NY: Cornell University Press, 1990).

15. See John Lambe, *Statement, by John Lambe, of the proofs brought against him for a rape, and of their invalidity; also of his own proofs in favour of his innocence*, May 9, 1624, London, National Archives, PRO, SP14/154/57. For a pamphlet account of his life, see *A briefe Description of the Notorious Life of John Lambe, Otherwise Called Doctor Lambe, Together with his Ignominious Death* (Amsterdam, 1628). For my discussion of the associations between magic and rape in the pamphlet, see Levine, "Wicked Mysteries and Notorious Conjurors: Magic, Rape and Violence in Two Early Modern Pamphlets," *Journal of Medieval and Early Modern Studies* 51, no. 3 (2021): 533–51.

16. Walker, "Rereading Rape," 3.

17. For Campana, Arthur's rescue of Red Cross articulates the central problem of identifying "with abject masculinity." Although Arthur spares neither "long paines" nor "labors manifold" to rescue Red Cross, the pity he is pierced with creates horror. "The danger of compassion inheres in a threat to the inviolable masculinity of subjectivity," and Arthur responds with "defensive violence" (Campana, *The Pain of Reformation*, 65).

18. I differ from Bahr in my reading of the battle between Orgoglio and Arthur as a kind of duel or contest between versions of masculinity, where Bahr, because of the feminine pronouns which describe the castle to which Orgoglio is compared, sees the battle as Arthur's rape of Orgoglio. I differ as well in my reading of the stripping of Duessa as a performance for Red Cross rather than an action on his part.

19. Walker, "Rereading Rape," 15.

## 7. Danger in Words

I would like to thank Charles Donahue, Paul A. Freund Professor of Law at Harvard (quoted herein) for his exhaustive and extremely generous comments on earlier drafts of this chapter. All faults are my own.

1. Christopher Marlowe, *Doctor Faustus A- and B-texts (1604–1616)*, ed. David Bevington and Eric Rasmussen (Manchester: Manchester University Press, 1993). All quotations are taken from the A text.

2. See Austin, *How to Do Things with Words*. Of "I do," "I name this ship," "I give and bequeath," and "I bet," Austin says: "In these examples it seems clear that to utter the sentence (in, of course, the appropriate circumstances) is not to *describe* my doing of what I should be said in so uttering to be doing or to state that I am doing it: it is to do it" (6). In this essay, I make use of Austin's initial distinctions of "constative" and "performative," as these have tended to circulate in previous discussions of the play.

In fact, Austin ultimately problematizes these very terms, replacing them first with a discussion of "locutionary" and "illocutionary forces" and ultimately with the notion of "more general *families* of related and overlapping speech acts" (150). One resonance between Austin and some of the demonological materials of the period is, in fact, the way that, after skeptical critique of the notion of an efficacious word, both he and they seem to reverse themselves and reify in utterances the belief of performativity.

3. Thus Genevieve Guenther sees Marlowe's "brilliant strategy" as "exploit[ing] the reformist understanding of magic as at once theatrical spectacle and theological instrument" (49). For Guenther, the crux of the argument of the "reformers" is that "magical language has no intrinsic spiritual efficacy" (47) but that "the devil does, in fact, come when the magician calls him" (52), performing "his false conjuration as a theater piece" (53) that inclines the spectators toward false belief. See Genevieve Guenther, "Why Devils Came When Faustus Called Them," *Modern Philology* 109 (2011): 46–70. For an earlier argument that the play "challenges the notion . . . that words bear an intrinisic power . . . subject[ing] this idea to an iconoclastic analysis" (63), see Daniel Gates, "Unpardonable Sins: The Hazards of Performative Language in the Tragic Cases of Francesco Spiera and *Doctor Faustus*," *Comparative Drama* 38, no. 1 (2004): 59–81. In contrast, and at times in response, see Andrew Sofer, "How to Do Things with Demons: Conjuring Performatives in *Doctor Faustus*," *Theatre Journal* 61, no. 1 (2009): 1–21, for the claim that "*Faustus* traffics in performative magic not in the service of skepticism . . . but to appropriate speech's performative power on behalf of a glamorous commercial enterprise, the Elizabethan theater itself." For Sofer, *Faustus* continually challenges Austin's distinction between "efficacious" (successful) performatives and "hollow" (unsuccessful) theatrical quotations of them: "Austin's distinction breaks down whenever a speech act in the world of the play makes a material difference in the world of the playhouse" (3). For David Hawkes's claim that "performative signs constituted a demonically inspired alienation, or 'sale' of the soul, inspir[ing] the earliest versions of the Faust myth," see *The Faust Myth: Religion and the Rise of Representation* (New York: Palgrave Macmillan, 2007). For an earlier version of the argument in this chapter, see Laura Levine, "Danger in Words: Faustus, Slade and the Demonologists," 47–60 in *Magical Transformations on the Early Modern English Stage*, ed. Lisa Hopkins and Helen Ostovich (Farnham, UK: Ashgate, 2014). Finally, for Jay Zysk's depiction of Faustus's "priest envy" ("while Doctor Faustus does not desire to become a priest he wants to participate in a linguistic economy in which to say something is to do something"), see his argument in *Shadow and Substance: Eucharistic Controversy and English Drama Across the Reformation Divide* (Notre Dame, IN: University of Notre Dame Press, 2017), 128–29 and more generally 119–54. For his discussion of the way "the missal's rubrics are designed to ward off . . . errors in the performance of liturgical ceremony" as the kinds of infelicities Austin describes in Lectures II and III, see 138–39.

4. See Leah S. Marcus, "Textual Indeterminacy and Ideological Difference: The Case of *Doctor Faustus*" in Renaissance Drama, New Series 20 (1989), 1–29.

5. In looking at early modern law as a lens through which to view *Faustus*, I am anticipated by Luke Wilson's fine book, *Theaters of Intention: Drama and the Law in Early Modern England* (Stanford, CA: Stanford University Press, 2000). In a series of important arguments, Wilson documents both the intricacies of Slade's case and his reading of their implications for Marlowe's play. My argument differs from his both in what it

seeks to explain in *Faustus* and in what it reads Slade's case *for*: where Wilson seeks to establish the growing emphasis on "intention" as one of the implications of Slade's case, and to identify notions of "subsequence" and "temporality" implicit in the idea of a promise as another, I read Slade's case for the specific tensions created by competing notions of contractual obligation. Where he reads *Faustus* as "generat[ing] . . . a web of intentional action dense enough to create the appearance that agency of any kind can in fact be made visible" (201), and where he reads Faustus himself as one of a number of "dramatic characters presented as imagining themselves distended in time" (205), I read *Faustus* for its response to the epistemological anxiety generated by these conflicting notions of obligation. Finally, I invoke the phrases "promise" and "breach of promise" as ways of visualizing *assumpsit*.

For Graham Hammill's landmark reading of the "commodification" of Faustus's soul and his rejection of the "theology of the gift," see "Faustus's Fortunes: Commodification, Exchange, and the Form of Literary Subjectivity," *English Literary History* 63, no. 2 (1996): 309–36.

6. Among the numerous critics who have commented on Faustus' various omissions and misconstructions of the texts he cites, see in particularly David Riggs and Edward Snow. For Riggs's analysis of the way "the devil's syllogism exposed a grave contradiction in Calvinist doctrine" (241) and (more broadly) his discussion of the way Faustus' mistranslations and truncations of texts are part of a larger demystification of Calvinist theology, see *The World of Christopher Marlowe* (New York: Henry Holt, 2004), 236–49. For Edward Snow's discussion of what "being and not being" connotes for Faustus (not "the metaphysical and ontological" issues at the heart of ancient Greek philosophy, "but merely the formal, scholastic paradigms by which logical disputation is taught and mastered"), see "Marlowe's *Doctor Faustus* and the Ends of Desire," 70–110, especially 76, in *Two Renaissance Mythmakers: Christopher Marlowe and Ben Jonson*, ed. Alvin B. Kernan (Baltimore: Johns Hopkins University Press, 1977). For the claim that the "specialized idioms of metaphysics, logic, ethics, medicine, law and Christian theology" each imply "its own world and world view" and for the way Faustus's translation (or mistranslation) of these seems "to have no point of view of its own, no commitment to any particular world view or governing set of values," see 75.

7. For Marjorie Garber, Faustus's "anagrammatising" of the name of God is effectively an instance of "unwriting," since in contrast to either English or German characters, "Hebrew writing is backward, its characters inscribed from right to left upon the page" (311). See Garber's "Here's Nothing Writ: Scribe, Script and Circumscription in Marlowe's Plays," *Theatre Journal* 36, no. 3 (1984): 301–20.

8. James VI, *Daemonologie*, 16–17.

9. See David Ibbetson, "Sixteenth Century Contract Law: Slade's Case in Context," 302–3 and more generally 295–318, *Oxford Journal of Legal Studies* 4, no. 3 (Winter 1984). See John Baker, "New Light on *Slade's Case*," *Collected Papers on English Legal History*, Cambridge: Cambridge University Press (2013), 1161–62 and more generally 1129–75, for a more detailed description. See too Allen D. Boyer, *Sir Edward Coke and the Elizabethan Age* (Stanford, CA: Stanford University Press, 2003) for a discussion of some of the same events. Suggestively Boyer points out a concern on Coke's part for "aligning the assumptions on which the law operated with the assumptions on which commerce functioned," 131–34.

10. See Coke's claim "that every contract executory importeth in it self an *Assumpsit*" in Slade's case *The Selected Writings of Sir Edward Coke*, vol. 1, ed. Steve Sheppard (Indianapolis, IN: Liberty Fund, 2003), 121.

11. David Harris Sacks argues: "Since there was no allegation of subsequent promise by the defendant, it was necessary for Slade's lawyers to collapse together the contract and the promise to perform it, thereby treating the making of a contract as the equivalent of a speech act" (36). But David Ibbetson gives a more sweeping analysis of the way the requirement for a subsequent promise went in and out of focus even in the decades before *Slade's Case*. As early as the 1560s, the Court of Common Pleas and the King's Bench differed in their attitudes toward whether it was necessary for the existence of a subsequent promise to be proved, in order to sue in *assumpsit*, Common Pleas requiring proof that the subsequent promise had been made, the King's Bench requiring only proof of a contract. Because of this polarization, Ibbetson says that "a certain wooliness of thinking" came to characterize legal arguments in the 1570s. By the 1580s, the issue of whether *assumpsit* required an express promise gradually replaced the issue of whether *assumpsit* required a subsequent promise. Paradoxically, within five years of *Slade's Case*, the case itself came to be associated with the issue of subsequent promises again, even though this was not what the two courts argued about. See Sacks's "The Promise and the Contract in Early Modern England: Slade's Case in Perspective," in *Rhetoric and Law in Early Modern Europe*, ed. Victoria Kahn and Lorna Hutson (New Haven, CT: Yale University Press, 2001) and Ibbetson, 297, 315 and 316.

12. Baker says, "The essence of the Common Pleas' objection to the indiscriminate use of actions on the case was that they were (by definition) special remedies, to be brought into operation only in cases where the general writs in the Register were inappropriate," 1152.

13. The original statute is presumably Westminster II, c.24. See Baker's discussion, 1152.

14. Baker comments, "The former was not uncommon, but the latter would 'confound' the *Register*," 1154.

15. See Ibbetson, who says the King's Bench "questioned the premise that no two forms of action could flow from the same cause of action," 298.

16. Baker comments, "It is unlikely that the debate was principally motivated by the jealous preservation of jurisdictional boundaries for the sake of revenue from fees," 1150.

17. Sacks, "The Promise and the Contract," 36.

18. Private communication with Charles Donahue, Paul A. Freund Professor of Law at Harvard.

19. Sacks, citing this passage, includes Coke's words, "And these words *assumpsit*, *promisit* and *agreeavit* are all synonymous and of one signification. Would you have every plain man use the proper words 'I assume' and 'I take upon myself'? It is not necessary" (Sacks, 36).

20. See Austin, *How to Do Things with Words*, 69–73.

21. Ibbetson says that "the significant point of *Slade's Case* was not that it allowed an action on an implied promise, but that it did not insist on a separation between the causes of action in debt and *assumpsit*," 315.

22. On the lack of unanimity in the final decision, see Ibbetson, who says, "Despite the impression given by the reports of the judgment that this was a unanimous opinion, it appears that it was in fact reached by a simple majority of six to five" (303) and Baker, who says, "Coke related the decision as being that of all the judges of England, and the same impression was conveyed by Chief Justice Popham in his curt announcement of 9 November 1602. Nevertheless, searches have failed to reveal any intimation by the judges of the Common Pleas that they had reversed their former opinions, or even that they had reluctantly decided not to press their views. What is more, the Statutory Exchequer Chamber continued to reverse King's Bench judgments in *assumpsit* for debt while the informal assembly was considering *Slade's Case*," 1168–69. See Baker 1130, 1168, and 1172 for discussions of Coke's Report in relation to his own arguments and 1132 for his description of the "irresistible conclusion that Coke's report is in fact a polished redaction of his own speeches for the plaintiff."

23. Bodin, *Demonomanie*, 20, 56.

24. For Eire's discussions of Zwingli and Calvin on the human tendency to substitute a false god for God, see 84 and 208–9 respectively.

25. Interestingly, Austin arrives at a similar sentiment at the end of lecture 11 about both performatives and constatives—that they are in fact ideals or abstractions. "What then finally is left of the distinction of the performative and constative utterance?" he asks. See Austin, *How to Do Things with Words*, 144–45, and chapter 2, note 6 for my discussion of Austin's answer.

## 8. Paulina and the Theater of Shame

1. All quotations taken from *The Winter's Tale: The Oxford Shakespeare*, ed. Stephen Orgel (Oxford: Oxford University Press, 1996). For a fuller account of Scot's "position," see chapter 3.

2. For the landmark essay on *The Winter's Tale* as "a study of skepticism—that is, as a response to what skepticism is a response to" and its claim that "its second half must be understandable as a study of its search for recovery," recovery consisting not in refutation but in "reconceiving," see Stanley Cavell's "Recounting Gains, Showing Losses: Reading in *The Winter's Tale*" in *Disowning Knowledge*, 2nd ed. (Cambridge: Cambridge University Press, 2003), 193–221.

3. See Orgel's brilliant comments on these lines and the "myself unbreeched" passage as "a particularly subversive view of [the] fantasy of freedom, the return to childhood" in "The Performance of Desire," 15–16. See too his fascinating "Mankind Witches," both in *Impersonations: The Performance of Gender in Shakespeare's England* (Cambridge: Cambridge University Press, 1996), 10–30 and 106–36. For other treatments of *The Winter's Tale* which in one way or the other identify patriarchy's misogynistic construct of women in the play as witches, see David Schalkwyk, "'A Lady's "Verily" Is as Potent as a Lord's': Women, Word, and Witchcraft in *The Winter's Tale*," *English Literary Renaissance* 22, no. 2 (1992): 242–72, for the claim that the designation "witch" is an "act of political violence perpetrated upon those, especially women, who threaten the patriarchal state and its metaphysics of blood" (267), and Kirstie Gulick Rosenfield, "Nursing Nothing: Witchcraft and Female Sexuality in *The Winter's Tale*," *Mosaic* 35, no. 1 (2002): 95–112. See as well D'Orsay W. Pearson's "Witchcraft in *The Winter's Tale*: Paulina as

'Alcahueta y vn Poquito Hechizera," *Shakespeare Studies* 12 (1979): 195–214 for the depiction of Paulina as an "urban witch." For a fascinating reading of the gendering of ghosts, see Frances E. Dolan, "Hermione's Ghost: Catholicism, the Feminine, and the Undead," in *The Impact of Feminism in English Renaissance Studies*, ed. Dympna Callaghan (New York: Palgrave Macmillan, 2007), 213–37.

4. See Orgel's influential discussion of the inconsistencies between III.ii and V.iii. For him these are evidence "not that at the play's conclusion, Hermione really is a statue come to life (we have the word of Hermione herself that this is not the case), but that Shakespearian drama does not create a consistent world. Rather it continually adjusts its reality according to the demands of its developing argument" (*The Winter's Tale: The Oxford Shakespeare*, 36). Other critics have imagined a Shakespeare who only allows us to participate "emotionally" but not cognitively in that argument. See Verna A. Foster, "The 'Death' of Hermione: Tragicomic Dramaturgy in *The Winter's Tale*," *Cahiers Élisabéthains: Late Medieval and Renaissance Studies* 43 (1993): 43–56. Among the many other critics who deal with anxious masculinity in the play, see particularly Janet Adelman, *Suffocating Mothers: Fantasies of Maternal Origin in Shakespeare's Plays*, Hamlet to The Tempest (New York: Routledge, 1991), 220–36, and Valerie Traub, "Jewels, Statues, and Corpses: Containment of Female Erotic Power in Shakespeare's Plays," *Shakespeare Studies* 20 (Jan. 1, 1988), 215–38, especially 228–33.

5. "Is this nothing? / Why, then the world and all that's in't is nothing" (I.ii.289–90), Leontes says in an almost direct echo of Troilus. For the anomalousness of Paulina as a female advisor, see Carolyn Asp, "Shakespeare's Paulina and the *Consolatio* Tradition," *Shakespeare Studies* 11 (1978): 145–58.

6. Two influential treatments of Paulina's and Hermione's speech in the play which have tended to focus on both the citational and fallible nature of words are David Schalkwyk's analysis of the "crisis of semiosis" generated by Leontes's inability to trust the word of women and what Lynn Enterline calls "the dream of a voice so persuasive it can effect the changes of which it speaks" (40), a dream destined to fail, at least partially. Enterline's reading ironizes at least to some extent Neely's claim that "Paulina's spell then effects the final transition from stillness to motion. . . . Language coerces reality; the statue is Hermione; art is nature" (254). See Carol Thomas Neely, "*The Winter's Tale*: The Triumph of Speech," in *The Winter's Tale: Critical Essays*, ed. Maurice Hunt (New York: Garland Publishing, 1995), 243–57; and Lynn Enterline, "'You Speak a Language That I Understand Not': The Rhetoric of Animation in *The Winter's Tale*," *Shakespeare Quarterly* 48, no. 1 (1997): 17–44. See also Howard Felperin on the problem of "linguistic indeterminacy" in the play in "'Tongue-tied, our queen?': The Deconstruction of Presence in *The Winter's Tale*," in *Shakespeare and the Question of Theory*, ed. Patricia Parker and Geoffrey Hartman (London: Methuen, 1985), 3–18.

7. Neely says of Hermione: "She has, in a sense, become an actor in a play directed by Leontes; but neither history nor drama can reveal the truth about her 'past life' or the depth of her present grief. . . . Language having doubly failed Hermione, it is her persistent hope and faith that she be *seen*" (Neely, "*The Winter's Tale*," 247).

8. Among the many treatments of the play which in one way or another articulate the case Shakespeare makes for theater in the statue scene, see Enterline on the role the idea of the living statue plays in "Shakespeare's claims for the theater" in "'You Speak a Language,'" as well as Kenneth Gross's discussion to which Enterline alludes. Kenneth Gross, *The Dream of the Moving Statue* (Ithaca, NY: Cornell University Press, 1992), 114–

15. For the claim that *The Winter's Tale* offers a "defense" of theater, see Rosenfield, "Nursing Nothing." For important arguments on other ways in which the scene celebrates the powers of art, see Bruce R. Smith's insightful comparison of sculpture to theater in "Sermons in Stones: Shakespeare and Renaissance Sculpture," *Shakespeare Studies* 17 (1985): 1–23 and Leonard Barkan's landmark essay "'Living Sculptures': Ovid, Michelangelo, and *The Winter's Tale*," in *English Literary History* 48, no. 4 (1987): 639–67. Finally, see Julia Reinhard Lupton's beautiful treatment of the way "the statue scene is, sublimely, both a metatheatrical and an antitheatrical moment . . . metatheatrical insofar as Shakespeare breaks Leontes' illusion and ours in the same gesture [but] . . . more deeply and more essentially, *antitheatrical*, insofar as Hermione's personifying of the statue allows her to reclaim and maintain, to distill and transmit, a quotient of that reserve she had regained in her wintry seclusion" in *Thinking With Shakespeare: Essays on Politics and Life* (Chicago: University of Chicago Press, 2011), 180. See too Lupton's earlier treatment of the way that just as Giulio Romano appears as "the fashioner of *theatrical spaces for sculpture*," the evocation of his name in the play prepares us to "take the actor's living body as the stony replica of Hermione" in *Afterlives of the Saints: Hagiography, Typology, and Renaissance Literature* (Stanford, CA: Stanford University Press, 1996), 213.

## Epilogue

1. All quotations taken from *The Tempest: The Oxford Shakespeare*, ed. Stephen Orgel (Oxford: Oxford University Press, 1998).

2. Among those critics who read Prospero's reversal as inauthentic or in some other way call it into question, Stephen Orgel describes Prospero forgiving his brother in act 5 as "enunciated . . . and qualified at once . . . reconsidered as more crimes are remembered . . . all but withdrawn . . . and only then confirmed through forcing Antonio to relinquish the dukedom, an act that is presented as something he does unwillingly" (11). "Prospero," Orgel says, "has not regained his lost dukedom, he has usurped his brother's . . . giving away Miranda is a means of preserving his authority, not of relinquishing it" (12). See Orgel, "Prospero's Wife," *Representations* 8 (1984): 1–13, especially 11–12. Differently, Harry Berger says of the "With my nobler reason 'gainst my fury / Do I take part" speech that Prospero is "selecting, rather than experiencing, his response. And the next statement is not so much a sententious commonplace as it is the critical musing of an artist or playwright aiming at the right touch." Of "The rarer action is / In virtue than in vengeance," Berger says, "His attention here is to the dramatic moment: it will make a better effect, because unexpected." Harry Berger Jr., "Miraculous Harp: A Reading of Shakespeare's *Tempest*," *Shakespeare Studies* 5 (1969): 253–83, especially 274. Brian Sutton (in the context of comparing Prospero to Joseph in the Old Testament) concludes that characters throughout the play are not ultimately repentant. See Sutton's "'Virtue Rather Than Vengeance': *Genesis* and Shakespeare's *The Tempest*," *The Explicator* 66, no. 4 (2008): 224–29.

Among the proliferation of critics who read the reversal as genuine, see particularly Margareta de Grazia's claim that "Gonzalo's importance especially can hardly be overstated, for it is Ariel's report chiefly describing him that moves Prospero to decide to forgive, and it is the sight of Gonzalo himself that moves him actually to forgive" (261), in de Grazia, "*The Tempest*: Gratuitous Movement or Action without Kibes and Pinches," *Shakespeare Studies* 14 (1981): 249–65. See also Michael Neill's "Remembrance and Revenge: *Hamlet, Macbeth* and *The Tempest*," in *Jonson and Shakespeare*, ed. Ian Donaldson (London: Palgrave Macmillan, 1983), 35–56, especially 47, in which Prospero is "a reformed revenger who finds 'the rarer action is / in virtue than in vengeance.'" For Orgel's response to de Grazia, see 22, footnote 1 in his edition of *The Tempest*.

3. For Neill, "The whole play might be read as a gloss on Donne's luminous aphorism 'the art of *salvation*, is but the art of *memory*'" ("Remembrance and Revenge," 45–46). He calls the usurped in revenge plays the "remembrancer," a "representative of the old order, whose duty is to recuperate history from the infective oblivion into which his antagonist has cast it" (36). Prospero is a remembrancer "whose very name suggests hope for the future" (46). In a very different way, Berger connects Prospero's "excessive idealism" with "the longing for the golden age, a state of mind based on unrealistic expectations" (258).

4. For Barbara Mowat, not the suddenness of this part of the renunciation but the suddenness of Prospero's renunciation of magic makes him "reminiscent of such commedia dell'arte magicians as the magician-hero in 'Pantaloonlet,' who after having used his magic to bring about a happy ending for himself, his friends and his daughter, abruptly declares that 'he does not wish to practice his magic art any longer.'" Barbara A. Mowat, "Prospero, Agrippa, and Hocus Pocus," *English Literary Renaissance* 11, no. 3 (1981): 281–303, especially 292.

5. Orgel says of the "they being penitent" speech, "The assertion opens with a conditional clause whose conditions are not met: Alonso is penitent, but the chief villain, the usurping younger brother Antonio, remains obdurate. Nothing, not all Prospero's magic, can redeem Antonio from his essential badness. . . . Perhaps, too, penitence is not what Prospero's magic is designed to elicit from his brother" (10). Berger says, "Ariel has said nothing about their being penitent; he said they were distracted, that is enchanted" ("Miraculous Harp," 273). Berger adds, "Prospero's 'they being penitent' is also an unwarranted inference which tells us less about the inner state of his enemies than about the state he wants to produce in them by his magical spectacles and illusions" (274). "Neither Antonio nor Sebastian gives any sign of remorse" (275).

6. For Sarah Beckwith, Prospero's vulnerability is always compromised: "It is as if he can reveal himself in his vulnerability as the one wronged only when [others] cannot see him, when they cannot therefore acknowledge him as the one they have wronged" (169). Sarah Beckwith, *Shakespeare and the Grammar of Forgiveness* (Ithaca, NY: Cornell University Press, 2011), 147–72.

7. For other arguments that take up the topic of anti-theatricality in relation to *The Tempest*, see Heather James, "Dido's Ear: Tragedy and the Politics of Response," *Shakespeare Quarterly* 52, no. 3 (Fall 2001): 360–82, though James is primarily concerned with anti-theatrical anxiety in relation to Miranda. See also Reut Barzilai's "'In My Power': *The Tempest* as Shakespeare's Antitheatrical Vision," *Shakespeare* 15, no. 4 (2019): 379–97. Barzilai doesn't account for Prospero's disclosure of his illusions as illusions.

8. Mowat cites the narrative tradition of the repentant wizard, the friar who "cries out upon himself," in which tradition she locates Greene's Bacon, although even she acknowledges that the "real-life Friar Roger Bacon never admitted that his 'magic' studies were evil." See "Prospero, Agrippa, and Hocus Pocus," 291.

9. Mowat makes this point in a different context. "Although the magician is here summoning a spirit, we are clearly not in the world of spirit-summonings inhabited

by 'callers and conjurors of wicked and damned Sprites'"; Prospero "is Ariel's 'great master'; Ariel is Prospero's industrious 'Servant,' 'correspondent to command'" ("Prospero, Agrippa, and Hocus Pocus," 293). In both this essay and in "Prospero's Book" (*Shakespeare Quarterly* 52, no. 1 [2001]: 1–33), Mowat makes the case for Prospero as eluding the rigid boundaries of either the "Renaissance philosopher-magus" or the "damned sorcerer" ("Prospero, Agrippa, and Hocus Pocus," 282). Toward the end of the earlier article she makes a case for the relationship between Prospero and Ariel as that of a master and "servant boy ready for his freedom" and even more specifically for the relationship between the "art-Magician" or "Jugler" and his assistant (297, 300–303). "Prospero's Book" imagines the book Prospero might have consulted and ultimately promised to drown through two grimoires (that contained in Reginald Scot's book 15 and the Folger's MSVb26). Mowat says, "Prospero's book leads us neither to Neoplatonic/Cabalistic magic nor to witchcraft, the two kinds of magic that are most often described in *The Tempest*. Instead, his book as grimoire takes us to a tremendously important third category, that of 'magician' or 'necromancer'" ("Prospero's Book," 25). See Stephen Orgel's "Secret Arts and Public Spectacles: The Parameters of Elizabethan Magic," *Shakespeare Quarterly* 68, no. 1 (2017): 80–91, for his response and for the argument that "Magic in the play may be a metaphor, for authority, power, literacy. But in this society, it is also magic, and magic books are in themselves magic (they don't simply teach you how to do it)" (83). For his claim that "the transition from *Doctor Faustus* to *The Tempest* in only two decades records something like a paradigm shift," see "Tobacco and Boys: How Queer Was Marlowe?" in *GLQ: A Journal of Lesbian and Gay Studies* 6, no. 4 (Sept. 1, 2000), 555–76.

10. See chapter 3 and chapter 5 of this work.

11. In many ways the scene draws on notions of conjuring in the ways that James describes conjuring in book 1, chapter 5 of *Daemonologie*. Describing the circles that conjurors draw, Epistemon says there are four principal parts to conjuration: the person of the conjuror, the action of conjuration, the words and rites used, and the spirits who are raised. We see three of these things in V.i.—the person of the conjuror in Prospero, the action of conjuration, and the words and rites used (the former borrowed from Ovid's *Medea*). But although Prospero addresses various elves and minor spirits in this scene, he doesn't exactly invoke them. In any case, no spirits arrive. Ariel, who is not a devil, is already there. And although Sebastian says "the devil speaks" in Prospero, no devils appear.

12. To this set of circles, Berger adds Sycorax's hoop and de Grazia adds the concentric circles of Prospero's cape, cell, "line-grove," and the island itself. She says that "on the island, [Prospero's] magic . . . hems him in with four concentric circles. . . . By breaking or untying his spell . . . he begins to free himself also from self-containing magic, thereby averting the fate of Sycorax who 'with age and envy / Was grown into a hoop'" ("Gratuitous Movement," 261). Berger says of Prospero's magic circle, "The magic circle is a pastoral kingdom . . . a version of what Erik Erikson calls the microsphere, 'the small world of manageable toys' which the child establishes . . . to 'play at doing something that was in reality done to him'" (261).

# Bibliography

Adelman, Janet. *Suffocating Mothers: Fantasies of Maternal Origin in Shakespeare's Plays, Hamlet to the Tempest.* New York: Routledge, 1991.
Aers, David, and Sarah Beckwith. "The Eucharist." In *Cultural Reformations: Medieval and Renaissance in Literary History*, edited by James Simpson and Brian Cummings. Oxford: Oxford University Press, 2010.
Almond, Philip C. *England's First Demonologist: Reginald Scot & The Discoverie of Witchcraft.* London: I. B. Tauris, 2014.
Anglo, Sydney. "Evident Authority and Authoritative Evidence: The *Malleus Maleficarum*." In *The Damned Art: Essays in the Literature of Witchcraft*, edited by Sydney Anglo. London: Routledge, 1977.
———. "Reginald Scot's *Discoverie of Witchcraft*: Scepticism and Sadduceeism." In *The Damned Art: Essays in the Literature of Witchcraft*, edited by Sydney Anglo. London: Routledge, 1977.
Asp, Carolyn. "Shakespeare's Paulina and the *Consolatio* Tradition." *Shakespeare Studies* 11 (1978): 145–58.
"Assumpsit in Lieu of Debt." In *Baker and Milsom Sources of English Legal History.* 2nd ed. Compiled by John Baker. Oxford: Oxford University Press, 2010.
Aston, Margaret. *England's Iconoclasts, Volume 1: Laws against Images.* Oxford: Oxford University Press, 2003.
Austin, J. L. *How to Do Things with Words.* 2nd ed. Edited by J. O. Urmson and Marina Sbisà. Cambridge, MA: Harvard University Press, 1975.
Bahr, Stephanie. "'Ne spared they to strip her naked all': Reading, Rape, and Reformation in Spenser's *Faerie Queene*." *Studies in Philology* 117, no. 2 (2020): 285–312.
Baker, John. "New Light on *Slade's Case*." *Collected Papers on English Legal History.* Cambridge: Cambridge University Press (2013): 1129–75.
Barkan, Leonard. "'Living Sculptures': Ovid, Michelangelo, and *The Winter's Tale*." *English Literary History* 48, no. 4 (1987): 639–67.
Barzilai, Reut. "'In My Power': *The Tempest* as Shakespeare's Antitheatrical Vision." *Shakespeare* 15, no. 4 (2019): 379–97.
Beckwith, Sarah. *Shakespeare and the Grammar of Forgiveness.* Ithaca, NY: Cornell University Press, 2011.
———. "Stephen Greenblatt's *Hamlet* and the Forms of Oblivion." *Journal of Medieval and Early Modern Studies* 33, no. 2 (2003): 261–80.
Belsey, Catherine. *The Subject of Tragedy: Identity and Difference in Renaissance Drama.* London: Methuen, 1985.

Berger Jr., Harry. "Archimago: Between Text and Countertext." *Studies in English Literature* 43, no. 1 (Winter 2003): 19–64.

———. "Miraculous Harp: A Reading of Shakespeare's *Tempest*." *Shakespeare Studies* 5 (1969): 253–83.

Blair, Ann. *The Theater of Nature: Jean Bodin and Renaissance Science*. Princeton, NJ: Princeton University Press, 1997.

Bodin, Jean. *De la Demonomanie des Sorciers*. Paris: Chez Iacques du-Puys, 1587. https://archive.org/details/BodinDemonomanieBNF1587/page/n1/mode/2up.

———. *On the Demon-Mania of Witches*. Translated by Randy A. Scott. Toronto: Centre for Reformation and Renaissance Studies, 1995.

Boyer, Allen D. *Sir Edward Coke and the Elizabethan Age*. Stanford, CA: Stanford University Press, 2003.

Bray, Gerald, ed. *Documents of the English Reformation*. 3rd ed. Cambridge: Lutterworth Press, 1994.

*A briefe Description of the Notorious Life of John Lambe, Otherwise Called Doctor Lambe, Together with his Ignominious Death*. Amsterdam [i.e., London], 1628.

Broedel, Hans Peter. *The Malleus Maleficarum and the Construction of Witchcraft*. Manchester: Manchester University Press, 2003.

Bucer, Martin, Jacobus Bedrotus, and William Marshall. "A Treatise Declarying and Shewing . . . That Pyctures & Other Ymages . . . Ar in No Wise to Be Suffred in the Temples or Churches of Christen Men." *Letters and Papers, Foreign and Domestic, of the Reign of Henry VIII*, IX nos. 357–58. Edited by J. S. Brewer. J Gairdner, and R. H. Brodie. London: 1892–1910. STC 24238-9.

Campana, Joseph. *The Pain of Reformation: Spenser, Vulnerability, and the Ethics of Masculinity*. New York: Fordham University Press, 2012.

Cavanagh, Sheila. *Wanton Eyes and Chaste Desires*. Bloomington: Indiana University Press, 1994.

Cavell, Stanley. *Disowning Knowledge*. 2nd ed. Cambridge: Cambridge University Press, 2003.

Certeau, Michel de. *The Possession at Loudon*. Translated by Michael B. Smith. Chicago: University of Chicago Press, 2000.

Clark, Stuart. "Inversion, Misrule and the Meaning of Witchcraft." *Past and Present* 87 (1980): 98–127.

———. "King James's *Daemonologie*: Witchcraft and Kingship." In *The Damned Art: Essays in the Literature of Witchcraft*, edited by Sydney Anglo, 156–81. London: Routledge, 1977.

———, ed. *Languages of Witchcraft: Narratives, Ideology and Meaning in Early Modern Culture*. New York: St Martin's Press, 2001.

———. "The Scientific Status of Demonology." In *Occult and Scientific Mentalities in the Renaissance*, edited by Brian Vickers, 351–74. Cambridge: Cambridge University Press, 1984.

———. *Thinking with Demons: The Idea of Witchcraft in Early Modern Europe*. Oxford: Oxford University Press, 1999.

———. *Vanities of the Eye: Vision in Early Modern European Culture*. Oxford: Oxford University Press, 2007.

Coke, Edward. *The Selected Writings of Sir Edward Coke*. Vol. 1. Edited by Steve Sheppard. Indianapolis, IN: Liberty Fund, 2003.

Culler, Jonathan. "Convention and Meaning: Derrida and Austin." *New Literary History* 13, no. 1 (1981): 15–30.
Darr, Orna Alyagon. *Marks of an Absolute Witch: Evidentiary Dilemmas in Early Modern England*. Burlington, VT: Ashgate, 2006.
Daston, Lorraine, and Katharine Park. *Wonders and the Order of Nature 1150–1750*. New York: Zone Books, 1998.
De Grazia, Margareta. "The Tempest: Gratuitous Movement or Action without Kibes and Pinches." *Shakespeare Studies* 14 (1981): 249–65.
DeNeef, A. Leigh. *Spenser and the Motives of Metaphor*. Durham, NC: Duke University Press, 1982.
Dolan, Frances E. *Dangerous Familiars: Representations of Domestic Crime in England, 1550–1700*. Ithaca, NY: Cornell University Press, 1994.
——. "'Gentlemen, I have one more thing to say': Women on Scaffolds in England 1563–1680." *Modern Philology* 92, no. 2 (1994): 157–78.
——. "Hermione's Ghost: Catholicism, the Feminine, and the Undead." In *The Impact of Feminism in English Renaissance Studies*, edited by Dympna Callaghan. New York: Palgrave Macmillan, 2007
——. "Reading, Writing and other Crimes." In *Feminist Readings of Early Modern Culture: Emerging Subjects*, edited by Valerie Traub, M. Lindsay Kaplan, and Dympna Callaghan, 142–67. Cambridge: Cambridge University Press, 1996.
——. "'Ridiculous Fictions': Making Distinctions in the Discourses of Witchcraft." *Differences* 7, no. 2 (1995): 82–110.
——. *Whores of Babylon: Catholicism, Gender, and Seventeenth-Century Print Culture*. Ithaca, NY: Cornell University Press, 1999.
Duffy, Eamon. *The Stripping of the Altars: Traditional Religion in England 1400–1580*. New Haven, CT: Yale University Press, 1992.
Eggert, Katherine. "Spenser's Ravishment: Rape and Rapture in *The Faerie Queene*." *Representations* 70 (Spring 2000): 1–26.
Eire, Carlos M. N. *Reformations: The Early Modern World, 1450–1650*. New Haven, CT: Yale University Press, 2016.
——. *War against the Idols: The Reformation of Worship from Erasmus to Calvin*. Cambridge: Cambridge University Press, 1986.
Enterline, Lynn. "'You Speak a Language That I Understand Not': The Rhetoric of Animation in *The Winter's Tale*." *Shakespeare Quarterly* 48, no. 1 (1997): 17–44.
Estes, Leland L. "His *Discoverie of Witchcraft*: Religion and Science in the Opposition to the European Witch Craze." *Church History* 52 (1983): 444–56.
Evennett, H. Outram. *The Spirit of the Counter-Reformation*. Edited by John Bossy. Notre Dame, IN: University of Notre Dame Press, 1970.
Felperin, Howard. "'Tongue-tied, our queen?': The Deconstruction of Presence in *The Winter's Tale*." In *Shakespeare and the Question of Theory*, edited by Patricia Parker and Geoffrey Hartman. London: Methuen, 1985.
Fischlin, Daniel. "'Counterfeiting God': James VI (I) and the Politics of *Dæmonologie* (1597)." *The Journal of Narrative Technique* 26, no. 1 (1996): 1–29.
Floyd-Wilson, Mary. *Knowledge, Science and Gender on the Shakespearean Stage*. Cambridge: Cambridge University Press, 2013.

Foster, Verna A. "The 'Death' of Hermione: Tragicomic Dramaturgy in *The Winter's Tale*." *Cahiers Élisabéthains: Late Medieval and Renaissance Studies* 43 (April 1993): 43–56.
Foucault, Michel. *Discipline and Punish: The Birth of the Prison*. Translated by Alan Sheridan. New York: Vintage Books, 1977.
———. *The Order of Things: An Archaeology of the Human Sciences*. New York: Vintage Books, 1973.
Frazier, Sir James George. *The Golden Bough*. New York: Macmillan, 1960.
Gallagher, Catherine, and Stephen Greenblatt. *Practicing New Historicism*. Chicago: University of Chicago Press, 2000.
Garber, Marjorie. "Here's Nothing Writ: Scribe, Script and Circumscription in Marlowe's Plays." *Theatre Journal* 36, no. 3 (1984): 301–20.
Gaskill, Malcolm. "Witches and Witnesses in Old and New England." In *Languages of Witchcraft: Narratives, Ideology and Meaning in Early Modern Culture*, edited by Stuart Clark. New York: St Martin's Press, 2001.
Gates, Daniel. "Unpardonable Sins: The Hazards of Performative Language in the Tragic Cases of Francesco Spiera and *Doctor Faustus*." *Comparative Drama* 38 (2004): 59–81.
Gibson, Marion. "Understanding Witchcraft? Accusers' Stories in Print in Early Modern England." In *Languages of Witchcraft: Narrative, Ideology and Meaning in Early Modern Culture*, edited by Stuart Clark. New York: St. Martin's Press, 2001.
Gilman, Ernest B. *Iconoclasm and Poetry in the English Reformation: Down Went Dagon*. Chicago: University of Chicago Press, 1986.
Ginzburg, Carlo. *Ecstasies: Deciphering the Witches' Sabbath*. Translated by Raymond Rosenthal. Chicago: University of Chicago Press, 1989.
———. *The Night Battles: Witchcraft and Agrarian Cults in the Sixteenth and Seventeenth Centuries*. Translated by John Tedeschi and Anne C. Tedeschi. Baltimore, MD: Johns Hopkins University Press, 1983.
Goldberg, Jonathan. *Endlesse Worke: Spenser and the Structures of Discourse*. Baltimore, MD: Johns Hopkins University Press, 1981.
Goodare, Julian. "The Scottish Witchcraft Panic of 1597." In *The Scottish Witch-Hunt in Context*, edited by Julian Goodare. Manchester: Manchester University Press, 2002.
Gosson, Stephen. *Playes Confuted in five Actions*. In *Markets of Bawdrie: The Dramatic Criticism of Stephen Gosson*. Edited by Arthur F. Kinney. Salzburg Studies in Literature, vol. 4, 138–200. Salzburg: Institut für Englische Sprache und Literatur, 1974.
———. *The School of Abuse, containing a Pleasant Invective against Poets, Pipers, Players, Jesters, &c*. London: Shakespeare Society, 1841. First published 1579.
Gough, Melinda J. "'Her filthy feature open showne' in Ariosto, Spenser and *Much Ado about Nothing*." *Studies in English Literature, 1500–1900* 39, no. 1 (1999): 41–67.
Greenblatt, Stephen. "Loudon and London." *Critical Inquiry* 12 (Winter 1986): 326–46.
———. "Shakespeare Bewitched." In *New Historical Literary Study: Essays on Reproducing Texts, Representing History*, edited by Jeffery N. Cox and Larry J. Reynolds. Princeton, NJ: Princeton University Press, 1993.
———. *Shakespearean Negotiations: The Circulation of Social Energy in Renaissance England*. Berkeley: University of California Press, 1988.
Gross, Kenneth. *The Dream of the Moving Statue*. Ithaca, NY: Cornell University Press, 1992.

———. *Spenserian Poetics: Idolatry, Iconoclasm & Magic.* Ithaca, NY: Cornell University Press, 1985.

Guenther, Genevieve. "Why Devils Came When Faustus Called Them." *Modern Philology* 109, no.1 (2011): 46–70.

Hammill, Graham. "Faustus's Fortunes: Commodification, Exchange and the Form of Literary Subjectivity." *English Literary History* 63, no. 2 (1996): 309–36.

Hanson, Elizabeth. *Discovering the Subject in Renaissance England.* Cambridge: Cambridge University Press, 1998.

Hawkes, David. *The Faust Myth: Religion and the Rise of Representation.* New York: Palgrave Macmillan, 2007.

Herzig, Tamar. "Fear and Devotion in the Writing of Heinrich Institoris." In *Emotions in the History of Witchcraft*, edited by Laura Kounine and Michael Ostling. Houndmills, UK: Palgrave Macmillan, 2016.

———. "Witches, Saints and Heretics: Heinrich Kramer's Ties with Italian Women Mystics." *Magic, Ritual and Witchcraft* 1, no.1 (2006): 24–55.

Hutson, Lorna. *The Invention of Suspicion: Law and Mimesis in Shakespeare and Renaissance Drama.* Oxford: Oxford University Press, 2007.

Ibbetston, David. "Sixteenth Century Contract Law: Slade's Case in Context." *Oxford Journal of Legal Studies* 4, no. 3 (Winter 1984): 295–318.

Institoris, Henricus (Heinrich Kramer), and Jacobus Sprenger. *Malleus Maleficarum, Vol. 1: The Latin Text.* Edited by Christopher Mackay. Cambridge: Cambridge University Press, 2006.

———. *The Malleus Maleficarum.* Translated by the Rev. Montague Summers. New York: Dover Publications, 1971.

James, Heather. "Dido's Ear: Tragedy and the Politics of Response." *Shakespeare Quarterly* 52, no. 3 (Fall 2001): 360–82.

James VI. *DÆMONOLOGIE, IN FORME of a Dialogue Diuided into three Bookes. EDINBVRGH, Printed by Robert Walde-graue, Printer to the Kings Majestie. An. 1597.* The Bodley Head Quartos. Edited by G. B. Harrison. New York: E. P. Dutton, 1924.

———. *Minor Prose Works of King James VI and I.* Edited by James Craigie. Edinburgh: Scottish Texts Society, 1982.

Johnson, Kimberly. *Made Flesh: Sacrament and Poetics in Post-Reformation England.* Philadelphia: University of Pennsylvania Press, 2014.

Kapitaniak, Pierre. "Reginald Scot and the Circles of Power: Witchcraft, Anti-Catholicism and Faction Politics." In *Supernatural and Secular Power in Early Modern England*, edited by Marcus Harmes and Victoria Bladen. Farnham, UK: Ashgate, 2015.

———. "Spectres, fantômes et revenants dans le théâtre de la Renaissance anglaise." PhD diss., Paris-Sorbonne University, 2001.

Kieckhefer, Richard. *Magic in the Middle Ages.* 2nd ed. Cambridge: Cambridge University Press, 2014.

Klaits, Joseph. *Servants of Satan: The Age of the Witch Hunts.* Bloomington: Indiana University Press, 1985.

Krier, Theresa. *Gazing on Secret Sights: Spenser, Classical Imitation, and the Decorums of Vision.* Ithaca, NY: Cornell University Press, 1990.

## BIBLIOGRAPHY

Lambe, John. *Statement, by John Lambe, of the proofs brought against him for a rape, and of their invalidity; also of his own proofs in favour of his innocence.* May 9, 1624. London: National Archives, PRO, SP 14/164/57.

Langbein, John H. *Torture and the Law of Proof: Europe and England in the Ancien Régime.* Chicago: University of Chicago Press, 1977.

Laqueur, Thomas W. "Crowds, Carnival and the State in English Executions, 1604–1868." In *The First Modern Society: Essays in English History in Honour of Lawrence Stone*, edited by A. L. Beier, David Cannadine, and James M. Rosenheim. Cambridge: Cambridge University Press, 1989.

Larner, Christina: *Witchcraft and Religion.* Oxford, UK: Basil Blackwell, 1984.

Levack, Brian P. *The Devil Within: Possession & Exorcism in the Christian West.* New Haven, CT: Yale University Press, 2013.

——. *The Witch-Hunt in Early Modern Europe.* London: Longman, 1987.

Levine, Laura. *Men in Women's Clothing: Antitheatricality and Effeminization 1579–1642.* Cambridge: Cambridge University Press, 1994.

——. "Wicked Mysteries and Notorious Conjurors: Magic, Rape, and Violence in Two Early Modern Pamphlets." *Journal of Medieval and Early Modern Studies* 51, no. 3. (2021): 533–51.

Lupton, Julia Reinhard. *Afterlives of the Saints: Hagiography, Typology, and Renaissance Literature.* Stanford, CA: Stanford University Press, 1996.

——. *Thinking With Shakespeare: Essays on Politics and Life.* Chicago: University of Chicago Press, 2011.

Macfarlane, Alan. *Witchcraft in Tudor and Stuart England.* London: Routledge, 1970.

Maitland, Frederic W. and Francis C. Montague. *A Sketch of English Legal History.* Ed. James F. Colby. New York: G.P. Putnam's Sons, the Knickerbocker Press, 1915.

Marcus, Leah. "Textual Indeterminacy and Ideological Difference: The Case of 'Doctor Faustus.'" *Renaissance Drama* 20 (1989): 1–29.

Marlowe, Christopher. *Doctor Faustus A- and B-texts (1604–1616).* Edited by David Bevington and Eric Rasmussen. Manchester: Manchester University Press, 1993.

Maus, Katharine Eisaman. *Inwardness and Theater in the English Renaissance.* Chicago: University of Chicago Press, 1995.

Monter, E. William. "Inflation and Witchcraft: The Case of Jean Bodin." In *Action and Conviction in Early Modern Europe*, edited by Theodore K. Rabb and Jerrold E. Seigel. Princeton, NJ: Princeton University Press, 1969.

Mowat, Barbara A. "Prospero, Agrippa, and Hocus Pocus." *English Literary Renaissance* 11, no. 3 (1981): 281–303.

——. "Prospero's Book." *Shakespeare Quarterly* 52, no. 1 (2001): 1–33.

Mullaney, Steven. *The Place of the Stage: License, Play, and Power in Renaissance England.* Chicago: University of Chicago Press, 1988.

Neely, Carol Thomas. "*The Winter's Tale*: The Triumph of Speech." In *The Winter's Tale: Critical Essays*, edited by Maurice Hunt. New York: Garland Publishing, 1995.

Neill, Michael. "Remembrance and Revenge: *Hamlet, Macbeth* and *The Tempest*." In *Jonson and Shakespeare*, edited by Ian Donaldson. London: Palgrave Macmillan, 1983.

*NEWES FROM SCOTLAND declaring the damnable life and death of DOCTOR FIAN, a notable SORCERER (1591).* Edited by G. B. Harrison. London: John Lane, Bodley Head Ltd., 1922–26. https://www.sacred-texts.com/pag/kjd/kjd11.htm.

Normand, Lawrence, and Gareth Roberts, eds. *Witchcraft in Early Modern Scotland: James VI's Demonology and the North Berwick Witches*. Liverpool: Liverpool University Press, 2000.
Orgel, Stephen. *Impersonations: The Performance of Gender in Shakespeare's England*. Cambridge: Cambridge University Press, 1996.
———. "Prospero's Wife." *Representations* 8 (Autumn 1984): 1–13.
———. "Secret Arts and Public Spectacles: The Parameters of Elizabethan Magic." *Shakespeare Quarterly* 68, no. 1 (2017): 80–91.
———. "Tobacco and Boys: How Queer Was Marlowe?" *GLQ: A Journal of Lesbian and Gay Studies* 6, no. 4 (2000): 555–76.
Parker, Pat. *Inescapable Romance: Studies in the Politics of a Mode*. Princeton, NJ: Princeton University Press, 1979.
Pearson, D'Orsay W. "Witchcraft in *The Winter's Tale*: Paulina as 'Alcahueta y vn Poquito Hechizera." *Shakespeare Studies* 12 (1979): 195–214.
Poole, Kristen. *Supernatural Environments in Shakespeare's England*. Cambridge: Cambridge University Press, 2011.
Popkin, Richard H. *History of Scepticism*. Rev. ed. Assen: Von Gorcum, 1964.
Purkiss, Diana. *The Witch in History: Early Modern and Twentieth-Century Representations*. London: Routledge, 2002.
Read, Sophie. *Eucharist and the Poetic Imagination in Early Modern England*. Cambridge: Cambridge University Press, 2013.
Riggs, David. *The World of Christopher Marlowe*. New York: Henry Holt, 2004.
Roper, Lyndal. *Oedipus and the Devil: Witchcraft, Sexuality and Religion in Early Modern Europe*. London: Routledge Press, 1994.
Rose, Jonathan. "Learning to Be a Legal Historian." *Journal of Legal Education* 51, no. 2 (June 2001): 294–304.
Rose, P. L. "Bodin's Universe and Its Paradoxes: Some Problems in the Intellectual Biography of Jean Bodin." In *Politics and Society in Reformation Europe*, edited by E. I. Kouri and Tom Scott. New York: St. Martin's Press, 1987.
Rosenfield, Kirstie Gulick. "Nursing Nothing: Witchcraft and Female Sexuality in *The Winter's Tale*." *Mosaic* 35, no. 1 (2002): 95–112.
Rushton, Peter. "Texts of Authority: Witchcraft Accusations and the Demonstration of Truth in Early Modern England." In *Languages of Witchcraft: Narratives, Ideology and Meaning in Early Modern Culture*, edited by Stuart Clark, 21–39. New York: St. Martin's Press, 2001.
Sacks, David Harris. "The Promise and the Contract in Early Modern England: Slade's Case in Perspective." In *Rhetoric and Law in Early Modern Europe*, edited by Victoria Kahn and Lorna Hutson. New Haven, CT: Yale University Press, 2001.
Schalkwyk, David. "'A Lady's "Verily" Is as Potent as a Lord's': Women, Word, and Witchcraft in *The Winter's Tale*." *English Literary Renaissance* 22, no. 2 (1992): 242–72.
Scot, Reginald. *The Discoverie of Witchcraft*. Edited by Brinsley Nicholson. Totowa, NJ: Rowman and Littlefield, 1973. First published in 1584.
Shakespeare, William. *The Tempest: The Oxford Shakespeare*. Edited by Stephen Orgel. Oxford: Oxford University Press, 1998.
———. *The Winter's Tale: The Oxford Shakespeare*. Edited by Stephen Orgel. Oxford: Oxford University Press, 1996.

Sharpe, James. *Instruments of Darkness: Witchcraft in England 1550–1750.* London: Hamish Hamilton, 1996.
Simpson, A.W.B. "The Place of *Slade's Case* in the History of Contract." In *Law, Liberty and Parliament: Selected Essays on the Writings of Sir Edward Coke,* edited by Allen D. Boyer. Indianapolis, IN: Liberty Fund, 2004.
Skinner, Quentin. "Meaning and Understanding in the History of Ideas." *History and Theory* 8, no. 1 (1969): 3–53.
Smith, Bruce R. "Sermons in Stones: Shakespeare and Renaissance Sculpture." *Shakespeare Studies* 17 (1985): 1–23.
Snow, Edward. "Marlowe's *Doctor Faustus* and the Ends of Desire." In *Two Renaissance Mythmakers: Christopher Marlowe and Ben Jonson.* Edited by Alvin B. Kernan. (Baltimore: Johns Hopkins University Press, 1977): 70–110.
Sofer, Andrew. "How to Do Things with Demons: Conjuring Performatives in *Doctor Faustus.*" *Theatre Journal* 61 (2009): 1–21.
Spenser, Edmund. *The Faerie Queene.* Edited by A. C. Hamilton with text edited by Hiroshi Yamashita and Toshiyuki Suzuki. Rev. 2nd ed. London: Routledge, 2013.
Stephens, Walter. *Demon Lovers: Witchcraft, Sex, and the Crisis of Belief.* Chicago: University of Chicago Press, 2002.
Stubbes, Philip. *The Anatomie of Abuses.* Netherlands: Da Capo Press, 1972. First published in 1593.
Sutton, Brian. "'Virtue Rather Than Vengeance': *Genesis* and Shakespeare's *The Tempest.*" *The Explicator* 66, no. 4 (2008): 224–29.
Thomas, Keith. *Religion and the Decline of Magic: Studies in Popular Beliefs in Sixteenth- and Seventeenth-Century England.* Oxford: Oxford University Press, 1997.
Traub, Valerie. "Jewels, Statues, and Corpses: Containment of Female Erotic Power in Shakespeare's Plays." *Shakespeare Studies* 20 (Jan. 1, 1988): 215–38.
Walker, D. P. *Spiritual and Demonic Magic from Ficino to Campanella.* Liechtenstein: Kraus Reprint, 1969. First published 1958 by Warburg Institute, University of London (London).
Walker, Garthine. "Rereading Rape and Sexual Violence in Early Modern England." *Gender and History* 10, no.1 (1998): 1–23.
Willis, Deborah. *Malevolent Nurture: Witch-Hunting and Maternal Power in Early Modern England.* Ithaca, NY: Cornell University Press, 1995.
———. "Shakespeare and the English Witch-Hunts." In *Enclosure Acts: Sexuality, Property and Culture in Early Modern England,* edited by Richard Burt and John Michael Archer. Ithaca, NY: Cornell University Press, 1994.
Wilson, Luke. *Theaters of Intention: Drama and the Law in Early Modern England.* Stanford, CA: Stanford University Press, 2000.
Wofford, Susanne Lindgren. *The Choice of Achilles: The Ideology of Figure in the Epic.* Stanford, CA: Stanford University Press, 1992.
Wooton, David. "Reginald Scot / Abraham Fleming, / The Family of Love." In *Languages of Witchcraft: Narrative, Ideology and Meaning in Early Modern Culture,* edited by Stuart Clark, 119–38. New York: St. Martin's Press, 2001.
Zika, Charles. *The Appearance of Witchcraft: Print and Visual Culture in 16th-Century Europe.* London: Routledge, 2007.
Zysk, Jay. *Shadow and Substance: Eucharistic Controversy and English Drama Across the Reformation Divide.* Notre Dame, IN: University of Notre Dame Press, 2017.

# Index

accuser (accusatory system): 12, 21, 63, 103, 147n13
acknowledged fact, 3, 32, 34, 66
Adelman, Janet, 160n4
affect: among demonologists and examiners, 7–8, 60, 66, 69, 78; and King James VI and I, 65, 71; and Leontes (*The Winter's Tale*), 114; pamphleteer, 76; of Prospero (*The Tempest*), 129; and David Seaton, 68, 84
Almond, Philip, 144n2
Ambrose of Milan, 134n17
Anglo, Sydney, 132n7, 137n3, 140n12, 145n4, 149n5
antitheatricality, 5, 27, 162n7; in *Demonomanie*, 4; in *The Faerie Queene*, 154n11; in Levine's earlier work, 132n10, 139n5, 152n11; in *The Tempest*, 121–25
apostasy, 139n6
Asp Carolyn, 160n5
Aston, Margaret, 6, 133n13
*assumpsit*, 97–99, 157n5, 158nn10–11, 158n19, 158n21, 159n22
Augustine of Hippo, Saint, 48, 134n17
Austin, J. L., 156n3; on constatives, 39, 142n6; illocutionary and perlocutionary acts, 142n6; performatives, 4–5, 37, 92, 100, 143n9, 155n2; problematizing original terms, 156n2, 159n25; on "statements," 4, 143n7, 145n3; "total speech situation," 136n24. *See also* performatives; performativity

Bahr, Stephanie, 82, 89, 154n6, 155n18
Baker, John, 98, 157n9
Barkan, Leonard, 161n8
Barzilai, Reut, 162n7
Beckwith, Sarah, 135n17, 162n6
Belsey, Catherine, 138n4
Berger, Harry, Jr., 82, 161n2, 162n3, 162n5, 163n12

Bevington, David, 155n1
Blair, Ann, 144n11, 144n14
Bodin, Jean, 2–9, 25–38, 132n7, 141n4, 142n6, 143n8, 144nn10–11; and *The Discoverie of Witchcraft*, 46, 49, 55, 146n7, 148n14; and *Doctor Faustus*, 100, 159n23; hierarchy of evidence, 66
bootes, 78. *See also* torture
Boyer, Allen D., 157n9
Broedel, Hans Peter, 137n1–2, 139n6, 140n10
Bucer, Martin, 6, 134n14

Calvin, John, 146n5, 157n6, 159n24
Campana, Joseph, 82, 153n2, 155n13, 155n17
Carmichael, James, 150n1
Cavanagh, Sheila, 153n3, 154n10
Cavell, Stanley, 159n2
certainty, 8, 136n21; and *Daemonologie*, 58, 64, 66, 68; and *Demonomanie*, 35–37; and *The Faerie Queene*, 82–85, 88, 90; and *Malleus Maleficarum*, 15; and *Newes from Scotland*, 74, 78–79, 150n3; and *The Winter's Tale*, 104, 107, 112. *See* doubt; uncertainty
Certeau, Michel de, 146n7
charms, 9, 39–42, 45, 47, 50, 53–56, 134n17; and *Daemonologie*, 56; in *Demonomanie*, 142n6; in *Doctor Faustus*, 100; in *The Tempest*, 121–22, 126
Clark, Stuart, 5, 7, 10, 60, 132n9, 135nn18–19, 136n24, 143n6, 148n1, 149n5; on Jean Bodin, 132n7, 141n4, 144n11; on *Daemonologie*, 149n6, 150n9, 152n13; on Michel Foucault, 132n6; on "inviolability," 63; on *Macbeth*, 10, 131n2; on *Malleus Maleficarum*, 137nn2–3; on Reginald Scot, 145n4, 147n10
Coke, Sir Edward, 97–100, 157n9, 158n10, 158n19, 159n22

173

# INDEX

conjurations, 9; in *Daemonologie*, 57, 163n11; in *The Discoverie of Witchcraft*, 40, 42, 45–46, 48–52; in *Doctor Faustus*, 93–94, 100, 156n3

conjuror's circles, 5, 9, 57, 94, 127

consideration, 98–99

contracts, 8–9, 135n18; in *Daemonologie*, 94; in *Doctor Faustus*, 92–100, 158nn10–11; in *Malleus Maleficarum*, 141n14. See also *Slade's Case*

counterperformance, 9, 13, 24, 73, 129, 138n4

Court of Common Pleas, 98–100, 158n11. See also *Slade's Case*

Craigie, James, 70, 152n10

Culler, Jonathan, 136n24

Cunningham, John. *See* Doctor Fian

curiosity, 55–61, 90, 95, 125; as a passion, 56; titillation of, 57–58

curses, 4; in *Demonomanie*, 27, 32, 142n6; in *Discoverie of Witchcraft*, 50–52; in *Malleus Maleficarum*, 23

*Daemonologie*, 55–64, 84; conjurors' circles, 57, 163n11; and curiosity, 55–58, 61, 95; and *Doctor Faustus*, 94–95; entresse, 61–63, 105, 150n9; and narrative, 63; relationship to Reginald Scot, 56, 58, 61, 103, 104, 129, 148n4; and *The Tempest*, 124–25, 129; and Weyer, 58, 148n2; and *The Winter's Tale*: 103–7, 109–10, 119; witch of Endor, 1–2, 7, 58–59, 103–5. See also King James VI/I

Darcy, Brian, 146n7

Darr, Orna Alyagon, 151n7

deed of gift, 95–96

demonological texts, 2, 8–11, 37, 60, 109, 119, 129, 136n24

demonology, 5–7; 60–62; 135n19, 144n2, 148n1, 149nn5–6, 156n2

demoniac, 7, 31, 42, 60, 146n7

demonic pact, 84–85, 94, 135n18, 136n25

*Demonomanie* (Jean Bodin), 2–5, 9, 25–38, 55, 66, 100, 131n3, 132n7; and Reginald Scot, 43, 46, 49

DeNeef, A. Leigh, 154n5

devil's mark, 7–8, 88; contrast with Michel Foucault, 151n7; in *Daemonologie*, 61–62; in *Demonomanie*, 31, 37; and *Newes from Scotland*, 67–71, 75, 77, 144n13. See also Geillis Duncane; Doctor Fian; Agnes Sampson; Agnes Tompson

devil's syllogism, 157n6

*Discoverie of Witchcraft, The*, 1–2, 5, 9, 39–54, 56–61, 85, 102–3, 112–14, 117, 129; 132n7, 141n14, 144n10, 144n2, 145n4, 146n5, 148n14; and analogies with witchmongers, 50–54; and biblical interpretation, 47–49; and exorcism, 50; and repetition of charms, 39–41; and theatricality, 42–46; and translation and mistranslation, 46–47; and ventriloquism, 2, 45; and witch of Endor, 44–49

dispossession, 51, 127–28. See also exorcism; possession

dittays, 68–70, 75–77, 152n8, 152n10, 152n13, 152n17, 153n23. See also indictments

*Doctor Faustus*, 8, 9, 92–93, 124, 126, 163n9; and bequests, 95–96; and Bodin, 100; and conjuring, 91, 93; consideration, 98–99; contract, 92–100; and *Daemonologie*, 94, 95; efficaciousness, 93, 100, 101; efficacy, 92; ideology, 92, 98; indeterminacy, 92; promise, 96–99, 157n5, 158n11, 158n17, 158n21; repetition, 92; and *Slade's Case*, 97–100; and speech-act theory, 91, 92, 100–101

dogmatism, and *Daemonologie*, 7, 58, 60, 104–07; and *The Winter's Tale*, 109, 116

Dolan, Frances, 138n4, 141n14, 143n8, 148n14

Donahue, Charles, 99, 158n18

doubt, 7–9, 135n21; and *Daemonologie*, 56–64, 84, 104, 149n5; and *Demonomanie*, 36–37; and *Newes from Scotland*, 66–72, 78–79; as skepticism, 60, 149n5; as uncertainty, 36–37, 56–64; and *The Winter's Tale*, 104, 106–14. See also uncertainty

Duffy, Eamon, 6, 132n11, 134n17, 138n3

Duncane, Geillis, 2, 7, 26, 65, 84–85; devil's mark, 67–77

Edward VI, King, 6, 134n14

effeminization, 88, 132n10, 154n12

efficaciousness, 5–6, 9, 17, 42, 73, 134n17, 143n6; in *Doctor Faustus*, 92–93, 100–101, 127, 156nn2–3

efficacy: of images, 6, 129; of words, 5, 9, 28, 41, 91–94, 100, 129, 134n17, 156n3

Eggert, Katherine, 153n3

Eire, Carlos, 6, 134nn15–17, 159n24

Elizabeth I, Queen, 6, 133n14, 146n7, 152n17

## INDEX

Endor, witch of, 1–2, 5, 9–10, 131n2, 147n8, 147n10; in *Daemonologie*, 58–59; in *The Discoverie of Witchcraft*, 44–48; related to *The Winter's Tale*, 103, 111–14
Enterline, Lynn, 160n6, 160n8
entresse, 61–63, 105, 150n9
Estes, Leland L., 145n4
Eucharist, 134n16–17, 156n3
evidentiary procedures, 65, 70, 74–75, 79
exorcism, 51, 127–29, 134n17, 146nn6–7

faerie, 148n14
*Faerie Queene, The*: and certainty, 82, 84–85, 90; and effeminization, 88, 154n12; and *Malleus Maleficarum*, 81, 84–85; and masculinity, 82, 86–90; and *Newes from Scotland*, 81, 84–85, 88, 90; and penetration, 82, 89; and rape, 82, 90, 153nn3–4; and stripping, 82–84, 86, 88
Fian, Doctor (John Cunningham), 3, 7–8, 67, 90, 153n23; and spectacle, 26; and *The Tempest*, 125; torture and execution of, 74–80
Fischlin, Daniel, 150n9
Floyd-Wilson, Mary, 132n6
Foster, Verna W., 160n4
Foucault, Michel, 8, 13, 141n3; concept of episteme, 3, 131n6, 141n3; critiques of, 132n6, 138n4; "penal arithmetic," 66, 71, 138n4, 150n3
Frazier, Sir James George, 152n14
Frye, Susan, 153n3

Garber, Marjorie, 157n7
Gaskill, Malcolm, 150n2
Gates, Daniel, 156n3
Gibson, Marion, 135n18, 147n13, 150n2
Gilman, Ernest B., 154n5
Ginzburg, Carlo, 135n18
Goldberg, Jonathan, 154n7
Goodare, Julian, 149n5, 150n9
Gosson, Stephen, 86, 132n10, 154n12
Gough, Melinda J., 154n6
Grazia, Margareta de, 161n2, 163n12
Greenblatt, Stephen, 10, 135n17, 136n23, 145n4, 146nn6–7
Gross, Kenneth, 153n5, 160n8
Guenther, Genevieve, 149n6, 156n3

Hammill, Graham, 157n5
Hanson, Elizabeth, 138n4
Hawkes, David, 156n3
Henry VIII, King, 133n14

Herzig, Tamar, 140n12
Hutson, Lorna, 138n4

Ibbetson, David, 157n9, 158n11, 158n15, 158n21, 159n22
iconoclasm, 6, 134nn15–16, 153n5
ideology, 38, 92, 98, 153n2
idolatry, 6, 153n5
image magic, 6, 72–4
incantations, 30, 39–42, 50, 53–54, 134n17
incubi, 62, 105
indeterminacy, 92, 101, 160n6
indictments, 66–68, 71, 74–79, 107, 147n13
inquisitorial system, 151n4
inquisitors, 2–4, 9–10, 129, 135n18; and *Daemonologie*, 61, 140n4; and *Demonomanie*, 25, 29, 43; and *Malleus Maleficarum*, 12–24, 85–86, 137n1, 137n3, 139n7, 140n9, 140n13
Institoris, Henricus. See *Malleus Maleficarum*
instrumental view of language, 5.

James VI/I, King, 1–5, 7–9, 26, 84, 132n7, 141n14, 154n9; and *The Discoverie of Witchcraft*, 44, 145n2; and *Doctor Faustus*, 94, 157n8; and *Newes from Scotland*: 65, 69, 71, 73–74; and *The Tempest*: 121, 124–26, 129, 163n11; and *The Winter's Tale*: 102–03, 109–10, 119. See also *Daemonologie*
James, Heather, 162n7
Johnson, Kimberly, 134n17
judicial procedure: in *Malleus Maleficarum*, 12–15, 24, 138n4. See also judicial strategy
judicial strategy, 32–33
Junius, Johannes (tortured burgomaster), 139n7

Kapitaniak, Pierre, 146n7, 147n8
Karlstadt, Andreas, 6, 134n15
King's Bench, court of the, 98, 158n11, 158n15, 159n22. See also *Slade's Case*
Kinney, Arthur F., 132n10
Klaits, Joseph, 139n7
knowledgelessness, 8, 136n21
Kramer, Heinrich (Henricus Institoris). See *Malleus Maleficarum*
Krier, Theresa, 155n14

Lambe, John, 88, 155n15
Langbein, John H., 66–67, 140n10, 151n4
Laqueur, Thomas W., 138n4
Larner, Christina, 139n7, 143n8

# INDEX

Levack, Brian, 146n7, 151n4
Levine, Laura, 132n10, 139n5, 149n7, 152n10, 153n18, 154n12, 155n15, 156n3
Lupton, Julia, 161n8
Luther, Martin, 134n15

*Macbeth*, 9–10, 123, 131n2, 147n8
Macfarlane, Alan, 147n13
Mackay, Christopher S., 136, 139nn6–7, 140n9, 140n13
maleficium, 68, 71, 137nn2–3
*Malleus Maleficarum*, 2, 9, 10, 46, 81, 85–86, 119; authorial contributions of Henricus Institoris (Heinrich Kramer) and Jacobus Sprenger, 137n1; confessions, 14, 21, 141n3; counterperformance, 13, 24; incantatory vs. nonreferential language, 19; judicial theatricality, 1, 13, 15, 21; precautions, 13, 20–24; scripts, 15–19, 20–21; workload, 13, 17–19, 22–24. *See also* possession
Marcus, Leah S., 92, 96, 156n4
Mary I, Queen, 6, 133n14
material change: ability of words to effect, 5, 23, 41–44, 47, 103, 143n6
Maus, Katharine Eisaman, 138n4, 142n5, 145n4
melancholics, 7, 52–53, 59, 104
melancholy, 49–54, 60
Mirandola, Pico della, 27, 140n12
Monter, E. William, 142n4
Morley, Humphrey (defendant in *Slade's Case*), 97
Mowat, Barbara A., 162n4, 162nn8–9

Neely, Carol Thomas, 160nn6–7
*Newes from Scotland*, 2, 7–9, 26, 64, 65–80, 85, 88, 90, 119, 125, 127, 131n5; and certainty, 66, 68, 74, 78, 79, 82; and confession, 66–71, 74, 76–79; and counterperformance, 73–74; and devil's mark, 67–71, 75, 77, 144n13; and narrative, 71–72, 75, 78; and possession, 75, 76, 78; and representation, 73, 74, 76; and spectacle and performance, 65, 68–69, 71, 73, 75–77, 80; and sympathetic magic, 73–76; and trial and examination records, 66–70, 74–75, 78–79, 151n6; and torture, 66–68, 70, 72, 74, 78; and uncertainty, 66, 69
Normand, Lawrence, 70, 76, 78, 144n2, 150n1, 151n7, 152nn8–10, 152n12, 152nn15–17, 153nn19–23
Noyon, sorcerer and bishop of, 37

Ontology, 7, 34
Oostsanen, Jacob Cornelisz van, 147n8
Orgel, Stephen, 111–12, 127, 131n1, 147n12, 159n1, 159n3, 160n4, 161n1–2, 161n5, 162n2, 162n5, 163n9

Parker, Pat, 154n7, 160n6
Pearson, D'Orsay W., 159n3
penetration, 23, 31, 62–63, 82–90, 105–10, 119, 154n6
performatives, 4–5, 45, 74–76, 92, 100, 134n17; versus constatives, 142n6, 155n2; and *Demonomanie*, 27–33, 37–39, 142n6, 143n9; and *Doctor Faustus*, 155n2, 156n3, 159n25; and *Malleus Maleficarum*, 23–24, 140n13
performativity, 24, 142n6, 156n2
pilliwinckes, 67–68
Pitcairn, Robert, 70, 152n10
Popkin, Richard H., 144n11, 148n3
possession, 3, 26, 43, 51, 60, 75–78, 126–28, 146n7, 149n5. *See also* dispossession; exorcism
precautions, 9, 13, 20–23, 79, 85–86, 119, 137nn2–3
presumption, 4, 32–33, 43, 140n13
prosecution, 7, 32, 59–60, 97, 104, 135n21, 138n4, 142n5, 152n7
Protestants, 6, 146n7, 147n8, 149n6, 149n9. *See also* Reformation; reformers
Purkiss, Diana, 145n4, 148n14, 149n5

Quilligan, Maureen, 153n3

Rasmussen, Eric, 155n1
Read, Sophie, 134n16
referential language, 4–5, 19, 27–28, 43–44
Reformation, 6, 92, 129, 134n17, 153n2. *See also* Protestants, reformers
reformers, 6, 101, 156n3. *See also* Protestants, Reformation
repetition, 5, 9, 11; in *Daemonologie*, 56, 58, 60–61, 149n6; in *Demonomanie*, 28–31, 36; in *The Discoverie of Witchcraft*, 40, 43, 52, 54; in *Doctor Faustus*, 92, 96, 99; in *The Faerie Queene*, 89, 132n10, 149n6; in *Malleus Maleficarum*, 16–18
representations, 28, 74, 76, 134n17, 151n6
rhetorical strategies, 11, 13, 112, 117, 119, 146n7
Riggs, David, 157n6
rites, 5–6, 55–57, 94, 127, 137n2, 163n11
Roberts, Gareth. *See* Lawrence Normand

Romano, Giulio, 161n8
Roper, Lyndal, 143n8
Rose, P. L., 142n4
Rosenfield, Kirstie Gulick, 159n3, 161n8
Rushton, Peter, 150n2

Sacks, David Harris, 98–99, 158n11, 158n17, 158n19
sacrament, 134n17, 137n2, 139n7
Sampson, Agnes (Agnis), 7–8, 70, 152n10; in *Newes from Scotland*, 67, 69–74, 85, 119, 152n8, 152n15, 152n17
Samuel (prophet) 1–2, 7; in *Daemonologie*, 58–59; in *The Discoverie of Witchcraft*, 44–48, 147n8; relation to *The Winter's Tale*, 103–04, 110–13
Schalkwyk, David, 159n3, 160n6
Scot, Reginald. See *The Discoverie of Witchcraft*
Seaton, David, 65–69, 71, 84, 143n8
Shakespeare, William, 1–2, 8–10; *Troilus and Cressida*, 114, 160n5. See also *Macbeth*; *The Tempest*; *The Winter's Tale*
Sharpe, James, 139n7, 145n4
shaving, 7, 20, 23, 70, 85, 119
Signs, 7, 84, 104, 106, 132n6, 132nn9–10, 134n17; in *Daemonologie*, 59–60, 64; in *Demonomanie*, 36, 46, 142n6, 144n13; in *Doctor Faustus*, 91, 93–95, 156n3, 158n19; and *Newes from Scotland*, 67–71, 76, 79
skepticism, 7–9, 33, 99, 110–12, 140n14, 149n5, 159n2; and *The Discoverie of Witchcraft*, 39, 50–54, 58, 60, 66, 145n4; and *Doctor Faustus*, 99, 156n3. See also dogmatism; doubt
Skinner, Quentin, 135n18
*Slade's Case*, 92; history, 97–98; legal strategies, 99–100; overlapping legal remedies, 98
Smith, Bruce R., 161n8
Snow, Edward, 157n6
Sofer, Andrew, 156n3
sorcerer, 29, 36–37, 79, 100, 163n9
sorcery, 2, 26, 75–76
speech act, 50, 99, 101, 142n6, 145n3, 156nn2–3, 158n11
Spenser, Edmund. See *The Faerie Queene*
Sprenger, Jacob. See *Malleus Maleficarum*
statemental ideal of language, 39, 143n7
Stephens, Walter, 11, 135n18, 136n25, 137n2, 139n7, 140n12
stripping, 8, 119; in *The Faerie Queene*, 81–90, 153nn2–3, 154n6, 155n14, 155n18; in *Malleus Maleficarum*, 20, 23

Stubbes, Philip, 132n10
succubi, 62, 105
Sutton, Brian, 161n2

*Tempest, The*, 9, 120–29; and *The Aeneid*, 123; and antitheatricality/theatricality, 123–25; and circles, 127–28; and *Daemonologie*, 124–25, 129; and exorcism, 129; and madness, 120–24; and possession/dispossession, 127; and spiritual change, 120, 126, 129
theatricality, 2–4, 135n21; in *Demonomanie*, 26, 32–33, 37–38, 141n3; in *The Discoverie of Witchcraft*, 42–43, 45, 49, 146n6; in *Doctor Faustus*, 156n3; in *The Faerie Queene*, 86, 154n11; in *Malleus Maleficarum*, 13–14, 19, 22–24, 138n4; in *Newes from Scotland*, 71–73, 77–79; in *The Tempest*, 123–25; in *The Winter's Tale*, 119, 121, 124–25, 161n8
Thomas, Keith, 6, 145n4, 148n13
thumbscrew, 7, 67. See also Pilliwinckes
Tompson, Agnes, 67, 70, 74, 79, 152n10. See also Agnes Sampson
torture, 7–9, 135nn20–21; in *Daemonologie*, 59; in *The Discoverie of Witchcraft*, 43, 49; and *The Faerie Queene*, 85, 90; in *Malleus Maleficarum*, 13, 137n3, 139n7, 140n10, 140n13; in *Newes from Scotland*, 66–72, 74, 78, 79, 151nn4–5, 151n7, 152n11; and *The Winter's Tale*, 104, 113. See also bootes; pilliwinckes; shaving; stripping
translation and mistranslation, 136n1; and *Faustus*, 157n6; and Reginald Scot, 46–49, 144n2
transubstantiation, 59, 105
Traub, Valerie, 160n4
*Troilus and Cressida*. See William Shakespeare
Trois-eschelles, 27, 31, 37

uncertainty, 7–9; and *Daemonologie*, 60, 66, 79; and *Demonomanie*, 36–37; and *Newes from Scotland*, 66, 79. See also certainty; doubt
utterances, 4–5, 30, 41, 134n17, 136n24, 142n6, 143n9, 145n3; in *Doctor Faustus*, 94, 99–101, 156n2, 159n25

Vairus, Leonard (Leonardo Vairo), 52
violability, inviolability, 63, 141n4, 149n9

Walker, D. P., 143n6
Walker, Garthine, 82, 88, 153n4

## INDEX

Weyer, Johann, 27, 46, 58, 129, 132n7, 149n5
Willis, Deborah, 138n4, 141n14, 143n8
Wilson, Luke, 156n5
*Winter's Tale, The*, 1–2, 8, 9, 102–19, 120–22; and counter-theater, 129; *Daemonologie*, 103–09, 112–19, 121; and dogmatism, 106–07, 116; and Endor, 110–14; and James VI/I, 102–4; and penetration, 105, 109, 119; Reginald Scot, 102–04, 110; and spiritual change, 116
Witch of Endor, 1–2, 10, 131n2; and *Daemonologie*, 58; and *The Discoverie of Witchcraft*, 44–48, 147n8, 147n10; and *The Winter's Tale*, 103, 110–14
Witch of Westwell, 42–43, 48
witches. *See* Geillis Duncane; Doctor Fian; Agnes Sampson; Agnes Tompson; Trois–eschelles; Witch of Endor; Witch of Westwell.
witnesses: and *Daemonologie*, 60; in *Demonomanie*, 32–34; and *The Discoverie of Witchcraft*, 42; and *Malleus Maleficarum*, 12–21; and *Newes from Scotland*, 66, 72, 77, 79, 150n2; and *The Tempest*, 129
Wofford, Susanne, 84, 153n5, 154n8, 154n11
Wooton, David, 145n4

Zika, Charles, 131n2, 147n8
Zwingli, Ulrich: concept of inner image and strange god, 6; iconoclasm and Eucharist, 134n16; substituting false god for God, 159n24
Zysk, Jay, 156n3

www.ingramcontent.com/pod-product-compliance
Lightning Source LLC
Chambersburg PA
CBHW020849160426
43192CB00007B/846